T0330794

ROUTLEDGE LIBRARY EDITIONS:
ACCOUNTING HISTORY

Volume 1

THE ACCOMPTANT'S ORACLE

THE ACCOMPTANT'S ORACLE

WARDHAUGH THOMPSON

Routledge
Taylor & Francis Group

LONDON AND NEW YORK

First published in 1984 by Garland Publishing, Inc.

This edition first published in 2021
by Routledge
2 Park Square, Milton Park, Abingdon, Oxon OX14 4RN

and by Routledge
52 Vanderbilt Avenue, New York, NY 10017

Routledge is an imprint of the Taylor & Francis Group, an informa business

British Library Cataloguing in Publication Data
A catalogue record for this book is available from the British Library

ISBN: 978-0-367-33564-9 (Set)
ISBN: 978-1-00-304636-3 (Set) (ebk)
ISBN: 978-0-367-51463-1 (Volume 1) (hbk)
ISBN: 978-1-00-305393-4 (Volume 1) (ebk)

Publisher's Note
The publisher has gone to great lengths to ensure the quality of this reprint but points out that some imperfections in the original copies may be apparent.

Disclaimer
The publisher has made every effort to trace copyright holders and would welcome correspondence from those they have been unable to trace.

The Accomptant's Oracle

Wardhaugh Thompson

GARLAND PUBLISHING, INC.
NEW YORK & LONDON 1984

For a complete list of the titles in this series
see the final pages of this volume.

This facsimile has been made from a copy in the library of
the Institute of Chartered Accountants
in England and Wales.

Only Volume II of *The Accomptant's Oracle*
has been reprinted for this edition.

Library of Congress Cataloging in Publication Data

Thompson, Wardhaugh.
The accomptant's oracle.

(Accounting history and the development of a profession)
Reprint. Originally published: The accomptant's
oracle, or, Key to science. Vol. II. York [North
Yorkshire] : Printed for the author by N. Nickson, 1777.
1. Accounting—Early works to 1800. I. Title.
II. Series.
HF5631.T46   1984   657   82-48385
ISBN 0-8240-6337-6 (alk. paper)

The volumes in this series are printed on
acid-free, 250-year-life paper.

Printed in the United States of America

THE

Accomptant's Oracle,

OR,

KEY to SCIENCE.

BEING A COMPLEAT PRACTICAL

SYSTEM of BOOK-KEEPING.

Together with the NATURE and USE of

BANKING BUSINESS;

And a plain, accurate, and concise Method, for MANUFAC-
TURERS to keep their Books

By DOUBLE ENTRY.

In TWO VOLUMES.

VOL. II.

By WARDHAUGH THOMPSON,
Many Years an ACCOMPTANT in LONDON.

YORK:
Printed for the AUTHOR, by N. NICKSON.

MD,CC,LXXVII,

PREFACE.

I Know it will be generally expected that I ſhould make ſome apology to the public, for writing on a ſubject which has ſo frequently been handled before me; whilſt at the ſame time they would deem it an unpopular freedom, ſhould I pretend to find fault with any of thoſe my predeceſſors. Strange inconſiſtancy! They expect an apology, and yet are diſpleaſed with the only true one, which any author ſo circumſtanced can poſſibly make; for however he may palliate the matter, it can be only one, or both of the following reaſons, which can induce him to take up the pen; namely, that he either thinks he has a ſuperior knowledge on the ſubject, or that he flatters himſelf he can communicate it in a more familiar and intelligible manner. The firſt of thoſe, from my practice in mercantile affairs, I hope I may (at leaſt) be allowed ſome pretentions to; and the laſt, I frankly confeſs, I am vain enough to think I have hit upon.

"And although (as Mr. *Saxby* obſerves in his "introduction to the Britiſh Cuſtoms) it be a "diſagreeable employment to animadvert on the "errors of others, yet a juſt regard to improve "and inſtruct, neceſſarily requires that ſome few "inſtances ſhould be pointed out wherein others "have been miſtaken." Thoſe I ſhall chiefly take notice of in the courſe of this work, are taken from Mr. *Mair*, who I not only think, but believe, is generally allowed our moſt methodical author on this ſubject.

After this declaration, it is natural enough for them to expect I ſhould tell them in what particulars I differ from others who have wrote before me,
and

and by way of bill of fare, to fay fomething of my plan in general. Firſt then, (in order to render this work as fimple and eafy as poſſible) I have omitted every thing which was not abſolutely neceſſary to the main end propoſed, namely, to give the learner a true and perfect knowledge of the Italian method of Book-Keeping by Double Entry; which however neceſſary others have thought it to enlarge upon, in my opinion only ſerves to puzzel and perplex them; and inſtead of facilitating, only retards their progreſs.

What I chiefly here elude to is, along and tedious deſcription of the form and uſe of all the ſubſidiary books which may be kept in the different branches of trade, ſuch as Litter-Book, Book of Sales, Invoice-Book, Ship-Book, &c. the forms of which are entirely arbitrary, every merchant not only keeping more or leſs at pleaſure, but alſo differs in the form of them according to fancy, or at beſt, ſutes the particular branch in which he is engaged.

Secondly, Inſtead of burthening the learner's memory with rules (to be got by rote) for making the Journal entries of the ſeveral caſes here introduced in the courſe of domeſtick trade, I have only given him a few of the principal ones, of which the others are compounded; and by a ſhort explanation at the bottom of every Journal entry, (refering to ſuch caſes) endeavoured to give him a ſatisfactory reaſon for every thing he does; for as innumerable caſes may occur in real buſineſs, which is impoſſible to foreſee in theory, ſo had I added to thoſe few, ten thouſand caſes and rules more, (which I ſhall ſuppoſe a perſon not only able to repeat by rote, but alſo to have a memory to retain) yet at the beſt, his knowledge would not only be limmited, but ſuperficial, whilſt he remain'd ignorant of the principles on which thoſe rules are founded.

ed. Memory and reafon are two different things, and where the latter is not confulted, they will receive but little, or no help from the former, efpecially in cafes which are new to them.

Thirdly, I have immediately under the debt fide of every Ledger accompt, told them what the debt and credit fide of the faid accompt contain. And under the credit fide, given them directions how to ballance the faid accompt, which having both immediately under their eye, will be more clear and inftructive to them then if in different parts of the book.

Fourthly, As there are feveral cafes which may be journalized differently, and all with equal propriety, I have in fome inftances fhewn how far the journalizing of any future tranfaction, relative to fuch entry, is affected, or determined, according to the choice which you made of the firft.

In order to give the young beginner (at leaft) fome general idea of the ufe and defign of Double Entry, I have made the firft fet of books to confift of only a few fimple tranfactions, and not more than he can journalize, poft, and ballance in one week: Whereas (according to the common mode) he is immediately introduced into a large field of bufinefs; fo that the diftance of time between any prime tranfaction, and any fucceeding one relative to it, together with the variety of frefh ones which fill up the intermediate fpace, makes him totally forget the dependence the one has upon the other, and confequently blunders through, without ever perceiving the ufe, defign, or end, of all his labour.

There are alfo many other material points in which I have taken the liberty to differ (and I hope with equal propriety) from thofe who are allowed our beft authors, which I fhall point out in the courfe of this work, and humbly fubmit it to the candid judgment of the public.

CONTENTS.

CONTENTS.

CHAP. I.

CHAP. II.

CHAP.

O F

BOOK-KEEPING

In GENERAL.

BOOK-KEEPING by Double Entry, or what is commonly called the Italian method of Book-Keeping, is the art of keeping our accompts in such a manner, as will not only exhibit to us our neat gain or loss upon the whole, but our particular gain or loss upon each article we deal in, by which we are instructed what branches to pursue, and which to decline; a piece of knowledge so very essential to every man in business, that without it a person can only be said to deal at random, or at best can be called but guess'd work.

Nor is this the only advantage we derive from it, for we can in a few hours, and with very little trouble, at any time, know the exact state of our affairs, viz. what goods of every fort we have in hand; what payments we have to make, and what cafh we can command; by which means we are timely apprized to prepare for any demands which can be made upon us, and can extend or curtail our trade as we find our capital will admit of, or the nature of our affairs require.

In fhort, it is a qualification fo abfolutely neceffary for every perfon in trade, that it may be truly faid, their fuccefs (if not wholly) in a great meafure depends upon it.

This affertion, however ftrange it may feem, is neverthelefs verified by numberlefs inftances, and we often fee people with this requifite improve very fmall capitals to exceeding large ones; whilft others, for want of it, are as frequently reduced from a confiderable fortune to the loweft ftate of indigence.

I know all who are unacquainted with this moft excellent art, will tell you, that all the advantages which I have above enumerated may be obtained by the common way of Book-Keeping, and therefore Double Entry only encreafes our labour to no purpofe;

pofe; but this argument, inftead of con-
cealing, only expofes their ignorance, for if
they are but half fo exact and accurate as
they pretend to be, their labour will not
only be much more, but after all, a mere
mafs of confufion, one thing having no dependence on, or any connection with another;
whereas by the Italian method, every account is chequered by another in fuch a
manner, that it is impoffible to commit the
leaft error, but it muft of neceffity fhew itfelf,
and by the nice dependence which one thing
has upon another, is eafily traced back to
its firft rife.

But to ftate the many ridiculous objections
made by thofe illiterate cavillers, or to at-
tempt to convince them of their errors by
mere dint of reafoning, would be fpending
my time to as little purpofe as they do,
fince it is impoffible for them to perceive the
propriety of any fingle part, without being
acquainted with the whole general fcheme.

My principal reafon, therefore, for taking any notice of them was, to foften (if
poffible) the prejudices of thofe who have
been weak enough to fuffer themfelves to be
impofed upon by fuch falacious arguments,
and to induce them to a candid perufal of
the following work: But before I proceed
further, I fhall beg leave to mention one ob-
jection more, which, as it feems to have

gained

gained moſt credit, ſo I think it incumbent in me to clear it up.

This grand argument is, that every merchant has a method of keeping his books to himſelf, ſo that a perſon however well acquainted he may be with the particular methods of thoſe whoſe books he has kept, yet ſay they, he is as much at a loſs the next compting houſe he goes into, as if he had never learned at all.

This (to any perſon who has the leaſt idea of the Italian manner of Book-Keeping) will appear too abſurd to deſerve an anſwer; but as I write as well for them who are totally ignorant of the matter, as for them who have acquired ſome knowledge of it, I thought fit to take off the weight of argument by telling them, that the general plan is not only the ſame throughout all Britain, but through all Europe, I mean in regular compting houſes, or by ſuch as are properly ſtiled merchants.

This notion probably has taken its riſe from the different manner in which the ſubſidiary books are kept, which as I obſerved in my preface, vary according to peoples particular humours; but thoſe do not in the leaſt affect the general plan, with which if a perſon be thoroughly acquainted, he can be at no loſs in any compting houſe in any
                                                    part

part of the world whatever, provided he underftand the language of the country. It would therefore be fpending much time and labour to no purpofe in giving the learner forms of books, which it is ten to one he ever has occafion for, or at leaft ever adheres to; for if he embarks in bufinefs for him-felf, he will foon difcover what books of that kind are neceffary, and confequently muft be the beft judge what form would beft anfwer his end.

If he acts as clerk to another merchant, where the number and forms of fuch books are already eftablifhed, it will require but a few hours to make himfelf acquainted with them. They are therefore fo far from be-ing effential, that (the Bill-book except-ed) I fhall not take the leaft notice of them, but leave every one to adopt what form he fhall find moft fitting and convenient.

I fhall next proceed to fhew the nature and ufe of the three principal books, which are the Wafte, the Journal, and the Ledger.

1ft. Of the WASTE-BOOK.

The Wafte-Book opens with an inven-tory of all the money, goods, and debts belonging to you, and alfo an exact ac-count of what debts you owe to others: After this is done, you next record every

tranfaction

tranfaction in trade in full, juft as it happens, with every particular circumftance
relating to it.

2d. Of the J O U R N A L.

In the Journal the above tranfactions are
properly digefted, and regularly formed into Debtor and Creditor, the better to prevent miftakes in pofting it from thence to
the Ledger.

3d. Of the L E D G E R.

In the Ledger you open an accompt for
every perfon or thing which is made Debtor
or Creditor in your Journal, which muft
confift of two oppofite parts, viz. on the
left hand fide you make it *Dr.* and on the
right fide, and the fame folio, you make it
Cre. to which you collect every tranfaction
relative to fuch accompt, which lie fcatter-
ed through the other books, and place them
under that particular head in your Ledger
to which they properly belong; which will
then exhibit to you, at one view, what
debts you owe; the debts that are due to
you; the quantity of every particular article you bought, and what it coft you; what
part of it you have fold, and at what price,
or how otherwife difpofed of; what cafh
you have in hand; and, in fhort, every thing
elfe neceffary to be known, in order to con-
duct your affairs with judgment and regu-
larity.   The

The form of the above three books will beſt appear by the books themſelves, and therefore I ſhall not give you any ſpecimen of them in this place.

CHAP I.

Of PROPER TRADE.

PROPER Trade is either Domeſtic or Foreign. Proper Domeſtic Trade is that which a merchant carries on by him-ſelf, without the help of a factor. Proper Foreign Trade is that which cannot be car-ried on without employing a factor.

SECTION FIRST.

Debtor and Creditor applied in proper Domeſtic Trade.

Proper Domeſtic Trade comprehends the inventory, buying, ſelling, receiving and paying of money. To each of theſe I ſhall aſſign a diſtinct problem; and to prevent burthening the learner's memory, I ſhall deliver the rules for journalizing the ſeveral caſes in as compendious a manner as poſſi-ble, giving under each head, the prime or leading caſes only; and in all other com-plex caſes which may happen in the courſe

of

of this work, (for the journalizing of which I have given no particular rule) fhall at the bottom of fuch Journal Entry, refer the learner to the feveral prime cafes of which that particular one is compound; and alfo at the bottom of the Journal Entry of every fimple or prime cafe, fhall refer him to that particular cafe and rule to which it properly belongs.

PROBLEM FIRST.

Debtor and Creditor applied to the inventory.

When you firft commence merchant, and take an inventory of your effects and debts you owe.

Rule. Sundries Debtor to ftock, viz.
Cafh for your ready money
Goods in hand for their refpective values.
Perfons for the debts they owe you,&c. &c.

2dly. Stock debtor to fundries, viz.
To the feveral perfons to whom you ftand indebted, &c.

PROBLEM

PROBLEM SECOND.

Debtor and Creditor applied in buying.

Cafe 1ft. When you buy goods with ready money.

Rule. Goods by their particular name, Debtor to cafh, *Nov.* 3, 1776.

Cafe 2d. When you buy goods on credit.
Rule. Goods Debtor to the feller.

Cafe 3d. When you buy goods and give the feller your draft upon any other perfon for the money.

Rule. Goods Debtor to the perfon on whom you gave the draft, *Nov.* 8, 1776.

Cafe 4th. When you barter goods for goods of equal value.

Rule. Goods received Debtor to goods delivered.

PROBLEM THIRD.

Debtor and Creditor applied in felling.

Cafe 1ft. When you fell goods for ready money.

Rule. Cafh Debtor to goods fold.

Cafe 2d. When you fell goods on credit.
Rule. The buyer Debtor to goods fold.

Cafe 3d. When you fell goods, for the payment of which the buyer gives you a draft upon another perfon.

Rule. Bills receivable Debtor to goods fold, *Nov.* 15, 1776.

Obfervation. Hence you may obferve, that the feveral cafes in felling, are juft the reverfe of the fame cafes in buying, from which few particular cafes may be deduced this

GENERAL RULE.

The thing received, or the receiver, is Debtor to the thing delivered, or the deliverer: Which general rule holds good in all cases of buying and selling whatsoever.

PROBLEM FOURTH.

Debtor and Creditor applied in receiving payment of debts, borrowing of cash, or receiving interest for money lent; in legacies left, wagers won, &c. &c.

Case 1st. When you receive cash in payment for goods formerly sold on credit, or on any other accompt, for which the person (who owed you on some other accompt) before stood debited in your Ledger; or if the said person remits you a bill at sight, or you draw upon him, for either of which you immediately receive cash.

Rule. Cash Debtor to the payer, remitter, or person on whom drawn, or thing which before stood debited.

Case 2d. When a person who owes you remits you a bill which is not presently due.

Rule. Bills receivable Debtor to the remitter.

Case 3d. When afterwards you receive cash in payment of the said bill, or for a bill immediately received upon selling goods.

Rule. Cash Debtor to bills receivable.

Case 4th. When you take goods in payment of a debt.

Rule. Goods received Debtor to the deliverer.

N. B. This is the very same thing as goods bought on credit.

Case

Cafe 5th. When you borrow money upon intereſt or otherwiſe.

Rule. Caſh Debtor to the lender.

Cafe 6th. When you receive intereſt for money lent, a wager won, a preſent, or legacy in caſh, or for any other thing for which nothing before ſtood debited in your Ledger, and for which you have no returns to make.

Rule. Caſh Debtor to profit and loſs.

PROBLEM FIFTH.

Debtor and Creditor applied in paying of debts, in lending of money, or paying intereſt for money borrowed; in paying expences of houſe-keeping, general charges on trade, &c. &c.

Cafe 1ſt. When you pay caſh for goods formerly bought on credit, or on any other ac-compt, for which the perſon (to whom you owed it on ſome other accompt) before ſtood credited in your Ledger; or if you remit the ſaid perſon a bill, or he draws upon you at ſight, for either of which you pay immediate caſh.

Rule. The perſon to whom paid, remitted, or drawn by, or thing which ſtood formerly credited, Debtor to caſh.

Cafe 2d. When the perſon to whom you ſtand indebted draws his bill upon you, payable a certain time after date, which you accept.

Rule. The drawer Debtor to bills payable, or bills accepted.

Cafe 3d. When you afterwards pay the ſaid bill.

Rule. Bills payable, or bills accepted, Debtor to caſh.

Cafe 4th. When the perſon to whom you

C 2   ſtand

ſtand indebted takes goods of you in payment of his debt.

Rule. The receiver Debtor to goods delivered.

N. B. This entry is the ſame as goods ſold on credit.

Caſe 5th. When you lend money, whether upon intereſt or not.

Rule. The perſon to whom lent, Debtor to caſh.

Caſe 6th. When you pày intereſt for money borrowed, a wager loſt, or make a preſent in caſh, or any other thing for which nothing before ſtood credited in your Ledger, and for which you expect no returns.

Rule. Profit and loſs Debtor to caſh.

Note 1ſt. But, if you do not immediately pay ſuch intereſt, wager, &c. &c. then Profit and loſs, Debtor to the perſon to whom due.

Note 2d. In paying clerks wages, warehouſe rent, poſtage of letters, &c. or any other thing which is a neceſſary expence on trade, and you cannot aſcertain exactly the particular ſhare of it which each article ought to be charged with, then it is better to make charges on trade, or charges on merchandize, Debtor to caſh, if paid; or to the perſon or perſons to whom due, if not paid.

Note 3d. For all money paid on account of houſe-keeping, &c. it is likewiſe better to erect a general accompt, by the title of houſhold expences; which accompt muſt be charged Debtor to caſh for all money paid on the ſaid account; or, if not paid, Debtor to the perſons to whom you ſtand indebted. By this

means

means you will fee, according to note firft, what are your neat gains or loffes by trade; and by note fecond, your neat expences in houfe-keeping diftinct from any thing elfe.

PROBLEM SIXTH.

Debtor and Creditor applied in particular cafes.

Cafe 1ft. When any perfon fails who owes you money, any goods proves damaged in your warehoufe, or elfewhere, or any kind of lofs whatever, for which you expect no returns; in all thofe cafes,

Rule. Profit and lofs Debtor to that particucular article, or thing, which ftood charged Debtor before, viz.

To the perfon who failed, to the goods damaged, or to the thing loft, for the lofs fuftained.

Cafe 2d. If afterwards you fhould chance to recover any part of a debt, or in any manner difpofe of thofe damaged goods, &c. which you had deem'd totally loft.

Rule. The thing received Debtor to profit and lofs for the fum recovered.

Note 1ft. If your legacy, wager, intereft, &c. be not immediately paid, then

The perfon from whom due (or executors of A. B.) Debtor to profit and lofs.

Note 2d. If you frequently infure fhips, goods, &c. for other people, then it is better (when you receive money as a premium for fuch infurance) to charge cafh Debtor to infurance accompt.

Cafe 3d. If a bill, which you draw upon any perfon who owes you money, fhould be protefted and returned, without good and fufficient
cient

cient reasons for the person on whom it was drawn refusing acceptance or payment of it, upon which you repay the value of the said bill, with charges of protest, postage, &c.

Rule. The person whom drawn Debtor to cash for value of the said bill, and charges. But if the person on whom drawn can shew good and sufficient reason for refusing acceptance or payment; such as, that he had (before your draft came to hand) remitted you in goods or bills which you had not received, then in that case,

Rule. Sundries Debtor to cash, viz.
The person on whom drawn for the value of the bill, and
Profit and loss for the charges.

Note. Both the above cases supposes you had credited the person on whom drawn, immediately upon drawing the said bill.

Case 4th. When any person who owes you money remits you a bill, which you immediately credit him for, and afterwards the person on whom it is drawn should refuse acceptance of the same, upon which you protest and return it.

Rule. The remitter Debtor to sundries, viz.
To bills acceptable for value of the bill, and
To cash, for charges of protest, postage, &c.

Note. If you negotiate either your own draft, or a draft remitted you by another person, with a bank or banker, which should happen to be return'd, they will not only charge you with the protest, postage, &c. but likewise interest for the value of the bill, from the time they gave you cash for it till you repay them, which interest you must also charge
the

the perfon on whom drawn, or the remitter, according to the circumftances of cafe third.

Cafe 5th. When in paying for goods formerly bought on credit, the perfon to whom you ftood indebted makes you any abatement.

Rule. The perfon (to whom paid) Debtor to fundries, viz.
To cafh for the fum paid, and
To profit and lofs for the fum abated.

Cafe 6th. When in receiving payment for goods formerly fold on credit you make any abatement.

Rule. Sundries Debtor to the payer, viz.
Cafh for the fum received, and
Profit and lofs for the abatement.

Note. Neither of the two laft cafes are prime ones, but each of them is compofed of two diftinct cafes, which are here refolved into one. However, I thought fit to give them a place, in order that I might refer to them, as the cafes (of which they are compofed) being general ones, I thought the learner might be at a lofs to know the particular circumftance in each of them, which included the above cafes fifth and fixth.

Cafe 7th. When you fend goods (which are not faleable at home) to any of your country correfpondents, without their particular order, defiring them to take them at a certain price.

Rule. Sufpence accompt Debtor to goods fent.

Cafe 8th. When you give any perfon cafh for a bill, for which he allows you difcount.

Rule. Bills receivable Debtor to fundries, viz.

To

To cafh for the money you gave for it, and
To profit and lofs for the difcount.

Cafe 9th. When any perfon difcounts you
a bill, for which you allow him difcount.

Rule. Sundries Debtor to bills receivable,
viz.
Cafh for the fum received, and
Profit and lofs for the difcount.

SECTION SECOND.

*Debtor and Creditor applied in proper Foreign
Trade.*

Proper Foreign Trade comprehends, firft,
The fhipping off goods to a factor; fecondly,
Advices concerning them from the factor;
thirdly, Returns made by the factor to you.

PROBLEM FIRST.

*Debtor and Creditor applied in fhipping off goods
to a factor.*

In all cafes in fhipping off goods, Voyage to
———— is Debtor, but the Creditor varies according to the following cafes:

Cafe 1ft. When you fhip off goods which
are already entered in your books.

Rule. Voyage to ———— Debtor to fun-
dries, viz.
To the refpective goods for their value,
To cafh for cuftom infurance and all other
charges, (if paid) or
To the perfons to whom due (if not paid).

Cafe 2d. When you buy goods with ready
money, and immediately fhip them off, without entering them in your books.

Rule.

Rule. Voyage to ———— Debtor to cafh for prime coft and charges.

Cafe 3d. If you buy goods on credit, and immediately fhip them off, without making any entry in your books.

Rule. Voyage to ———— Debtor to fundries, viz.

To the feller or fellers for value of the goods.
To cafh for charges at fhipping.

Note 1ft. Several others might be fuppofed, but as the journalizing of fuch may be eafily gathered from what has already been faid, I fhall therefore leave them for the exercife of the learner.

Note 2d. As voyage is to be debited for all charges, or whatever augments the coft, fo it muft be credited by whatever leffens the fame, fuch as drawbacks on re-exported goods, bounties on goods exported, &c. &c.

PROBLEM SECOND.

Debtor and Creditor applied upon receiving advice from your factor, A. B.

Before I proceed to the particular application of Debtor and Creditor in the feveral cafes of the firft advice from your factor, it may not be improper, firft to point out to you the three accompts which you may have occafion to keep with him, and to fhew you what the Debtor and Creditor fides of each of them contains; by which means the Journal Entry of the firft advice, will not only be rendered eafy to you, but you will alfo perceive the propriety of charging and difcharging any of the faid three accompts to and by each other, in all cafes of future advices. The three ac-

Vol. II.   D   compts

compts which you will have occasion to keep
with your factor, are the following, viz.

A. B. my accompt current.
A. B. my accompt of goods.
A. B. my accompt on time.

1ft. A. B. my accompt current.   This accompt is debited for neat proceeds of what
goods of yours your factor sells for ready money, for what cash he receives for goods formerly sold on credit, for what bills you ₹re-
mit, or cause to be remitted to him : It is credited for all returns he makes you, whether in
bills, goods, or cash, for all bills which you
draw upon him, and for all cash which he
pays on your account.

2d. A. B. my accompt of goods.   This
accompt is debited for the value of the goods
your factor receives from you : It is credited
as the goods are difpofed of, viz. by A. B. my
accompt current, if fold for ready money; or
by A. B. my accompt on time, if fold on
credit.

3d. A. B. my accompt on time.   This accompt is debited for the value of what goods
of yours the factor fells on credit : It is credited by A. B. my accompt current, when he
advifes you that he has received payment for
the faid goods.

The Cafes of the firft Advice.

In all cafes of the firft advice, Voyage to
——— is Creditor, but the Debtor varies according to the nature of the advice.

Cafe 1ft. If the firft advice be, that A. B.
has received your goods, but fold none of
them.

Rule. A. B. my accompt of goods Debtor
to

to voyage to ———— for the sum the said voyage stood formerly charged with.

Case 2d. If the first advice be, that A. B. has received your goods, and sold them all for ready money.

Rule. A. B. my accompt current Debtor to voyage to ———— for the neat proceeds.

Case 3d. If the first advice be, that the goods are received and sold on credit.

Rule. A. B. my accompt on time Debtor to voyage to ———— for neat proceeds.

Case 4th. If the first advice be, that the goods are not only received and sold, but a cargo shipped in return, and now at sea. Here are three varieties:

1st. If the value of the cargo shipped, with charges paid by your factor, be equal to the neat proceeds of your cargo out.

Rule. Voyage from ———— Debtor to voyage to ———— for the neat proceeds.

2d. If your factor over-ship the neat proceeds.

Rule. Voyage from ———— Debtor to sundries, viz.
To voyage to ———— for neat proceeds.
To A. B. my accompt current for the overplus.

3d. If your factor under-ship the neat proceeds.

Rule. Sundries Debtor to voyage to ————, viz.
Voyage from ———— for first cost and charges.
A. B. my accompt current for ballance in his hands.

Case 5th. If the first advice be, whether
from

from your factor or any other person, that the
ship and cargo is loft at fea, and your goods
were not infured, then the entry will be according to the rule for journalizing cafe firft
in problem fixth: But if the goods were all
infured.

Rule. Infurer Debtor to voyage to ——————

Or if you get prefent payment, then
Cafh Debtor to voyage.

Befides the foregoing cafes in this problem,
many more might be fuppofed; but as thofe
are the principal ones, of which all the others
are compounded, I thought it unneceflary to
particularize them. And as to

The Cafes of the fecond or fucceeding Advices, &c.

General Rule. Nothing further need be obferved, but that particular regard muft be
had to the entry that was made upon the advice immediately preceding, for whatever
then ftood charged Debtor muft now be credited.

PROBLEM SECOND.

*Debtor and Creditor applied when returns are
made you by your factor.*

Before your factor makes you any returns,
it is reafonable to fuppofe that he has received and difpofed of your outward bound cargo
for ready money, for the neat proceeds of
which, (if you have had any prior advice)
your accompt current with him ftood debited
in your books: In this cafe it muft therefore
be credited for all returns, whether in goods
or bills, but the Debtor varies according to
the following cafes:

Cafe

Cafe 1ft. For all returns in bills, whether your factor remits you bills at fight, or payable any time after date, or you draw upon him.

Rule. The entries will be the fame as their parallel cafes in proper Domeftic Trade; only that inftead of naming your factor fimply, as A. B. you fay A. B. my accompt current.

Cafe 2d. If your factor (by your order) fhips off goods for you, of which you received advice prior to the arrival of the fhip.

Rule. Voyage from ———— Debtor to A.B. my accompt current for coft and charges.

Cafe 3d. If your factor A. B. at *Amfterdam* (by your order) buys goods, and fhips them off for C. D. your factor at *Lifbon*, and advifes you thereof, by fending you a copy of the Invoice.

Rule. Voyage from *Amfterdam* to *Lifbon* Debtor to A. B. my accompt current for coft and charges.

Note. The entry is the fame as if he had bought the goods with his own money.

Cafe 4th. When your factor A. B. at *Amfterdam*, advifes you that (according to your order) he has fhipped off all, or part of your goods, (formerly confign'd to him) for your factor C. D. at *Lifbon*.

Rule. Voyage from *Amfterdam* to *Lifbon* Debtor to fundries, viz.

To A. B. at *Amfterdam*, my accompt of goods, for the fum the faid accompt ftood debited, and

To A. B. my accompt current, for charges paid in re-fhipping.

Note. The above cafe fourth fuppofes that you

you had received a prior advice from your factor A. B. at *Amsterdam*, acquainting you, that he had received your goods, but that on account of the markets being overstocked, there were little prospect of disposing of them to advantage, and therefore desired your further instructions; whereupon you gave him an order to ship all or part of the said goods off for your factor C. D. at *Lisbon*.

Case 5th. When goods arrive, of which you have had a prior advice of their being shipped for you.

Rule. Goods received *per* the ———— Debtor to sundries, viz.

To voyage from ———— for what the said voyage stood charged for, and
To cash for fresh charges paid here.

Case 6th. When goods arrive, of which you receive no advice prior to the arrival of the ship.

Rule. Goods received by the ———— Debto sundries, viz.

To A. B. my accompt current, for first cost and charges abroad, and
To cash for fresh charges paid here, as before.

Note 1st. The above fifth and sixth cases supposes the goods received to be all of one kind, as all sugars, all rum, &c. &c. but if the goods imported be of various kinds, then first discharge the voyage, or A. B. your accompt current, by making sundries Debtor to them, viz. The several kinds of goods for their respective costs and charges abroad: And then again debit each particular kind of goods, for their respective share of freight and other charges paid here.

Note

Note 2d. The foregoing firft, fecond, third, and fixth cafes in this problem, fuppofes that you had formerly received the accompt of fales from your factor, and that he had received payment of your goods, for the neat proceeds of which, A. B. my accompt current, ftood debited in your Ledger; upon which fuppofition the faid accompt current is credited in all the above-mentioned cafes. But if the advice prior to thofe of the firft, fecond, third, and fixth cafes, had been that the goods were fafe arrived, but none of them fold, or that they were even fold on credit, then (inftead of A. B. my accompt current) A. B. my accompt of goods, or A. B. my accompt on time, would have been credited. See the general rule in cafes of the fecond or fucceeding advices.

Note 3d. If any of the goods imported be of the fame kind with thofe which you before had by you, and for which accompts were already opened in your Ledger, as for inftance, fugars; yet notwithftanding that, open a frefh accompt, with this diftinction:
Sugars received by the ———— from ————
   Debtor.

By this method you will not only be able to judge from what markets you are beft fupplied with any of thofe particular commodities, but by adding the profits or loffes which appear in thofe refpective accompts together, you will then fee what you gained or loft upon the whole goods imported.

Cafe 7th. If you draw upon your factor A. B. payable to your factor C. D. or if your factor A. B. (by your order) remits a bill to your factor C. D.

Rule.

Rule. C. D. my accompt current Debtor to A. B. my accompt current.

Before I proceed further, I shall beg leave to point out one capital error, into which most of our writers on this subject have fallen, in making the Journal Entries of the above fifth and sixth cases. See Mr. *Mair*, *July* 9th and 10th.

According to his method, 1st. When the goods arrives, Voyage from *Jamaica* is charged Debtor to cash, for freight, duty, and other charges paid here.

2dly. He sells six barrels of his indigo upon the keys, for which he credits voyage from *Jamaica.*

3dly. He brings the remaining part of his goods into his warehouse, viz. five hogsheads of pimento, and five hogsheads of sugar, which he likewise charges Debtor to the said voyage, but only for their first cost, exclusive of all other charges paid on them, either by his factor abroad, or by himself here.

Now as the true intent and meaning of Double Entry is to shew what every particular article cost us, in order to direct us in the disposal of them, as well as to know exactly what we gain or lose by each, this method of Mr. *Mair's* can therefore in no measure answer the said end, but, on the contrary, only serve to mislead us: For if you look into the sugar and pimento accounts, you find the one only charged with 59 *l.* 17 *s.* and the other with 38 *l.* 7 *s.* 6 *d.* which (as I observed before) was only the prime cost, exclusive of any other charge either abroad or at home, which charges must have very considerably augment-

ed

ed the coſt of each; for ſuppoſing out of the
15*l*. 4*s*. 11*d*. charges abroad, and 97*l*, 12*s*.
paid here, 37 *l*. 16*s*. of it to belong to the ſix
barrels of indigo, (which is a large allowance,
being 1*s*. *per lb*.) there yet remains 75*l*. 0*s*.
11*d*. to be divided between the pimento and
ſugar; ſo that had he ſold thoſe two articles
together for 147*l*. 6*s*. 9*d*. it would have ap-
peared, by his method, that he had gained
49*l*. 2*s*. 3*d*. which is exactly 50 *per cent.*
whereas in reality he would have loſt 25*l*. 18*s*.
8*d*. this therefore (as I obſerved before) muſt
greatly miſlead the merchant; for, from a
ſeeming profit of 50 *per cent.* he is encou-
raged to continue importing thoſe goods, by
which he loſes very near 15*l*. A miſtake of no
leſs than 65 *per cent.* or thereabouts.

Again, if we look into his accompt of voyage from *Jamaica*, there it appears he has
loſt 34*l*. 1*s*. 11*d*. for it being charged Debtor
for the prime coſt and charges of the whole
goods abroad, as well as the whole charges
paid at home, and only credited by the pimento and ſugar at prime coſt, excluſive of all
other charges, there remains nothing to counterballance that difference, but the advanced
price which he ſold his indigo for, whereas
neither profit nor loſs ſhould have appear'd in
that accompt.

As to the indigo, he would find himſelf
greatly puzzled to know how, or in what manner, he had diſpoſed of it, (as he had opened
no accompt for it in his Ledger) except he
ſhould accidentally ſtumble upon the accompt
of voyage from *Jamaica*, or his memory ſhould
ſerve him ſo far as to recollect he had placed
it there, and even then he muſt ſearch through

all his Waſte-Book, to ſee what it coſt him a-
broad, and what charges he has paid on it
ſince, before he could tell whether he had
gained or loſt by it.

I ſhall now ſhew you how thoſe ſeveral accompts will ſtand, according to the rules I
have given for journalizing the afore-mentioned fifth and ſixth caſes.

1ſt. By charging the ſeveral articles imported Debtor to voyage from *Jamaica*, or to
A. B. your accompt current, for their reſpective firſt coſt and charges, as *per* invoice,
the voyage, or your factor's accompt current,
would then ſtand exactly ballanced; for there
can be neither profit or loſs upon the voyage
when the goods arrive ſaſe, no more than in
your factor's accompt current.

2dly. The ſeveral kinds of goods being a-
gain charged Debtor for their reſpective ſhares
of freight, duty, and other charges paid here,
their ſeveral accompts will then exhibit to you
the real ſum which every particular article
ſtands you in, and conſequently ſhew you what
you gain or loſe by each of them.

* * *

CHAP. II.

Debtor and Creditor applied in Factorage.

FACTORS, beſides a Waſte-Book, Journal, and Ledger, uſually keep two other
books, viz. an Invoice Book, and Book of
Sales. Into the firſt of thoſe they copy the
invoices of all their conſignments, to prevent
enumerating the ſeveral articles in the Waſte-
Book.

Book. A Sale-Book is not abfolutely neceffary, but may very well be difpenfed with, as it is the fame with your employer's accompt of goods in your Ledger, only narrated in a more full and minute manner. My bufinefs being therefore at prefent to fhew how factory accompts are managed in the Wafte-Book, Journal, and Ledger, I fhall proceed upon the fuppofition that neither of the two afore-mentioned books are kept.

PROBLEM FIRST.

Debtor and Creditor applied upon the receipt of goods.

Cafe 1ft. When you receive goods configned to you by your employer to fell for his accompt.

Rule. A. B. his accompt of goods *per* the ———— Debtor to cafh, for freight, cuftom, and other charges which you pay.

PROBLEM SECOND.

Debtor and Creditor applied in difpofing of your employer's goods.

Cafe 1ft. When you difpofe of all, or any part of your employer's goods.

Rule. Debtors to the fame as in proper domeftic trade, (according to the particular circumftance of fale) to A. B. his accompt of goods.

Cafe 2d. When all your employer's goods are difpofed of, then the faid accompt of goods muft be ballanced in this manner:

Rule. A. B. his accompt of goods Debtor to fundries, viz.

To profit and lofs for your commiffion.

E 2

To

To A. B. his accompt on time for the out-
standing debts.

To A. B. his accompt current for the employer's ready money in your hands.

Cafe 3d. When you receive payment for any
of your employer's goods formerly fold on
credit.

Rule. Cafh Debtor to the perfons of whom
received, the fame as if the goods had been
your own,

But if you are obliged to make any abatements, then

Sundries Debtors to the faid perfons, viz.

Cafh for the fum received, and

A. B. his accompt current for the fum abated.

Cafe 4th. When, after you have clofed your
employer's accompt of goods, and fent him
his accompt of fales, you pay perfons for wharf-
age, cartage, &c. &c.

Rule. The perfons to whom paid Debtors
to cafh, the fame as in proper trade; but if
they make you any abatement, this being your
employer's profit, not your own, charge

The perfons to whom paid Debtors to fundries, viz.

To cafh for the fum paid, and

To A. B. his accompt current for the fum a-
bated.

Note. For the very fame reafon A. B's accompt current is debited in cafe third, inftead
of profit and lofs, for the abatements you make.

Cafe 5th. When the debts are all paid in.

Rule. Ballance the accompt on time, by
charging it Debtor to your employer's accompt
current, for the fum of the debts now received,
and advife your employer thereof.

Cafe

Cafe 6th. When you cannot difpofe of your employer's goods to advantage, and thereupon (by his order) fhip them all off to another of his factors elfewhere.

Rule. A. B. his accompt of goods Debtor to cafh for charges on fhipping, and then clofe the faid accompt of goods, by making his accompt current Debtor to it for the ballance, and you have done with it; all future advices concerning them being fuppofed to be fent to to your employer.

Cafe 7th. But if your employer defires you to fhip off his goods for a factor of your own elfewhere.

Rule. The entry at fhipping the fame as in cafe third, making no more entries till you receive the accompt of fales, and then charge your factor at ———— his accompt current, or his accompt on time, (according to the circumftances of fale) Debtor to your employer's accompt of goods for neat proceeds; which two accompts are to be difcharged, the fame as in proper foreign trade, as returns are made you by him.

Cafe 8th. When your factor advifes you that the whole of your employer's goods are difpofed of, then ballance the faid accompt of goods in this manner:

Rule. A. B. his accompt of goods, Debtor to fundries, viz.

To profit and lofs for your commiffion.

To A. B. his accompt on time, for the ballance of the neat proceeds, not yet received from your factor, and

To A. B. his accompt current from what you have received.

Note

Note ıſt. When your factor has remitted you the whole of the neat proceeds, then ballance your employer's accompt on time as directed in caſe fifth.

Note 2d. According to this method your employer's accompt current will be credited immediately upon advice from your factor of the ſale of his goods, for the ballance of his accompt of goods; but as you are not obliged to make any remittances to your employer, till your factor has remitted you, you muſt therefore have recourſe to the credit ſide of your factor's accompt current, to ſee what money or bills you have received from him on your employer's accompt, and ſo much you are immediately accountable for, and no more.

Obſervation. Here I ſhall beg leave to make another remark on Mr. *Mair:* In making the Journal entry of caſe ſixth (if I underſtood him right) he has made a very groſs blunder. [See the latter part of his fourth note, page 49.] There he ſays (upon receiving advice from your factor of the ſales of your employer's goods) you ought to charge A. B's accompt current (meaning clearly from what follows) your employer's at ———— Debtor to ditto, his accompt of goods for the neat proceeds, and diſcharge A. B. his accompt current at ———— as returns are made to you by your factor. Here, it is plain, he ſubſtitutes one man's accompt for another, namely, the employer's for the factor's, ſo that your employer's accompt current, inſtead of ſhewing the true ſtate of affairs between your employer and you, exhibits only how matters ſtand betwixt you and your factor; then again he tells you, that

A.

A. B. his accompt current at —— muſt be
diſcharged as returns are made-you by your
factor; this circumſtance clearly implies that
by A. B's accompt current at——he means
your employer's : This therefore, being taken
for granted, it muſt be acknowledged, that
the ſaid accompt will exhibit the true ſtate of
affairs betwixt your factor and you, provided
nothing elſe was to come to the credit ſide of it
but the returns your factor makes you ; but Mr.
Mair ſeems to have forgot that your employer's accompt of goods remains yet unballanc-
ed, and that there ought to be ſome accompt
to ſhew how matters ſtand betwixt your employer and you.

Now, as your employer's accompt of goods
ſtood debited for all charges you were at on
receiving, re-ſhipping them, &c. and credited by
your employer's accompt current at ——
for the neat proceeds of the ſales, it would alſo
anſwer that purpoſe, and conſequently, ought
to be credited for all returns made to your
employer: But this would be a very ſtrange
way of proceeding, for who would ever think
of looking in the employer's accompt of goods
for that which ought to be found in his accompt current, namely, (as I before obſerved)
how matters ſtand betwixt your employer and
you. But even this method, cannot be what
Mr. *Mair* means ; for he ſays, you are to diſcharge A. B's (meaning ſtill your employer's
accompt current at ——) as returns are
made you by your factor; your employer's accompt of goods muſt therefore (as it ought)
be cloſed by making it Debtor to ſome other
accompt, and what other can it be made Debtor to, but your employer's accompt current

rent at ———? But this laſt ſtep totally coun-
teracts what we had before allowed the ſaid
accompt current to exhibit; for if it ſtood debited for the neat proceeds of ſales, as *per* advice from your factor, and now credited by
the difference between the debt and credit ſide
of your employer's accompt of goods, the
credit ſide will therefore be equal to the debt
ſide, except the charges which the afore-mentioned accompt of goods ſtood debited for, and
conſequently ſhew nothing but a maſs of con-
fuſion. I can therefore deviſe no method by
which one part of Mr. *Mair's* inſtructions can,
with reſpect to the ſaid caſe ſixth, be reconci-
led to another, but by ſuppoſing he opened an
accompt current with his employer at home,
diſtinct from his accompt current abroad, by
which he cloſed the accompt of goods: This,
perhaps, is ſuppoſing too much, but even
granting it to be ſo, it is at beſt but a very ir-
regular and confuſed method, as the one accompt might be eaſily miſtook for the other.

PROBLEM THIRD.

*Debtor and Creditor applied when you make re-
turns to your employer.*

Caſe 1ſt. In all caſes of returns of goods.
Rule. A. B. his accompt current Debtor to
ſundries, viz.
To caſh, if bought for ready money, and in
    all caſes for charges,
To accepter, if on bill.
To ſeller, if on truſt.
To goods, if your own, and
To profit and loſs, or commiſſion accompts
    for your commiſſion.

Caſe

Cafe 2d. In all cafes of returns in bills, whether you draw upon your employer or he draws upon you.

Rule. The Journal entry the fame as in proper trade, according to the feveral circumftances there enumerated, only inftead of mentioning your employer's name fimply, as A. B. you fay A. B. my accompt current.

✻✿✻✿✻✿✻✿✻✿✻✿✻✿✻✿✻✿✻✿✻✿✻✿✻

CHAP. III.

Of PARTNERSHIP or COMPANY.

THE accompt of the company's affairs may either be kept by one of the partners in his own books, along with the accompt of his own private bufinefs, or in feparate books allotted for that purpofe. The firft method is generally practifed in occafional or tranfient adventures, the latter is ufed by fixed companies, whofe trade is confiderable, or who have the profpect of dealing long that way.

Firft, I fhall fhew how the partner (who acts as the truftee for the company) keeps the company's accompts in his own books, along with the accompts of his own private bufinefs.

Secondly, I fhall explain the nature and ufe of the two accompts, which a partner (who does not act as truftee) has occafion for, refpecting his concerns in company.

Thirdly, I fhall teach the manner of keeping companies accompts in books which contain nothing elfe.

SECTION FIRST.

How the truſtee keeps the company's accompts in his own books.

A truſtee who keeps the company's accompts in his own books, has occaſion for the three Ledger accompts following, in which **A. B.** repreſents your partner's name.

Firſt, Goods in company with **A. B.**

This accompt is debited for the value of the goods bought into company, for all charges, and your commiſſion; it is credited as you diſpoſe of the goods in the ſame manner as if the goods were your own.

Secondly, **A. B.** his accompt in company.

This accompt is credited by your partner's in-puts, his ſhare of charges, and proportion of neat gains at the cloſing of the books; it is debited for his ſhare of neat proceeds, and his proportion of loſs, if any, when the company's accompts are finiſhed.

Thirdly, **A. B.** his accompt proper.

This is a perſonal accompt, which is debited and credited as ſuch for the mutual debts contracted, and payments made, betwixt you and partners.

Note. If the company deal in foreign trade, you, who act as truſtee, will have occaſion for other accompts, viz. Voyage in company, factor our accompt current, &c. all which are uſed the ſame way as their parallels in proper foreign trade.

Having thus deſcribed the accompts to be opened in the Ledger, by a truſtee, who keeps accompts for the company in his own books, I come in the next place to ſhew the application

tion of Debtor and Creditor in particular cafes.

PROBLEM FIRST.

Debtor and Creditor applied when goods are bought into company, according to the method generally taught.

In occafional adventures of this kind, it is not cuftomary to make up a certain capital to lodge in the truftee's hands, for the purpofe of buying goods, &c. but you·who act as manager, draw cafh out of the partners hands, juft as the emergency of affairs require.

Cafe 1ft. When you buy goods with ready money, of which your partners immediately pay down their refpective fhares of the purchafe, or you inftantly draw upon them for it, or when you buy your own fhare only, and your partners bring in each their particular fhare in goods, enter only once, viz.

Rule. Goods in company Debtor to fundries, viz.

To cafh for your own fhare, if bought for ready money, or to the feller, if on credit.

To each partner's accompt in company for their fhare.

Note 1ft. If your own fhare of goods brought into company were formerly entered in your books, then, inftead of cafh, or the feller, goods proper would be Creditor.

Cafe 2d. When you buy goods for ready money, on the company's accompt, of which your partners do not immediately pay down their refpective fhares, or any part of it, enter twice, viz.

F 2 *Rule*

Rule. Firſt, Goods in company Debtor to caſh, for the value.

Secondly, Each partner's accompt proper Debtor to his accompt in company, for his part of the purchaſe.

Caſe 3d. When you buy goods on credit, which is either from you, the truſtee, or from partner, or from a neutral perſon, enter twice, viz.

Rule. Firſt, Goods in company Debtor.

To goods proper, if bought of yourſelf, for the value of the goods.

To partner's accompt proper, if of a partner, for the value of the goods.

To ſeller, if of a neutral perſon, for the value of the goods.

Secondly, Each partner's accompt proper Debtor to his accompt in company, for his ſhare of the ſtock.

Note 2d. When you pay a neutral perſon for goods formerly bought on time, the entry will then be the ſame as in proper trade, according to the manner of payment, and there will be no ſecond entry; but, if he allow you diſcount, or make you any abatement, then you enter twice, viz.

Firſt, The perſon to whom paid Debtor to ſundries, viz.

To caſh, goods, bills, &c. for the value paid.

To goods in company, for the ſum abated, or diſcounted.

Secondly, Each partner's accompt in company Debtor to his accompt proper, for his ſhare of the ſum abated, or diſcounted.

Caſe 4th. If your partners ſhould lodge money

ney in your hands to buy goods, of which you do not make an immediate purchafe.

Rule. Cafh Debtor to fundries, viz.

To each partner's accompt proper, for the fum received of him, and no fecond entry till the goods are bought.

Cafe 5th When you buy the faid goods.

Rule. Firft, Goods in company Debtor to cafh, for value of the goods bought.

Secondly, Each partner's accompt proper Debtor to his accompt in company, for his fhare.

Note 3d. The above cafe fourth fuppofes, that either the quantity of goods to be bought were undetermined at the time your partners lodged the money in your hands, or that you were uncertain with refpect to the price they might be bought for; for if you had known thofe two particulars exactly, and your partners confequently paid in neither more nor lefs than their refpective fhares, then, inftead of your partners accompts proper, their accompts in company would have been credited, and there would have been no fecond entry when you bought the goods, the circumftances (in that cafe) being exactly the fame as in cafe firft, and the rule, of courfe, agreeable to it.

Hence you may obferve that a Double Entry is never neceffary but when your partners proper accompts are affected, which will always happen when they pay more or lefs than their refpective fhares. And although a great variety of other cafes might be fuppofed, yet I think thofe already given (if properly attended to) will prove fufficient to direct the learner's practice.

☞ But

☞ But, notwithftanding the rules laid down in the foregoing cafes for making the double Journal·Entry are according to the method generally taught, yet there are fome of them very improper, as your partners proper accompts will not (according to that manner of keeping them) exhibit truly what they ought, namely, the debt immediately due to, or by the partners, I fay immediately, becaufe nothing elfe ought to appear there but what is.

Perhaps you will fay, that I, as well as others, have defcribed it as a perfonal accompt, and therefore ought to exhibit the fame in common with fuch.

Indeed Mr. *Mair*, as well as other authors on the fubject, feems to have had the fame notion of it, and of courfe, moft of our teachers who implicitly follow their inftructions. But in moft cafes there is a very material difference between a partner's proper, or perfonal accompt, and that of a neutral perfon.

As for inftance: Suppofe you fell goods to a neutral perfon, at fix months credit; then, of courfe, the faid perfon will ftand debited in your Ledger for the value of the goods; but as the conditions of fale was fix months credit, you confequently have no right to the money before the expiration of that time, it being prefumed, that your profit was adequate to fuch credit; and if he even does not pay you for a confiderable time after the faid goods becomes due, yet you cannot by law recover any more than the original debt.

But a partner's accompt proper is very different; for the difference between the debt and credit fides of it, being what ready money the company has advanced for him, or he for
the

the company, in whofoever's favour, therefore, the ballance is found to be, they are intitled to intereft for it from the time fuch fum was advanced till the time it is paid; for it would be very unreafonable in one partner to expect a fhare of the profit, whilft the others advanced the money, as the partner· or partners who advanced it, might have lent out fuch fum to any other perfon at intereft, or employed it in any manner which they thought moft to their advantage.

Now, according to the preceding rules for making fome of the double Journal Entries, a partner's accompt proper can in no wife anfwer this end, as I fhall make clearly appear by the following inftances:

Firft, Let us fuppofe that you, the truftee, buy goods of a neutral perfon, for account of yourfelf, and A. B. your partner, at three months credit, to the amount of 300 *l*.

Here, (according to rule in cafe third) after having charged goods in company Debtor to the feller, you next, by a fecond entry, charge A. B. his accompt proper Debtor to ditto, his accompt in company for his half of the purchafe, which is 150 *l*.

Let us again fuppofe, that in a few days after you difpofe of all thofe goods for ready money, viz. for 340 *l*. Here, having firft charged cafh Debtor to goods in company with A. B. you again, by a fecond entry, charge A. B. his accompt in company Debtor to ditto, his accompt proper for his half of the fales, viz. 170 *l*.

Hence it will appear that by A. B's accompt proper, that you the truftee ftand only in-

debted

debted to him 20*l.* which is the fum the credit fide of the faid accompt is heavier then the debt fide; whereas, you in reality are immediately accountable to him for the whole 170*l.* for as you bought the goods at three months credit, he, as a partner, is intitled to the fame credit; and the goods being fold in a few days after for ready money, he is alfo directly intitled to his half of the fales.

Secondly, For another inftance, let us reverfe the above cafe, by fuppofing that you bought the goods with ready money, which you paid wholly yourfelf.

Here, (according to the rule in cafe fecond) after having firft charged goods in company Debtor to cafh, you next, by a fecond entry, charge A. B. his accompt proper Debtor to ditto, his accompt in company is one half, as before, viz. 150*l.*

We fhall next fuppofe you fold the faid goods in a few days, at three months credit.

And having firft charged the buyer Debtor to goods in company for the amount, we next, by a fecond entry, charge A. B. his accompt in company Debtor to ditto, to his accompt proper for his one half of the fales, which is 170*l.*

Note. In the firft inftance above the fecond entry in buying is wrong, and the fecond in felling right; and in the fecond inftance the reverfe.

It would then appear by your faid partner's accompt proper, that there was a ballance due to him from you of twenty pounds, which indeed would have been fo had the goods been fold for ready money; but as they were fold

at

at three months credit, you consequently are not accountable to him for his share of the sales, till you receive it from the person to whom you sold the goods: So that instead of you owing him 20*l.* as would appear by his accompt proper, he stands indebted to you 150*l.*

Hence it is evident, that a partner's accompt proper being immediately debited (in every circumstance of buying, except where he instantly pays down his own share) for his part of the goods bought, and credited under every circumstance of sale, that a very considerable ballance might appear against him, or in his favour, when in reality it may be the very reverse.

From what has been said, I think, there is scarce any person so stupid as not to perceive the impropriety of making the second Journal Entries as directed in the preceding cases, under the particular circumstances of buying, and selling, above recited, and such like; or any so obstinate, as not to acknowledge it: But allowing they do both, yet, perhaps they will say, it is easy to discover the true ballance.

This I grant, where there happens but to be a single entry on each side, but as every additional one renders it more perplext, it often becomes a matter of great difficulty: But besides, every personal accompt, when settled to any particular period, the accompt will of course, ballance to that time, so that you always know where to begin again, which will very seldom be the case with a partner's accompt proper kept in that manner; and therefore, every time you have occasion to ballance accompts between you, you will find it more and more intricate.

Others again, to remedy this inconvenience, make the fecond Journal Entry only when the goods are fold for ready money, but neglect it when they are fold on time; but neither does this mend the matter, for the very fame difficulties will arife here, which the firft inftance above clearly proves: But befides, the partner's accompts in company could not be properly clofed by this method.

I fhall alfo give one inftance of this; but firft, I fhall fhew you what the debt and credit fide of your partner's accompt in company contains.

The credit fide of your partner's accompt in company contains his fhare of all goods bought, and of charges, it is according to this method debited only for his fhare of what goods are fold for ready money, or his fhare of money paid you for goods formerly fold on credit, which fhare, he, your partner, does not immediately receive.

Now let us fuppofe the faid accompt to be credited for his fhare of goods bought into company 300*l.*

We fhall likewife fuppofe you, the truftee, fold the whole of thofe goods at fix months credit, before the expiration of which time, you have occafion to clofe your books.

The firft in company accompts to be ballanced, is that of goods in company. Now, this accompt ftanding debited for firft coft and charges of all goods bought, and credited for the whole fales, the difference therefore between the debt and credit fides of it, muft be the

the gain or lofs of the company on that particular article, we fhall therefore fuppofe the
gains to be 100*l*. confequently, in order to
ballance the accompt of goods in company,
you muft debit it, to your partner's accompt
in company, for his fhare of the gain, viz. 50*l*.
and alfo debit it to profit and lofs for your
own fhare, which is, alfo 50*l*.

Of courfe then, your partner's accompt in
in company, muft be credited by goods in
company, for his faid fhare of gain.

Now, as the goods were all fold on credit,
and not yet received for, there can therefore
(according to this laft method) be nothing
upon the debt fide of your partner's accompt
in company, and confequently muft be clofed
by ballance.

This method is therefore more abfurd than
the former, for the credit fide exhibits his
fhare of the profits, whilft it does not appear
by the debt fide, that the goods are yet fold.

But perhaps thofe who practice this method
will tell you, that they underftand how the
matter is themfelves, but this is not fufficient,
a merchant's books ought to be clear to every
body, at leaft to every good accomptant; and
therefore, to avoid confufion, (in cafe of
death, &c.) in whatever points he deviates
from common practice, he fhould write an
explanation of fuch at the beginning of his
book.

The method therefore I would recommend is, that which I have purfued in the fpe-
cimens of company accompts, given in this
work, with refpect to making the Double Entries, (when neceffary) and which, in the courfe
of my own practice, I have always found to be

the

the moſt clear and diſtinct. This is done by opening an accompt on time for every partner, beſides an accompt proper, and an accompt in company; which accompt on time, is made uſe of in the ſecond **Journal** Entries only (under particular circumſtances) inſtead of their accompt proper.

But in order that you may comprehend clearly the uſe and deſign of this method, it may not be improper to give you the conditions of agreement, uſually and indeed abſolutely neceſſary to be made between the parties, on the commencement of their partnerſhip, viz.

Firſt, If, when goods are bought for ready money, any one or more of the partners ſhould not immediately pay down his or their reſpective ſhare or ſhares, that the partner or partners who advances the ſame for him or them ſhall be intitled to intereſt for the ſame, at the rate of $5l.$ *per cent. per annum*, from the time ſuch ſum is advanced, till the repayment of it.

Secondly, If the goods for the company's accompt be bought of a partner on credit, for inſtance, at three months, and at the expiration of the ſaid time, the other partner or partners ſhould not pay him his or their reſpective ſhare or ſhares, that then it ſhall be deemed as ready money advanced, and bear intereſt at the above-mentioned rate, from the expiration of the ſaid three months, till the time ſuch ſum is diſcharged; and ſo in all caſes, where one partner advances money for another.

Theſe things being premiſed, I ſhall next proceed to ſhew in what particular caſes the
ſecond

fecond Journal Entry differ (according to this method) from thefe before given.

PROBLEM SECOND.

The way of making the fecond Journal Entries (when neceſſary) under particular circum-ſtances, inſtead of that ſhewn in problem firſt, and which method is purſued in the various ſpecimens of company accompts given in this work.

Caſe 1ft. The fame as the firft cafe in problem firft, and no fecond entry.

Caſe 2d. Both firft and fecond entries, alfo the fame with thofe in cafe fecond, problem firft.

Caſe 3d. Inftead of the firft and fecond entries in problem firft, make the following, viz.
Entry 1ft. Goods in company Debtor.
To goods proper, if bought of yourfelf, for the value of the goods.
To partner's accompt on time, if of a partner, for the value of the goods.
To feller, if of a neutral perfon, for the value of the goods.
Entry 2d. Each partner's accompt on time, Debtor to ditto, his accompt in company for his fhare.

Note 1ft. If, when the goods becomes due, each of you pay your refpective fhares, then the entry will be,
Seller, or partner's accompt on time Debtor to fundries, viz.
To cafh for your fhare.
To each partner's accompt on time, for his fhare.

Note

Note 2d. But if you, or any other partner
advance another partner's fhare for him, then
make the following two entries, viz.

Firft, Seller, or partner, his accompt on time
Debtor to fundries, viz.

To cafh for your own fhare, and partner's, if
    advanced by you.

To each partner (except him who did not pay)
    his accompt on time, for his own fhare, and

To the partner (who advances for another)
    his accompt proper, for the fum advanced.

Secondly, The partner (who did not pay)
his accompt proper Debtor to ditto, his accompt on time, for his fhare deficient.

Note 3d. If, when you pay either a neutral
perfon, or a partner, for goods formerly
bought on credit, (according to note firft in
this problem) and the feller fhould make you
any abatement, then enter twice, viz.

Firft, Seller, or partner's accompt on time,
Debtor to fundries, viz.

To cafh, for what you pay.

To each partner's accompt on time, for what
    he pays.

To goods in company, for the fum abated.

Secondly, Each partner's accompt in company Debtor to ditto, his accompt on time,
for his fhare of the abatement.

Note 4th. But if the payment be made according to note fecond, then enter thrice, viz.

Firft, Seller, or partner's accompt on time,
Debtor to fundries, viz.

To cafh, for what you pay on your own ac-
    compt, and partner's, if advanced by you.

To each partner (except him who did not pay)
    his accompt on time, for the fhare he pays.

To

To partner (who advances for another) his accompt proper, for the fum advanced.

To goods in company, for the fum abated.

Secondly, Each partner's accompt in company Debtor to ditto, his accompt on time, for his fhare of the abatement.

Thirdly, The partner (who did not pay) his accompt proper Debtor to ditto, his accompt on time, for his fhare deficient.

Cafe 4th. and 5th. The entries in both the fame as in problem firft.

Cafe 6th. If goods in company be damaged, deftroyed, or loft.

Here there are three varieties, in all of which enter fundries Debtor for the whole lofs, viz.

Each partner's accompt in company for his fhare, and

Profit and lofs for your own fhare, but the creditor varies according to the following circumftances:

Firft, If the goods be damaged or loft, whilft in your (the truftees) hands, then

To goods in company.

Secondly, If the goods be all, or part of them loft at fea, or in the company's factor's hands abroad, which he gives you an account of in his firft advice, then

To voyage to ———— in company.

Thirdly, If the factor's firft advice was, that the goods were fafe arrived and in good condition, and afterwards advife you that they are deftroyed or loft, then

To Factor our accompt of goods.

Cafe 7th. If after the factor has advifed you that he has fold all, or part of the company's goods on credit, he fhould, by another advice, inform

inform you that the perſon to whom he ſold them had failed, in this, or any other caſe of the ſame kind, enter

Sundries Debtors to factor, our accompt current, (or to the buyer, if ſold at home) viz.
Each partner's accompt on time, for his ſhare of the loſs.
Profit and loſs for your own ſhare.

Obſervation. In making the Journal Entry of caſe ſixth in this problem, Mr. *Mair* has committed a very palpable error, for without having reſpect to the ſeveral circumſtances which I have there taken notice of, in which the creditor varies, he has only given one rule for all, viz. Each partner's proper accompt Debtor to goods in company, for his reſpective ſhare of the loſs, and profit and loſs for your own ſhare.

Now, allowing ſuch loſs or damage to have happened, whilſt the goods remained (unſold) under the care of the partner's truſtee, (for otherwiſe, goods in company could not have been the Creditor) yet even in this caſe, he has miſtaken the Debtors, which ought to have been each partner's accompt in company, inſtead of his accompt proper.

In order to ſet this in as clear a light as poſſible, let us ſuppoſe, that of the goods bought into company, every partner immediately paid his own ſhare of the purchaſe : Here, according to the firſt caſe in both this and problem firſt, goods in company ſtand debited in your Ledger to ſundries, viz. To each partner's accompt in company, for his reſpective ſhare, and of courſe, each partner's accompt in company, credited by goods in company for the ſame.

In

In this cafe, there is nothing upon either the debt or credit fide of their proper accompts.

Let us next fuppofe, that (whilft thofe feveral accompts ftand in the above-mentioned fituation) the goods fhould be all loft or deftroyed.

In this cafe, it is plain that goods in company muft be credited by fomething for the fum it ftood debited for before, in order to clofe the faid accompt; but why each partner's proper accompt fhould be debited, is a myftery which Mr. *Mair* has not thought fit to reveal to us.

For if we now review the feveral accompts relative to the company (according to the above method) we fhall find they ftand thus: The accompt of goods in company will ftand ballanced, each partner's accompt proper being debited to the faid accompt of goods in company, (and nothing being on the credit fide) it would there appear that each partner owed you, the truftee, fo much money, whilft their accompts in company have not a fingle article on the debt fide of them. Now, admitting the goods loft to be the only article in which the faid partners were concerned with you in, and at purchafing of which they paid each their refpective fhares, in that cafe, it is therefore impoffible the partners can be in your debt; and befides, your partners accompts in company (which now fhould ftand clofed) yet remains open, without any other means left to ballance the fame, except making each of them Debtor to their accompts proper for the ballance, which is a round about way of going to work, and might be done at once, by making each partner's accompt in company Debtor to goods in company for his respective share of the loss.

Had the goods been sold either by you, the trustee, or by the company's factor abroad, on credit, and afterwards the person to whom they were sold had failed, then indeed Mr. *Mair* would have been right with respect to the Debtors, viz. each partner's accompt proper, but the Creditor (even in that case) would still have been wrong.

For, according to Mr. *Mair*'s method of making the second Journal Entry, in all cases of sales, whether for ready money or on credit, he immediately debits each partner's accompt in company to ditto, his accompt proper, for his share of the sales; and consequently (if a loss should happen afterwards, by the failure of the person to whom they were sold) each partner's accompt proper would be debited, not to goods in company, but to the person who failed, if sold by you, the trustee at home, or to factor's accompt current, if sold by him abroad.

There is therefore no case of loss which could possibly happen, in which Mr. *Mair*'s rule for journalizing case sixth will hold good with respect to both Debtor and Creditor, which he himself would have proved had he reduced this rule of his to practice, by introducing a case similar to it, which he has not done in the whole course of his work.

Note 5th. I shall also journalize and post one company accompt (according to Mr. *Mair*'s method and others, of making the second Journal Entry in some particular cases) in a place of this work apart from the rest, by which

which the learner will fee hów clear, according to my method, and how perplex'd, according to theirs, every partner's proper accompt will appear.

I might next proceed to fhew the application of Debtor and Creditor when goods in company are difpofed of: In payments betwixt you, the truftee, and partners, or betwixt one partner and another: In fhipping off goods in company: In receiving advices or returns from the company's factor, &c. &c. But as all thofe things may be eafily gathered from what has been already fhewn, it would only ferve to puzzle and perplex the young beginner; I therefore think it better to give an explanation of every entry immediately below it, and at the fame time refer him to fuch of thofe cafes already given, which it is either fimilar to, or the reverfe of.

SECTION SECOND.

How a partner keeps the accompts he has occafion for.

A merchant, concerned as a partner in company, muft keep the two Ledger accompts following, in which obferve, that A. B. reprefents the manager or truftee's name.

Firft, A. B. my accompt in company: This accompt is made Debtor for your inputs, and proportion of all charges, and credited for your fhare of neat proceeds.

Second, A. B. my accompt proper: This is a perfonal accompt, being charged and difcharged as fuch, for the mutual debts and payments betwixt you and the truftee.

Having

Having told you what the debt and credit fide of each of thofe two accompts contains, the particular application of Debtor and Creditor, in every cafe which can poffibly happen, will be eafily underftood, and therefore no further explanation I think is neceffary, befides what you will find at the bottom of every Journal Entry.

SECTION THIRD.

How company accompts are kept by themfelves in books allotted for that purpofe.

In large and fixed companies the capital is generally determined, of which every partner pays into the hands of the manager his proportion, according to the particular fhare which he holds in company.

In this cafe you will have occafion to open the fame accompts in your **Ledger** as in proper trade, with this difference only, that the diftinctive adjection in company is added to the title as ftock in company, cafh in company, profit and lofs in company, broad cloth in company, ballance in company, &c. &c. &c. in fhort, the books are kept in all refpects (and ballanced) the very fame way as in proper trade, provided your partners and you agree to continue your profits as an addition to your capital.

But if you (at the years end, or at the clofing of your books) refolve to withdraw each your fhare of the profit, then, inftead of clofing your profit and lofs accompt by ftock; (as hereafter directed in ballancing the accompts in proper trade) you muft open an accompt proper for each of your partners, as alfo for yourfelf, yourself, and when you have added up the debt and credit fide of your profit and lofs accompt, and found the difference, divide the faid difference according to your feveral fhares, and if the credit fide be heavieft, ballance it, by making the faid accompt Debtor to each of your proper accompts for your refpective fhares of the profit, and at the fame time give each of your proper accompts credit by profit and lofs in company; and when each of you is paid your fhare, make your accompts proper Debtor to cafh in company.

But if you would have every accompt to ftand ballanced in the old books, then you muft take up your fhares of the profits before you ballance the cafh in company, and clofe your profit and lofs accompt, by making it Debtor to cafh for each of your fhares of the profit received.

This method of keeping company accompts will appear fo clear and eafy to thofe who are thoroughly accquainted with the accompts of proper trade, that I think it needs no examples to illuftrate it; but if any of my readers fhould be difpleafed with the fimplicity of the above method, or are fond of difficulties, I refer fuch to Mr. *Mair*'s inftructions for keeping company accompts in feparate books; there he fuppofes a large and fixed company to commence bufinefs, without any eftablifhed fund or capital, which is now the cafe, and confequently has fhewed us the fame thing under two diftinct heads, or rather has made two diftinct heads of the fame thing; for if there be no real capital advanced, in what material circumftance can the books of a fixed company differ from thofe which he has defcribed

scribed under the head of a partner truftee, keeping the company's affairs in his own books, along with his own private bufinefs? None, he himfelf confeffes, except that the partner truftee in filling up the company's books, muft remember to do for himfelf the fame as he does for the reft of the partners: That, I think, would have occured to any perfon of common fenfe, or if he thought it at all neceffary to have been taken notice of, it might have been fignified in a note at the end of the former,

But to give this laft method of his, at leaft, an air of diftinction from the other, he tells us, that a ftock accompt (in large and fixed companies) is neceffary, but for what purpofe (where there is no joint ftock made up, no debts owing to, or due from the company) I cannot conceive, except it be to give occafion for a triple Journal entry, where even a double one was fuperfluous.

C H A P. IV.

Containing rules for pofting from the Journal to the Ledger, with the way of tranfpofing accompts.

First, Turn to the index, and fee whether the Debtor of the Journal poft be written there, if not, infert it under its proper letter, with the number of the folio to which it is carried.

Secondly, Turn to the faid folio, and at the head of the fpace allotted for the accompt,

compt, write the title in a large text hand, making it Debtor on the left fide of the folio, and Creditor on the right.

Thirdly, Having firft wrote the date in the column on the left hand margin, begin the poft with the word, *To*, and then write the name of the perfon or thing to be credited, and compleat the entry in one line, by giving a fhort hint of the nature and terms of the tranfaction, carrying the fum to the money columns, and infert the quantity, if it be an accompt of goods, &c. in the inner columns, and the figure in the folio column, refering to the folio where the faid Creditor ftands.

Fourthly, Turn next to the Creditor of the Journal poft, and proceed in the fame manner with it, both in the index and Ledger, with this difference only, that the entry is to be made upon the credit fide, and the word *By* be prefixed to it.

Note. If there be fundry Creditors to one Debtor, then immediately after the word *To*, on the Debtor fide, (inftead of the names of the feveral perfons, or to things to be credited) you write fundries as *per* Journal, and neglect the refering figures in the folio column; and in the fame manner after the word *By* on the Creditor fide, when there are fundry Debtors to one Creditor.

Fifthly, The Ledger poft being finifhed, return to your Journal, and in the margin, mark the folio when fuch Debtor and Creditor ftands in the Ledger, putting the Debtor folio above, and the Creditor below, with a fmall line drawn between them thus, ⅟ to fignify that fuch Journal entry is pofted to the Ledger: Thofe folio figures likewife ferve as

one

one index to the Ledger, and are of great ufe in examining the books.

SECTION FIRST.

How to tranfpofe an accompt from one folio of the Ledger to another.

When the fpace allotted for an accompt proves too little, the accompt muft be tranf- pofed to a new fpace, which (if a perfonal accompt , or fuch as have no inner columns) is done in this manner:

Firft, Add up both the Debtor and Creditor fide of the accompt; if the Debtor fide be heavieft, then ballance it, by charging the faid accompt Debtor to the new accompt for the difference; and confequently, the new accompt muft be credited by the old; infert- ing in the folio column of the new accompt, the number of the folio where the old ac- compt ftands, and in the old accompt folio column, the number of the new, and exactly the reverfe when the Debtor fide of the old accompt is heavieft.

But if it be an accompt of goods, &c. which have inner columns, then the beft way is, after adding up both fides of the accompt, to mark the faid accompt Debtor to the new for the total of the Creditor fide; and again, Creditor by the new, for the whole amount of the Debtor fide; by this means the old ac- compt will be exactly ballanced, and the new accompt will then exhibit on the Debtor and Creditor fide, the fame fums and quantity that the old one did before it was tranfpofed.

CHAP.

C H A P. V.

HAving fhewn you under the refpective Ledger accompts of proper domeftic trade, what the debt and credit of fuch accompts contains, and alfo how to ballance the fame, I fhall now proceed to fhew under their proper heads, what the debt and credit fides of the feveral accompts of factorage, proper foreign trade, domeftic company accompts, and company foreign trade contain, and likewife how the fame are to be ballanced.

S E C T I O N F I R S T.
Of Factorage Accompts.

1ft. A. B. or employer, his accompt of goods.

This accompt is debited for all charges paid on your employer's goods, and your commiffion: It is credited for the neat proceeds of the fales.

This accompt is always clofed when you have finifhed the fales, and advifed your employer thereof; in performing of which there are three varieties, viz.

Var. 1ft. When the whole remains in your hands undifpofed of at the time when you generally ballance your books.

Rule. Clofe the faid accompt, by crediting it by ballance for the amount of the debt fide.

Var. 2d. When only part are fold at the faid time.

Rule. Clofe it then by a double ballance, viz. make it Debtor to ballance for the a-

mount of the credit fide, and Creditor by ballance for the amount of the debt fide.

Var. 3d. When all are fold, and you have
advifed your employer thereof.

Rule. After firft charging it **Debtor** for
your commiffion, then clofe the faid accompt,
by making it **Debtor** to your employer's accompt current for the neat proceeds.

2d. **A. B.** or employer, his accompt current.

This accompt is debited for all bills your
employer draws upon you, for all fums paid
on his accompt, or remitted by you to him,
for goods fent him by his order, and, in fhort,
for all kind of returns whatfoever: It is credited by his accompt of goods for neat proceeds of fales, for all bills you draw on him,
and all remittances he makes to you, whether in bills or goods, by your order, and for
all money which he pays on your accompt.

This accompt is clofed by making it **Debtor** to, or **Creditor** by ballance for the difference.

SECTION SECOND.
Of Proper Foreign Trade.

1ft. Voyage to ————

This accompt is debited for firft coft and
charges of all goods exported: It is credited
under the feveral cafes of the firft advice, as
follows:

By neat proceeds of what are fold, viz. for
all returns, whether in bills, goods, or money,
for what part remains unremitted, and for
what goods continue in your factor's hands
undifpofed of at firft coft and charges.

In

In ballancing this accompt under every circumſtance which can poſſibly happen, there
are but two varieties.

Var. 1ſt. When you have received no advice of the arrival of the ſhip.

Rule. Cloſe the ſaid accompt by crediting
it by ballance for the amount of the debt ſide.

Var. 2d. Under every circumſtance of the
firſt advice (except that the goods are ſafe
arrived, but none of them diſpoſed of, in
which caſe this accompt would ſtand already
ballanced).

Rule. Then it is cloſed by charging it Debtor to, or Creditor by profit and loſs for the
difference of the two ſides.

N. B. If your employer's accompt of goods
ſtood formerly debited for all or any part of
the outward cargo, and you have ſince received advice from your factor that all or
part of them are ſold, then, before you cloſe
this accompt, firſt cloſe that of your employer's accompt of goods, as hereafter directed,
and then ballance the voyage accompt, according to the method ſhewn above. By this
method (if the whole are ſold which his accompt of goods ſtood charged with) the whole
profit or loſs will appear under the outward
voyage accompt; and if part of the afore-
mentioned goods are only ſold, the profit or
loſs will then only appear in two accompts,
viz. part under the voyage accompt in your
old books, and part under factor your accompt of goods in your new: Whereas, according to Mr. *Mair's* method, in the latter
caſe, part of the profit or loſs would come under the two accompts afore-mentioned, and
part under factor your accompt of goods in

I 2   the

the old books, except he clofed the factor's accompt of goods by a double ballance.

2d. Factor my accompt of goods.

This accompt is debited for firft coft and charges of goods which remain'd in your factor's hands on your firft advice: It is credited on any future advice for the neat proceeds of what part of them are fold.

In ballancing this accompt there are three varieties.

Var. 1ft. When none are fold.

Rule. Clofe the faid accompt by crediting it by ballance for the amount of the debt fide.

Var. 2d. When all are fold, and the outward voyage accompt ftill remains open.

Rule. Charge it Debtor to, or Creditor by the voyage accompt for the difference of the two fides, as obferved in the note under variety fecond, in fhewing how to ballance the faid voyage accompt.

Var. 3d. When only part of them are fold.

Rule. Firft give the faid accompt credit by ballance for what part remains unfold at firft coft and charges, and then make it Debtor to, or Creditor by voyage accompt for the difference of the two fides, and then clofe the faid voyage accompt as before directed.

3d. A. B. or factor, my accompt on time.

This accompt is debited for the amount of what goods of yours your factor has fold on credit: It is credited when he advifes you that he has received payment of the fame, and clofed by giving it credit for what remains unpaid.

4th.

4th. **A. B.** or factor, my accompt current.

This accompt is debited for neat proceeds of all goods, either immediately sold for ready money, or for those formerly sold on credit, which he has received payment for, (except remitted with the advice of the receipt of such money, either in goods, bills, or cash) as also for all bills drawn by him on you, or remittances made by you to him: It is credited by all bills you draw on him, or value of goods sent you by your order, and for every disbursment on your account.

This accompt is also closed by charging it Debtor to, or Creditor by ballance for the difference.

5th. **Voyage from** ———

This accompt is debited for all returns in goods shipped for you by your order, the creditor or creditors depending upon the circumstances of the advice, whether the first, second, third, &c. It is credited by the goods when received, which accompt will then close of itself; but if nothing appears upon the credit side, (which will be the case if the ship is not arrived) then it is closed by crediting the said accompt by ballance.

SECTION THIRD.

Of Domestic Company Accompts.

Where you act as trustee, and keep the accompts along with those of your own private trade.

1st. **Goods in company.**

This accompt is debited for first cost and charges of the goods bought into company: It is credited for the sales.

This

This is the firſt to be cloſed in company accompts, in performing of which there are four
varieties.

Var. 1ſt. When none are ſold, and your
partners agree to let them remain in your
hands till diſpoſed of.

Rule. Cloſe the ſaid accompt by crediting it
by ballance for the amount of the debt ſide.

Var. 2d. When none are ſold, and the partners agree to divide the goods amongſt them,
according to their reſpective ſhares which they
hold in company.

Rule. Then this accompt is to be cloſed by
crediting it by each partner's accompt in company for his reſpective ſhare of firſt coſt and
charges, and by ballance for your own ſhare.

Var. 3d. When all are ſold.

Rule. Make the ſaid accompt of goods in
company Debtor to, or Creditor by each partner's accompt in company for his ſhare of the
gain or loſs, and to or by profit and loſs for
your own ſhare.

Var. 4th. When only part are ſold, and the
remaining part continued in your hands till
diſpoſed of.

Rule. In this caſe it is beſt to cloſe it by a
double ballance, making it Debtor to ballance
for the amount of the credit ſide, and Creditor by ballance for the amount of the debt
ſide.

2d. Partner, or A. B. his accompt in company.

This accompt is credited for his ſhare of
firſt coſt and charges, and debited for his
ſhare of ſales.

The ballancing of this accompt depends
upon

upon the firſt and fourth variety, ſhewn in ballancing the accompt of goods in company.

Var. 1ſt. Cloſe this accompt by making it Debtor to ballance for the amount of the Creditor ſide.

Var. 4th. Cloſe it by a double ballance, as before directed.

Note. According to the ſecond and third variety of cloſing the accompt of goods in company, your partner's accompt in company will ſtand already evened.

Obſervation. In ballancing the accompts of goods in company, and partner his accompt in company, Mr. *Mair* has ſuppoſed that the goods were either all or none of them diſpoſed of before the time which you generally ballance the accompts of your own private trade, and in the latter caſe, at that period your partners and you agree to divide the goods amongſt you, which is very ſeldom done; but I think (if I remember right) that he has not ſhewn how the partners account in company, and goods in company are to be ballanced, when part of the goods remain undiſpoſed of at the afore-mentioned period, ſo as to be carried to your new books, and there appear clear and diſtinct.

3d. Partner, or A. B. his accompt of time. This accompt is debited for his ſhare of goods bought on credit: It is credited (when the payment of the ſaid goods becomes due) according to the particular circumſtance, and alſo for his ſhare of all goods ſold on credit.

If this accompt does not ſtand evened of itſelf, at the time you cloſe the accompts of your own private trade, and there ſhould appear ſomething on both ſides of the accompt, then

then clofe it by a double ballance, giving the
faid accompt credit for the particular fums of
the debt fide, and making it Debtor for the
particulars of the credit fide, mentioning the
time the faid refpective fum on each fide becomes due; but if there appears nothing on
one of the fides, it is to be clofed by a fingle
ballance.

4th. Partner, or A. B. his accompt proper.

This accompt is debited for your partner's
fhare of all goods bought for ready money,
and alfo for his fhare of thofe bought on credit, when payment becomes due, in either of
which cafes he did not immediately pay down
his refpective fhare; as alfo for intereft of fuch
fums, from the time of this accompt being
charged with them, till the time the fame is
difcharged: It is credited by his fhare of all
goods fold for ready money, (or thofe fold on
credit when payment is made) and he does
not immediately at the faid time receive his
refpective fhare, and alfo for the payment of
fuch fums as this accompt ftands charged with
on the Debtor fide.

SECTION FOURTH.
Of Foreign Trade in Company.

Where you act as truftee, and keep company accompts in the fame books with thofe
of your own private trade.

1ft. Voyage to ——— in company, factor
(or A. B.) our accompt of goods, ditto our
accompt of time, ditto our accompt current,
and voyage from ——— in company, contain the fame on both debt and credit fides,
as their fimilar accompts do in proper foreign
trade, and are ballanced in all refpects the
fame,

fame, except voyage to ——— in company,
and factor (or A. B.) our accompt in company, which are to be ballanced the fame as
goods in company are in domeftic company
accompts, according to the feveral varieties
there fhewn.

I have been the more full and explicit in
fhewing you what the debt and credit fides
contain in the feveral accompts in foreign and
domeftic company accompts, as I found it
impoffible to give examples of each, in the
courfe of this work, under the various circumftances which each will admit of; but thofe
inftructions properly attended to, I hope the
reader will find himfelf at no great lofs to ma-
nage the faid accompts, in all the cafes which
can poffibly happen.

I fhall now proceed to fhew you how the
general ballance is performed, in order finally
to clofe the old books, and from which to
form an inventory for opening the new.

SECTION FIFTH.

Shewing how the general ballance is performed,
in order finally to fhut the old books.

Having already ballanced every particular
accompt in your Ledger, as before directed,
except *Profit and Lofs*, *Stock*, and *Ballance*,
which till now are left open, take two loofe
fheets of paper, ruled the fame as your Ledger; on one write *Profit and Lofs Debtor, Contra Creditor;* and on the other, *Ballance Debtor, Contra Creditor;* then beginning with the
firft accompt in your Ledger, collect all the
profit or lofs, which you find in every accompt
throughout the whole, which have no date,

into the firft of thofe fheets, (except Stock accompt, the Profit and Lofs accompt, which yet remain open) placing 'thofe you find on the debt fide to the credit fide of the faid loofe fheet, and thofe you find on the credit fide in your books to that of the debt fide : As for inftance, in the accompt of *Yorkſhire Planes*, folio 8; there you fee Yorkſhire Planes is there Debtor to profit and lofs 10*l*. 18*s*. 2*d*. fo that oh the credit fide of the loofe fheet, you muft write, *By Yorkſhire Planes*, 10*l*. 18*s*. 2*d*. when you have collected the whole of your profit or lofs, write the fame into the fame accompt in your Ledger, viz. the articles on the debt fide of your loofe fheet on the debt fide in your Ledger, and thofe on the credit fide on your fheet to the credit fide in your Ledger. Then take your other loofe fheet, and collect all the ballance in the fame manner, which when you have done, open an accompt of ballance in your Ledger, into which copy the debt and credit fide of the faid ballance fheet.   Then

1ft. Begin with the firft of thofe three accompts, viz. Profit and lofs, and having added up the debt and credit fides of the faid accompt feparately, upon a piece of loofe paper or flate, and found the difference, (by fubtracting the one from the other) write on the deficient fide, *To* or *By Stock*, inferting the faid difference in the money columns, and then caft up each fide in the book, which you will then find equal.

2dly. Turn next to the Stock accompt, and on the contrary fide to that where you juft had wrote in the ballance accompt, viz. if on the credit fide of the ballance accompt, then on the debt fide of this, or if on the debt
fide

fide of the ballance accompt, then on the credit fide of this, write *To* or *By Ballance*, inferting the faid difference of the ballance accompt in the money columns: Add then up each fide of the ftock accompt feparately, upon a piece of paper, and having found the difference, write on the different fide, *To* or *By Ballance* for the neat proceeds of my eftate, inferting the faid difference, which two fides being then added up in the book, they will alfo be found equal.

Laftly. Turn to your Ballance accompt, and on the contrary fide of that where you wrote laft in your ftock accompt, write *To* or *By Stock* for the neat of my eftate, inferting the fum which you laft wrote in your ftock accompt; and if then, upon adding up the two fides of the ballance accompt, they are even, your books are all right, if not, they are wrong.

You have now been fhewn how the general ballance is performed, but as the reafon of thofe three accompts clofing in this manner, one by another, may not appear quite fo evident, I think it neceffary to give you the following explanation; and in order that I may be as clear and intelligible as poffible, it will be neceffary to note particularly what the debt and credit fides of each of thofe three accompts contain, and alfo what the difference of each of them are.

ift. The Stock accompt exhibits on the credit fide the whole of your effects in money, goods, and debts due from others to you : The debt fide fhews the debts due from you to others.

K 2

The

The difference therefore between thofe two fides is the neat of what you were then worth.

2dly. The Ballance accompt on the debt fide fhews the whole of your effects in money, goods, and debts, at this time : And the credit fide is an exact account of the debts due from you to others.

3dly. Your Profit and Lofs accompt contains on the credit fide your particular profits on the feveral articles fold, legacies left you, wagers won, intereft on money lent, &c. The debt fide is, in like manner, a particular account of your feveral loffes.

The difference therefore between thofe two fides is your neat gain or lofs, which fum muft be exactly equal to the difference between the neat of your flock accompt, when fubtracted from the neat of your ballance accompt.

The neat therefore of your gain or lofs being carried to your flock accompt, viz. to the credit fide, if gain, or to the debt fide, if lofs, the difference then between thefe two fides being carried to the deficient fide of your ballance accompt, the debt and credit fides of the latter muft of courfe come even: For it is felf-evident, that the neat of what you was worth when you begun trade, (which was the difference of your flock accompt) increafed by adding the neat of your gain to it, or diminifhed by fubtracting the neat of your lofs from it, will then be equal to your prefent neat worth, which is the difference between the debt and credit fide of your ballance accompt; confequently then, fuch fum or difference being carried to the deficient fide of your ballance accompt, the two fides of the said

said accompt will then be equal, and finally close the whole.

Or, in brief, thus: The whole of your stock (which is the credit side of the said accompt) when you begun trade, your neat gain, (which is the difference of your profit and loss accompt) and the debts you now owe, (which is the credit side of your ballance accompt) being all added together, the sum will be equal to the sum of the debt you owed when you begun trade, (which is the debt side of your stock accompt) and your present stock, (which is the debt side of your ballance accompt) and on the contrary when you lose by trade. Then the debts you owed when you begun trade, your neat loss, together with your present stock, will be equal to your stock when you began trade, and the debts you now owe.

✦✖✦✖✦✖✦✖✦✖✦✖✦✖✦✖✦✖✦✖✦✖✦✖

CHAP. VI.

Of examining the Ledger, in order to discover the errors, (if any) and to shew how the same are to be corrected.

THIS necessary part of the business, I would recommend to you to perform by piecemeal, at your leisure hours, and to be thoroughly finished before you ballance a single accompt, by which means it will be much more easy, and be corrected with far less trouble, than when it is put off till the general ballance, when all the accompts are cast up and closed.

The most common errors are the following:
1st.

1ft. When you charge any one accompt Debtor, and omit crediting one or more accompts at the fame time for the value.

This accompt is corrected by only crediting the accompt or accompts fo omitted: And the contrary, when you credit any accompt, and omit charging fome one or more accompts Debtor at the fame time for the faid value.

2dly. When you poft to the debt fide inftead of the credit, or to the credit fide inftead of the debt.

This error is corrected by firft writing on the contrary fide, *To* or *By Error*, which counterballances the wrong entry on the other fide, and then charge it right, by pofting it on the fame fide on which you wrote the error.

3dly. When you happen to poft any thing to a wrong accompt.

Correct this by difcharging the wrong poft on the contrary fide, faying *To* or *By Error*, as before, and then turn to the accompt where it had been omitted, and poft it there.

4thly. When you enter different fums on the debt and credit fides of the refpective accompts you poft to.

Firft difcharge the whole of the wrong fum, by writing *To* or *By Error*, as before directed, and then charge the fum as it ought to be, on the fame fide where the wrong fum ftands.

SECTION FIRST.

When you examine your Ledger, begin with the firft article on the debt fide of the firft accompt in it, and obferving where its correfpondent credit ftands, (which you will
know

know by the referring figure in the folio column) turn to it, and see if it be right posted;
if it is, then opposite to the referring figure in
the said folio column, in both the Debtor and
Creditor, make a mark, thus, ✓ to signify
they are both examined.; if it be wrong, then
correct it as before directed.

Proceed then to the second article on the
debt side of the first accompt in your Ledger,
and examine it in like manner; when you have
finished the debt side, then go on with the
credit side of the same accompt, in the same
manner, and so on to the next accompt, going regularly through your Ledger till the
whole is finished.

Note. When you come to any accompt
which is debited to, or credited by, sundries,
(in which case there are no referring figures
in the folio columns, then turn to the same
date in your Journal, and finding (by the referring figures in the margin, opposite to the
sundry accompts debited or credited) where
the said accompts stand in your Ledger, turn
to the said accompt, and see if they are debited or credited for their respective sums, and
if the sum of the whole credits be equal to the
debt, or the sum of the whole Debtors be e-
qual to the credit, and, if right, mark them
all off, as before, thus, ✓ and so proceed, pass-
ing over those you find mark'd, as they have
been already examined, and taking notice
where you leave off, that you may know
where to begin again when you have another
opportunity.

When you have gone through the whole in
this manner, and find, when you come to the
general ballance, that the books will not close,
which

(which you fhould make upon loofe paper, and is commonly called a trial ballance) then you are fure the miftake lies either in cafting up the debt or credit fide of fome of the accompts, or that you have fubtracted wrong in finding the difference; when this is the cafe, you muft carefully examine the particular ballances through your Ledger, but of this you ought to be particularly careful, as it will then be very difficult to correct them without fcratching out, a thing cautioufly to be avoided in merchants books, efpecially in the Ledger.

CHAP. VII.

Obfervations with refpect to the forms in which the Wafte-Book, Journal, and Ledger, are to be wrote.

SECTION FIRST.

Of the WASTE-BOOK.

THE Wafte-Book is wrote in plain fimple language, with every circumftance of date, conditions, and amount of the tranfaction, the firft word of which muft always be wrote larger than the reft, as for inftance, Bought, Sold, Bartered, Paid, Received, &c. and each article (when there are more than one) to begin a new line, and their refpective amounts to be placed regularly under one another, fhort of the money columns, and the total fum to be carried into the money columns. See *December* 5th.

The

The various conditions to be done in the same manner. See *December* 20th.

SECTION SECOND.
Of the JOURNAL.

1ft. The Journal Entry, where there is but one Debtor and one Creditor, muft be always contained in one line, which muft be in a pretty large hand, and the amount immediately to follow the end of the faid line, on the inner fide of the money columns, and then a fhort reafon given in fmall hand for the faid entry, as full as you poffibly can, and in as few words, and then the fum put into the money columns. See *Nov.* 3d.

But what you find in fmaller type (after the word *Reafon* or *Obfervation*) at the bottom of each Journal Entry, is only in order to explain it more fully to the learner, but muft be omitted in real bufinefs.

2dly. When there are fundry Debtors to one Creditor, then the Creditor is only mentioned in the firft line, and the feveral Debtors are comprehended under the general head of fundries, but particularized in the following lines, each of which muft alfo be wrote in large hand, and the reafon then given in the fame line where the firft Debtor is mentioned. See *November* 7th.

3dly. When there are fundry Creditors to one Debtor, then the Debtor is only mentioned in the firft line, and the feveral Creditors reprefented under the title of fundries, which are likewife particularly expreffed in the following lines, preceded by the word *To*. See *November* 20th.

SECTION THIRD.

Of the LEDGER.

The Ledger Poft always begins with the word *To* or *By*, and muft never exceed one line, in which the tranfaction muft be as fully exprefled, as the length of the line will admit of.

The explanations given in the firft fet of books, under each accompt there, is only for the learner's inftruction, but are alfo omitted in real trade.

Thofe things with refpect to the form of the afore-mentioned books, I thought neceffary to take notice of, as the fize of this book will not admit of it being in the form it ought, particularly in the Journal and Ledger, where you will often find we are obliged to have two lines, for what ought to have been exprefled in one.

CHAP. VIII.

Shewing how a new inventory is to be formed from the old books, in order to open new ones.

THE inventory is raifed from the ballance accompt in your old Ledger : The debt fide of which is your ftock in trade of money, goods, and debts; and the credit fide, the debts you owe to others; which is to be wrote into your Wafte-Book, in the fame manner as you did at firft, as you will fee by the Wafte-Book of the fecond fet of books, beginning *January* 1ft, 1777.

WASTE-

WASTE-BOOK.

LONDON, the 1ſt of *January*, 1777.

---

		l.	*s. d.*
MY father having declined buſineſs, has this day made me a preſent of the remaining part of his ſtock in trade, conſiſting of money, goods, and debts; in conſequence of which, I ſtand engaged for all the debts he owes reſpecting the ſaid trade.			

An Inventory *of which follows, viz.*

	l. s. d.		
Caſh in the hands of my bankers, *I. C.*	500 00 0		
Alſo 24 pieces of *Yorkſhire* foreſt cloths, quantity 490 yards, at 4*s.* 6*d. per* yard,	110 05 0		
15 pieces of *Scots* lawns, at 4*l.* 10*s. per* piece,	67 10 0		
30 pieces of fuſtians, at 2*l.* 2*s. per* piece, and 20 ditto, at 4*l.* 10*s. per* piece,	113 00 0		
20 dozen of ſilk hoſe, at 6*l.* 6*s. per* dozen,	126 00 0		
25 pieces of velvet, quantity 450 yards, at 8*s. per* yard,	180 00 0		
John Martin of *Barnet* owes me, due the 10th inſtant,	50 07 6		
James Tomlinſon of *Hatfield*, on demand,	28 04 6		
		1175 06 06	

I owe as follows.

To *James Gray* of *Leeds*, due the 24th inſtant,	35 10 0		
To *Samuel Wilkinſon* of *Bolton*, due the 10th inſtant,	55 00 0		
To *William Webſter* of *Mancheſter*, due the 1ſt of *December* next,	73 00 0	163 10 00	

L 2   *Jan.*

		l.	s.	d.
	———————*January* 3d.———————			
✓	Bought with ready money, 1 *cwt.* 2 *qrs.* indigo at 3 *s.* per lb. ———	25	04	00
	————————5th.————————			
✓	Bought of *James Thornton* from *Wigan*, 10 pieces, quantity 250 yards of printed cotton, at 2 *s.* 8 *d. per* yard, to pay in six weeks, ———	33	06	08
	————————8th.————————			
	Bought of *Robert Smith* 120 gallons of rum, at 8 *s.* 6 *d. per* gallon, for which I have given him my draft on *John Martin* of *Barnet*, payable at three days, for	48	00	00
	————————10th.———————			
✓	Sold for ready money, 6 dozen pair of my silk hose, at 7 *l. per* dozen, comes to ——— ———	42	00	00
	————————12th.———————			
✓	Sold *John Martin* of *Kingston* my 20 pieces of best fustians, at 3 *l. per* piece, to pay in one month, ———	60	00	00
	————————15th.———————			
✓	Sold *David Johnston* of *Stamford*, 20 pieces of *Yorkshire* forest cloths, quantity 386 yards, at 5 *s. per* yard, for which he has given me his draft on *Stephen Ramsey*, payable in 10 days, for ——— ———	96	10	00
	————————17th.———————			

		l.	s.	d.			
✓	Sold *James Wilks* of St. *Edmonds Bury*, 15 pieces of velvet, quantity 270 yards, at 9 *s.* 6 *d. per* yard.						
	Received of him in part, ——— ———	60	00	0			
	Rest due in one month, ——— ———	68	05	0	128	05	00

		l.	s.	d.			
	————————20th.———————						
✓	Bought of *Thomas Simpson* from *Manchester*, 20 dozen of men's hats, at 6 *l. per* dozen.						
	Paid him ——— ———	60	00	0			
	The other half I am to pay him in 3 months,	60	00	0	120	00	00

		l.	s.	d.			
	————————23d.———————						
	Bought of *Ralph Cook* from *Wakefield*, 25 pieces of *Yorkshire* planes, quantity 525 yards, at 4 *s. per* yard.						
✓	Paid him in part, ——— ———	40	00	0			
	Given him my draft on *James Tomlinson* at sight, for ——— ———	28	04	0			
	The remainder I am to pay in 4 months, being ——— ———	36	16	0	105	00	00

Jan.

		l.	s.	d.
————————January 25th.————————				
✓ Remitted *James Gray* of *Leeds*, in full, by the hands of *Thomas Scott* Waggoner, in cash ———		35	10	00
————— 26th.———				
✓ Paid *Samuel Wilkinson* from *Bolton*, in full, ———		.55	00	00

✓ Sold *James Forster* in *Smithfield*, 10 pieces of *Scots* lawns, at 5 l. 5 s. per piece.

	l.	s.	d.			
Received of him in part, ———	20	00	0			
Given me his draft on *Smith* and *Co.* Lombard Street, at 15 days, for ———	20	00	0			
The rest he is to pay me in six weeks,	12	10	0			
				52	10	00

✓ *James Thornton* of *Wigan*, has drawn his bill on me, payable to *Charles Stevenson*, or order, at 20 days, for ——— ——— ——	33	06	08
✓ Received for *David Johnston's* draft on *Stephen Ramsey*,	96	10	00
———————30th.———			
✓ Bartered with *Thomas Green* from *Sturbridge*, my 120 gallons of rum, at 10 s. per gallon, for 10 pockets of hops, weight 10 cwt.. 2 qrs. 24 lb. at 5 l. 12 s. per cwt. ———	60	00	00

————————*February* 1st.————

Paid *William Webster* of *Manchester*, in full, as follows:

	l.	s.	d.			
✓ Sold him my 1 cwt. 2 qrs. of indigo, at 3 s. 6 d. per lb. comes to ———	29	08	0			
The ballance I have paid him in cash being	43	12	0			
				73	00	00

————————3d.————

	l.	s.	d.			
✓ Bartered with *Thomas Lee* from *Stockton*, my remaining 8 dozen of silk hose, at 7 l. 10 s. per dozen, for 10 barrels of pickled pork, at 4 l. 4 s. per barrel, comes to	42	00	0			
The ballance I have received in cash, being	18	00	0			
				60	00	00

Received

		l.	*s.*	*d.*
———————February 5th.———————				

✓ Received of *John Martin* of *Barnet*, the ballance of his accompt ———   ———   2   7   6

✓ Sold for ready money the following goods, viz.

	l.	*s.*	*d.*
4 pieces of *Yorkshire* forest cloths, quantity 104 yards, at 5 *s.* 3 *d. per* yard, —	27	06	0
5 pieces of *Scots* lawns, at 5 *l. per* piece,	25	00	0
10 ditto of common fustians, at 2 *l.* 9 *s. per* piece,	24	10	0

     76   16   00

———————8th.———————

✓ Bought of *Samuel Rich* from *Norwich*, the following goods, to pay in 6 months, viz.

	l.	*s.*	*d.*
15 pieces of *Norwich* crapes, quantity 310 yards, at 2 *s. per* yard, ———	31	00	0
10 ditto of ditto stuffs, quantity 200 yards, at 1 *s.* 4 *d. per* yard,	13	06	8

     44   06   08

———————10th.———————

✓ Bought of *Daniel Bradshaw* in *Thames Street*, the following goods, viz.

	l.	*s.*	*d.*
200 gallons of rum, at 8 *s. per* gallon ———	80	00	0
10 anchors of brandy, at 4 *l.* 10 *s. per* anchor ———	45	00	0

	l.	*s.*	*d.*
Paid him in part, — — —	60	00	0
The rest I am to pay in 3 months, — —	65	00	0

     125   00   00

✓

———————11th.———————

Sold *John Martin* of *Barnet*, the following goods, to pay in 4 months, viz.

	l.	*s.*	*d.*
10 pieces of my common fustians, at 2 *l.* 8 *s. per* piece, — — — —	24	00	0
10 ditto of velvets, quantity 180 yards, at 10 *s. per* yard, — — —	90	00	0

     114   00   00

James

	L	s.	d.
——————————*February* 12th.———————			

James Tomlinson of *Hatfield*, has given me an order
for the following goods, which I have this day sent
him by the waggon, viz.

✓ 8 pieces, quantity 200 yards of printed cottons, at 3 s. per yard } 30 00 0

10 pieces of *Norwich* crapes, quantity 206 yds, at 2 s. 6 d. per yd } 25 15 0

L. s. d.

Remitted me at the same time, a draft on
Coats and *Co.* in *Lombard Street*, at } 20 00 0
fight, which I have received for —

The remainder he promises to pay in two } 35 15 0
months, — — — —

| | 55 | 15 | 00 |

✓ *John Martin* of *Kingston*, has remitted me a bill drawn
by *James Fletcher*, on *Richard Brooks* in the *Strand*,
due the 21st instant, which he has accepted for

| | 60 | 00 | 00 |

——————————14th.———————

✓ Received for *Forster's* draft on *Smith* and *Co.* —

| | 20 | 00 | 00 |

✓ *James Wilks* of St. *Edmonds Bury*, has remitted me
his draft on *Maxwell* and *Co.* in the *Strand*, due in
16 days, which they have accepted for — —

| | 68 | 05 | 00 |

———————15th.———————

/ Paid *James Thornton's* draft on me to *Charles Stevenson*,

| | 33 | 06 | 08 |

———————18th.———————

Received from *James Thornton* of *Wigan*, as per my
order, dated the 29th of *January*, the following
goods, viz.

L. s. d.

30 pieces printed cottons, quantity 655 } 81 17 6
yards, at 2 s. 6 d. — —

20 pieces of ditto linens, quantity 420 } 63 00 0
yards, at 3 s. per yard, — — —

| | 144 | 17 | 06 |

———————20th.———————

Bought of *Jacob Ratcliff*, 20 pieces of fine *Devonshire*
planes, quantity 500 yards, at 5 s. 6 d. per yard.

L. s. d.

Paid him in cash, — — — — — 66 15 0

Given him *James Wilks's* draft on *Maxwell* } 68 05 0
and *Co.* — — — —

| | 135 | 00 | 00 |

Upon

	l.	*s.*	*d.*
—————————*February* 21ft.———————			
✓ Upon fearching my pocket-book for *Fletcher's* bill on *Brooks*, due this day, I found I had loft it; I immediately fent to *Brooks* to ftop payment of it, but my clerk was informed that they had difcounted it for one who figned his name *Watfon*, the 18th inftant.			
✓ Received from *William Webfter* of *Manchefter*, as *per* my order to him the 1ft inftant,			
10 pieces of velvets, quantity 280 yards, at 7 *s. per* yard, — — — — —	98	00	00
✓ Received alfo from *Thomas Burges* of *Paifley*, as *per* my order, the 27th of *January*,			
20 pieces of lawns, at 5 *l. per* piece, — —	100	00	00

————————22d.————————

	l.	*s.*	*d.*		*l.*	*s.*	*d.*
✓ Sent *John Martin* of *Kingfton*, as *per* his order, the 12th inftant,							
5 pieces of printed cottons, quantity 125 yards, at 3 *s.* 2 *d. per* yard, —	19	15	10				
10 ditto of *Yorkfhire* planes, quantity 215 yards, at 4 *s.* 6 *d. per* yard, —	48	07	06		68	03	04

————————23d.————————

	l.	*s.*	*d.*		*l.*	*s.*	*d.*
✓ Sent *James Wilks* of St. *Edmonds Bury*, as *per* his order, dated the 13th inftant, the following goods, viz.							
3 pieces of *Yorkfhire* planes, quantity 78 yards, at 4 *s.* 8 *d. per* yard, —	18	04	0				
5 pockets of hops, weight 4 *cwt.* 3 *qrs.* 26 *lb.* at 1 *s.* 4 *d. per lb.* — —	37	02	0				
4 pieces printed linens, 86 yards, at 3 *s.* 6 *d. per* yard, — —	15	01	0		70	07	00

James

———————*February* 24th.——————   *l.* | *s.* | *d.*

James Forster of *Smithfield,* has paid me in full of
what he owed me, being — — —   12 | 10 | 00

✓ Sold him at the same time, the following goods, to pay
in 2 months:

                                   l.   *s.*   *d.*

10 pieces of printed linens, quantity 208 } 36   8   0
   yards, at 3 *s.* 6 *d. per* yard,   —

15 pieces of ditto cotton, quantity 330 } 55   00   0
   yards, at 3 *s.* 4 *d. per* yard,   —

5 ditto of *Scots* lawns, at 5 *l.* 10 *s. per* piece, 27   10   0
                                          118 | 18 | 00

✓ Sold for ready money, the following goods, viz.

                                  l.   *s.*   *d.*

80 gallons of rum, at 9 *s.* 6 *d. per* gallon,   38   00   0

5 anchors of brandy, at 5 *l.* 5 *s. per* anchor, 26   5   0
                                          64 | 05 | 00

———————25th.——————

✓ Sold my 10 barrels of pork, (being a little damaged)
at 3 *l.* 16 *s. per* barrel ready money, comes to   —   38 | 00 | 00

———————26th.——————

✓ Sent *James Gibson* of *Stilton* my remaining 10 pieces
of common fustians, desiring him to take them at
2 *l.* 2 *s. per* piece; if not, to return them at my ex-
pence   —   —   —   —   21 | 00 | 00

Sold *John Kirkman* of *Richmond* the following goods,
to pay in three months, viz.

                                  l.   *s.*   *d.*

✓ 6 pieces of my second velvets, quantity 168 } 71   8   0
   yards, at 8 *s.* 6 *d. per* yard   —

2 pieces of best printed cottons, quantity 50 } 8   6   8
   yards, at 3 *s.* 4 *d. per* yard   —   —

4 pieces of *Yorkshire* planes, quantity 88 } 20   10   8
   yards, at 4 *s.* 8 *d. per* yard —————
                                          100 | 05 | 04

———————27th.——————

Sold *Robert Lamb* of *Yarmouth* the following goods, to
pay in 2 months, viz.

                                  l.   *s.*   *d.*

5 pockets of hops, weight 5 *cwt.* 2 *qrs.* } 28   2   8
   26 *lb.* at 1 *s.* 4 *d. per lb.*   —

60 gallons of rum, at 9 *s.* 3 *d. per* gallon — 27   15   0
                                          55 | 17 | 08

| | | *L.* | *s.* | *d.* |

———————— *February* 28th.————————

Bought with ready money the following goods, viz.

l. s. d.

✓ 50 pieces of fine jeans, quantity 1000 } yards, at 2 *s.* 4 *d. per* yard ——— }	116 13 4			
20 dozen pair of men's thread hofe, at } 1 *l.* 4 *s. per* dozen ——— }	24 0 0			
400 pair of men's fhoes, at 4 *s. per* pair	80 0 0			
		220	13	04

Sold *Cuthbert Euſtage* of *Stamford* the following goods, to pay in 4 months, viz.

l. s. d.

✓ 5 pieces of *Norwich* crapes, quantity 104 } yards, at 2 *s.* 9 *d. per* yard ——— }	13 17 0			
200 yards of *Devonſhire* planes, at 6 *s.* } 6 *d. per* yard ——— }	65 0 0			
		78	17	00

John Martin of *Kingſton* has fail'd, and I have compounded his debt, being 68 *l.* 3 *s.* 4 *d.* for 15 *s.* in the pound.

l. s. d.

✓ The compofition which I have received is	51 2 6			
The fum loft is ———	17 0 10			
		68	3	04

✓ Paid clerks wages, warehoufe room, and other expences on trade, for thefe two months paft —		20	00	00

✓ Paid alfo for my board, which together with pocket expences, as *per* petty cafh-book, amounts to		8	00	00

✓ My father being pleafed with my affiduity in bufinefs, in order to extend it further, has made me a prefent of ———		10000	00	00

J O U R N A L.

JOURNAL.

LONDON, the 1ſt of *January*, 1777.

		l.	*s.*	*d.*
	Sundries Drs. to Stock, 1157 *l.* 6 *s.* 6 *d.*			
1	Caſh in the hands of my banker, I. C.	500	0	0
1	*Yorlſhire* foreſt cloths, for 24 pieces, quantity 490 yds. at 4 *s.* 6 *d. per* yd.	110	5	0
2	*Scots* lawns for 15 pieces, at 4 *l.* 10 *s.* per piece	67	10	0
2	Fuſtians for 30 pieces, at 2 *l.* 2 *s. per* piece	63	0	0
2	Ditto for 20 ditto, at 2 *l.* 10 *s. per* piece	50	0	0
2	Silk hoſe for 20 dozen pair, at 6 *l.* 6 *s. per* dozen	126	0	0
3	Velvets for 25 pieces, quantity 450 yards, at 8 *s. per* yard	180	0	0
3	*John Martin* of *Barnet* owes me, due the 10th inſtant	50	7	6
3	*James Tomlinſon* of *Hatfield* on demand	28	4	0
4		1175	06	06

See Prob. 1ſt, Sect. 1ſt, Chap. 1ſt.

Reaſon. As every particular article of which your ſtock conſiſts, as well as thoſe perſons who owe you money, muſt each (in their reſpective accompts in your Ledger) be charged Debtor to ſomething for their ſeveral ſums; ſo if you conſider that the ſtock accompt on the credit ſide, (after your inventory is poſted) exhibits to you the whole of your effects, they muſt therefore neceſſarily be made each of them Debtor to ſtock, and conſequently ſtock Creditor by each of them.

Stock

		l.	s.	d

————January 1st.————

4 | Stock Dr. to fundries, 163 l. 10 s.

		l.	s.	d.
4	To *James Gray* of *Leeds*, due the 4th inst.	35	10	0
4	To *Samuel Wilkinson* of *Belton*, due the 10th inftant	55	0	0
5	To *William Webfter* of *Manchefter*, due the 1ft of *February* next	73	0	0

163 10 00

See Prob. 1ft, Sect. 1ft, Chap. 1ft.

Reafon. As the credit fide of your ftock accompt in your Ledger exhibits the whole of your effects, fo the debt fide of it fhews the whole of what you owe, and therefore muft be charged Debtor to the feveral perfons to whom you ftand indebted, and confequently each of thofe perfons (in their refpective accompts in your Ledger) muft be credited by ftock for the fums due to them.

————3d.————

5 | Indigo Dr. to cafh, 25 l. 4 s.
1 | Paid for 1 *cwt.* 2 *qrs.* at 3 s. *per lb.* ——

25 04 00

See Cafe 1ft, Prob. 2d, Sect. 1ft, Chap. 1ft.

Reafon. The indigo being the thing received, it is plain it muft be charged Debtor, in order to fhew the quantity you bought, and what it coft you; and cafh being the thing parted with, muft of courfe be credited, to fhew that you have paid fo much money away.

————5th.————

5 | Printed cottons Dr. to *James Thornton* of *Wigan* 33 l.
6 | 6 s. 8 d.
  | Bought of him 10 pieces, quantity 250 yards, at 2 s. 8 d. *per* yard, to pay in fix weeks ——

33 06 08

Cafe 2d, Prob. 2d, Sect. 1ft, Chap. 1ft.

Reafon. The cottons are here charged Debtor for the very fame reafon that the indigo was; but as you bought them on truft, it is evident that the perfon of whom you bought them, muft ftand credited in your Ledger, to fhew that you owe him for the faid cottons.

————8th.————

3 | Rum Dr. to *John Martin* of *Barnet* 48 l.
1 | Given my draft on him at 3 days to *Robert Smith,*
6 | for 120 gallons bought of faid *Smith,* at 8 s. 6 d. *per* gallon ——

48 00 00

Cafe 3d, Prob. 2d, Sect. 1ft, Chap. 1ft.

Reafon.

Reason. Here it is plain, according to all the particular
cases in buying, and also the general rule, that sum being
the thing received, it muft be charged Debtor; but the reafon
why *John Martin* becomes the Creditor may not appear quite
fo plain, as according to the faid general rule, he is not immediately the deliverer: But if you confider that *John Martin*
ftood debited in your Ledger to ftock for 50 l. 7 s. 6 d. it then
will appear reafonable, that now, when you have drawn upon
him, he fhould be credited for the value of your draft. And
again : Altho', as I obferved before, he was not immediately
the deliverer, yet he is really fo in fact; for as you gave *Robert Smith* a draft on him for the fum, *Smith* could not be the
Creditor ; and therefore it is the fame thing as if *Martin* had
paid you the value of the faid draft in fum, in which fenfe he
may alfo be confidered as the deliverer.

	l.	s.	d.

-------------*January* 10th.-------------
$\frac{1}{2}$ Cafh Dr. to filk hofe, 42 l.
    Received for 6 dozen pair, at 7 l. *per* dozen   —
    Cafe 1ft, Prob. 3d, Sect. 1ft, Chap. 1ft.   42 | 00 | 00

Reason. As the filk hofe ftood debited to your ftock at o-
pening of your books, they muft therefore now be credited for
what are fold, in order to know in what manner they are difpofed of, and what you gain or lofe by them; and cafh being
the thing received is charged Debtor to them, to fhew you
have received fo much money.

$\frac{6}{2}$ -------------12th.-------------
John Martin of *Kingfton* Dr. to fuftians, 60 l.
    For 20 pieces of my beft ditto, at 3 l. *per* piece, to
    pay in one month   ——
    Cafe 2d, Prob. 3d, Sect. 1ft, Chap. 1ft.   60 | 00 | 00

-------------15th.-------------
$\frac{7}{1}$ Bills receivable Dr. to *Yorkfhire* foreft cloths, 96 l. 10 s.
    Sold *David Johnfton* 20 pieces, quantity 386 yards,
    at 5 s. *per* yard, for which I have received his
    draft on *Stephen Ramfay*, payable in 10 days for   96 | 10 | 00
    Cafe 3d, Prob. 3d, Sect. 1ft; Chap. 1ft.

Reason. Here it might appear reafonable to charge *Stephen
Ramfay* Debtor; but in order to avoid opening an accompt
for every perfon on whom in the courfe of trade you may
chance to have bills upon, and with whom perhaps you may
never have any future tranfactions, you therefore (inftead of
charging *Stephen Ramfay* Debtor) open a general accompt of
bills receivable, under which head you bring all the bills you
receive. Hence you may obferve, that however the perfon or
                                  thing

thing to be charged Debtor may vary according to circumftances, the Creditor, according to the general rule, is ftill the
fame, viz. the goods fold: For as they formerly ftood debited
in your Ledger to fomething or other for their coft, fo they
muft now be credited by fome other thing for the value you
fold them for, in order to fhew what returns they have made,
and what you have gain'd or loft by difpofing of them.

——————————17th.——————————

Sundries Dr. to velvets, 128 *l.* 5 *s.*

<table>
<tr><td></td><td></td><td>*l.*</td><td>*s.*</td><td>*d.*</td><td></td></tr>
<tr><td>3</td><td>Cafh in part for 15 pieces, quantity 270 yards, at 9 *s.* 6 *d.* per yard —</td><td>60</td><td>0</td><td>0</td><td></td></tr>
<tr><td>7
3</td><td>*James Wilks* in *St. Edmond's Bury* for the reft, due in 1 month — —</td><td>68</td><td>5</td><td>0</td><td>128 | 05 | 00</td></tr>
</table>

Obfervation. As the circumftances attending the fale of
the above goods are reduceable to two diftinct cafes, namely,
goods fold for ready money, and goods fold on credit; fo the
above Journal entry is a compound of the refpective Journal
entries belonging to the faid two cafes, in both of which the
goods fold is the common Creditor.

——————————20th.——————————

7
1 Hats Dr. to fundries, 120 *l.*

<table>
<tr><td></td><td></td><td>*l.*</td><td>*s.*</td><td>*d.*</td><td></td></tr>
<tr><td></td><td>To cafh in part for 20 dozen, at 6 *l.* per doz.</td><td>60</td><td>0</td><td>0</td><td></td></tr>
<tr><td>8</td><td>To *Thomas Simpfon* of *Manchefter* for the reft in three months —</td><td>60</td><td>0</td><td>0</td><td>120 | 00 | 00</td></tr>
</table>

Obfervation. This entry is alfo reduceable to two diftinct
cafes, namely, goods bought for ready money, and goods
bought on credit; the debtors therefore are the fame with thofe
of the refpective entries belonging to the faid two cafes, and
the Creditor here common to both.

N. B. This is exactly the reverfe of this entry above.

——————————23d.——————————

8
1 *Yorkfhire* planes Dr. to fundries, 105 *l.*

<table>
<tr><td></td><td></td><td>*l.*</td><td>*s.*</td><td>*d.*</td><td></td></tr>
<tr><td></td><td>To cafh in part for 25 pieces, quantity 525 yards, at 4 *s.* per yard —</td><td>40</td><td>0</td><td>0</td><td></td></tr>
<tr><td>3</td><td>To *James Tomlinfon* for my draft on him at fight for — —</td><td>28</td><td>4</td><td>0</td><td></td></tr>
<tr><td>8</td><td>To *Ralph Cock* of *Wakefield* for the reft, to pay in 4 months — —</td><td>36</td><td>16</td><td>0</td><td>105 | 00 | 00</td></tr>
</table>

Obfervation.

Observation. The conditions of buying here taking in the
several circumſtances of three diſtinct caſes, viz. of *January*
the 3d, 5th, and 8th, conſequently the above entry is compoſed of the reſpective Journal entries belonging to the ſaid
three caſes; the reaſon for which entry you will find there
recited.

l. | s. | d.

—————————*January* 25th.—————————

4 | *James Gray* of *Leeds* Dr. to caſh, 35 *l.* 10 *s.*
— | Remitted him in full by the hands of *Thomas Scott,*
1 | waggoner ———————————— ———— 35 | 10 | 00
| Caſe 1ſt, Prob. 5th, Sect. 1ſt, Chap. 1ſt.

Reaſon. As *James Gray* ſtood credited in your Ledger by
your ſtock accompt, it is therefore plain that (now when you
have paid him) he muſt be made Debtor, in order to ſhew he
is paid; and caſh being the thing delivered, it is equally rea-
ſonable that it ſhould be credited to ſhew what caſh you have
paid.

—————————26th.—————————

4 | *Samuel Wilkinſon* of *Bolton* Dr. to caſh, 55 *l.*
1 | Paid him in full ——————— ———— 55 | 00 | 00

The reaſon of this entry is the ſame with that of the entry
above.

—————————————————————

Sundries Dr. to *Scots* lawns, 52 *l.* 10 *s.*

l. | s. | d.

1 | Caſh received in part for 10 pieces, at } 20 0 0
| 5 *l.* 5 *s. per* piece ——————— }
7 | Bills receivable for *Forſter* on *Smith* and } 20 0 0
| Co. at 15 days, for ——— }
9 | *James Forſter* of *Smithfield* for the reſt, } 12 10 0
— | due in ſix weeks ——————— }
2 | —————— 52 | 10 | 00

Obſervation. The Waſte-Book caſe of this entry takes in
thoſe of the 10th, 12th, and 15th of *January*, and therefore this Journal entry is compoſed of the reſpective Journal
entries belonging to the afore-mentioned thre caſes, in each
of which the goods ſold is Creditor, and caſh, bills receivable,
or the perſon to whom they were ſold, Debtors.
Note. This entry and its caſe in the Waſte-Book, as alſo
the three ſeveral ones to which it refers, are exactly the re-
verſe of the Journal entry, and its Waſte Book caſe the 23d of
January, and thoſe three ſeveral caſes to which the ſaid entry (23d of *January*) refers.

James

		L.	s.	d.

—————January 28th.—————

6 James Thornton of *Wigan* Dr. to bills payable, 33 *l.*
6 *s.* 8 *d.*

9 Drawn his bill on me to *Charles Stevenson*, or order,
at 14 days, which I have accepted ——— **33 06 08**
Cafe 2d, Prob. 5th, Sect. 1st, Chap. 1st.

Reason. Here it would have been equally proper to have
made *James Thornton* Debtor to *Charles Stevenson*, since by
that means *Thornton's* accompt would have stood discharged
the same as by the above entry, and *Charles Stevenson*, to
whom the bill was payable, would then have become the Creditor in his place: But for the reasons before recited at the
bottom of the Journal entry the 15th of *January*, it is more
convenient to open a general accompt under the title of bills
payable.

1 Cash Debtor to bills receivable, 96 *l.* 10 *s.*
—— Received for *David Johnston* on *Stephen Ramsay* **96 10 00**
7 Cafe 3d, Prob. 4th, Sect. 1st, Chap. 1st.

Reason. Here it is evident that as bills receivable was
charged Debtor to *Yorkshire* forest cloths, the 15th of *Janua-*
ry, that now you have received payment of the said bill, that
the accompt of bills receivable must be credited for the same
sum; and cash (which you received for it) be made Debtor in
its place, to shew how much your cash is increased.
Observation. But had you on the said 15th of *January* (instead of bills receivable) charged *Stephen Ramsay*, on whom
the bill was drawn, Debtor, then the above entry would have
been cash Debtor to *Stephen Ramsay.* This shews you the
nice dependance which one thing has upon another, and how
the Debtor or Creditor of any present Journal entry is affected
or determined, according to the Journal entry you have made
of the last transaction relative to it.

—————30th.—————

9 Hops Dr. to rum, 60 *l.*
—— Received 10 pockets, weight 10 cwt. 5 *st.* 10 *lb.*
6 at 5 *l.* 10 *s.* per cwt. in barter for 120 gallons of
rum, at 10 *s.* 6 *d.* per gallon ——— **60 00 00**
Cafe 4th, Prob. 2d, Sect. 1st, Chap. 1st.

Reason. In the Waste-Book entry of this, we find buying
and selling blended in one transaction, and therefore the
Journal entry must be common to both, that is to say, (according to the general rule) hops being the thing bought must
be charged Debtor, and rum being the thing sold Creditor.

February

		l.	s.	d.

5 *William Webfter* of *Manchefter* Dr. to fundries, 73 *l.*

		l.	s.	d.			
5	To indigo, for 1 *cwt.* 2 *qrs.* at 3 *s.* 6 *d.* per *lb.*	} 29	8	0			
1	To cafh for the ballance — —43	12	0				

Paid him in full in goods and money ———— | 73 | 00 | 00 |

Obfervation. This alfo comprehends the Journal entries of two diftinct cafes, namely, the paying a debt, and the felling of goods; fo that *William Webfter* is charged Debtor to indigo, the fame as if any other indifferent perfon had bought it of you; and alfo Debtor to cafh for what money you paid him. By this means you will find (when this is pofted to the Ledger) that *Webfter's* accompt will ftand ballanced; the credit fide of the indigo accompt, will fhew that it is fold, and what you have gained or loft by it; and the credit fide of your cafh accompt inform you what way you have difpofed of your money.

———————— 3d. ————————

Sundries Dr. to filk hofe, 60 *l.*

		l.	s.	d.
10	Pickled pork, for 10 barrels, at 4 *l.* 4 *s.* per barrel	} 42	0	0
1	Cafh for the ballance — 18	0	0	

| | | 60 | 00 | 00 |

2 Received in barter for 8 dozen of filk hofe at 7 *l.* 10 *s.* per dozen.

Obfervation. This likewife is compofed of two diftinct cafes, namely, goods bartered for goods of equal value; and goods fold for ready money, the reafon for which two entries has already been explained.

———————— 5th. ————————

1	Cafh Dr. to *John Martin* of *Barnet*, 2 *l.* 7 *s.* 6 *d.*			
—	Received the ballance of his accompt —			
3	Cafe 1ft, Prob. 4th, Sect. 1ft, Chap. 1ft.	2	07	06

The reafon of this entry is fo evident, that it needs no further explanation.

		l.	s.	d.

——————————February 5th. ——————————

1 | Cash Dr. to sundries, 76 l. 16 s.

		l.	s.	d.
1	To *Yorkshire* forest cloths, for 4 pieces, quantity 104 yards. at 5 s. 3 d. *per* yd.	27	6	0
2	To *Scots* lawns, for 5 pieces, at 5 l. *per* piece	25	0	0
2	To fustians, for 10 pieces, (common sort) at 2 l. 9 s. *per* piece	24	10	0

Sold the above goods for ready money.   76 | 16 | 00

——————————8th.——————————

Sundries Dr. to *Samuel Rich* of *Norwich* 44 l. 6 s. 8 d.

		l.	s.	d.
10	*Norwich* crapes, for 15 pieces, quantity 310 yards, at 2 s. *per* yard	31	0	0
10 10	*Norwich* stuffs, for 10 pieces, quantity 200 yards, at 1 s. 4 d. *per* yard	13	6	8

Bought the above goods at six months credit.   44 | 06 | 08

——————————10th.——————————

Sundries Dr. to *Daniel Bradshaw* in *Thames-street*, 125 l.

		l.	s.	d.
6	Rum, for 200 gallons, at 8 s. *per* gallon	80	0	0
11 11	Brandy, for 10 anchors, at 4 l. 10 s. *per* anchor	45	0	0

125 | 00 | 00

11 | *Daniel Bradshaw* Dr. to cash 60 l.

1 | Paid him in part of the above goods   60 | 00 | 00
The ballance which is 75 l. I am to pay in 3 months.

Observation. In order to render this transaction clear, it was necessary to make the two distinct Journal entries above, although it is only a single transaction in the Waste-Book. Had there been sundry Debtors to one Creditor, or sundry Creditors to one Debtor, then it might have been performed in one entry. But as there are two Debtors and two Creditors, if you had made a single entry of it, it would have been sundries Debtors to sundries, which would have made it appear very complex and intricate. But by dividing it into two as above, *Bradshaw* will stand credited by the whole amount of the goods, and debited for what cash you paid him, so that the difference of the two sides will shew you what remains due to him.

February

——————————————————February 11th.—————————— *l.* | *s.* | *d.*

3 | John Martin of *Barnet* Dr. to fundries, 114 *l.*

 | | *l.* | *s.* | *d.* |
2 | To fuftians, for 10 pieces, (common) at 2 *l.* 8 *s. per* piece ——————— } 24 0 0
3 | To velvets, for 10 pieces, quantity 180 yds. at 10 *s.* per yard ——————— } 90 0 0

114 | 00 | 00

Sold the above goods at 4 months credit.

——————————————12th.——————

3 | James Tomlinfon of *Hatfield* Dr. to fundries, 55 *l.* 15 *s.*

 | | *l.* | *s.* | *d.* |
5 | To printed cottons, for 8 pieces, quantity 200 yards, at 3 *s. per* yard —— } 30 0 0
10 | To *Norwich* crapes, for 10 pieces, quantity 206 yards, at 2 *s.* 6 *d. per* yard —— } 25 15 0

55 | 15 | 00

1 | Cafh Dr. to *James Tomlinfon,* 20 *l.*
3 | Received for his draft on *Coats* and Co. ——— 20 | 00 | 00
| The ballance being 25 *l.* 15 *s.* he is to pay in 2 months.

Reafon. The fame as that given for the two entries the 10th inftant.
Note. The reafon why bills receivable was not charged Debtor, is becaufe you immediately received cafh for his bill.

7 | Bills receivable Dr. to *John Martin* of *Kingfton,* 60 *l.*
6 | Remitted me a bill drawn by *James Fletcher,* on *Richard Brooks,* in the *Strand,* due the 21ft inftant, for —— —— —— 60 | 00 | 00
| Cafe 2d, Prob. 4th, Sect. 1ft. Chap. 1ft.

Reafon. As *John Martin* ftood debited in your Ledger for 60 *l.* it is evident, that now, when he has remitted you a bill for the faid fum, that his accompt muft be credited in order to difcharge the fame, and bills receivable be made Debtor in *Martin's* ftead.

—————————————14th.——————

1 | Cafh Dr. to bills receivable, 20 *l.*
7 | Received for *Forfter's,* on *Smith* and Co. —— 20 | 00 | 00

		l.	*s.*	*d.*

—————————*February* 14th.—————————

7 | Bills receivable Dr. to *James Wilks* of *St. Edmonds* *Bury*, 68 *l.* 5 *s.*
— |
7 | Remitted me his draft on *Maxwell* and *Co.* in the *Strand*, due the 30th inftant, which they have accepted —————— —————— —————— | 68 | 05 | 00

—————————15th.—————————

9 | Bills payable Dr. to cafh, 33 *l.* 6 *s.* 8 *d.*
— |
1 | Paid *James Thornton's* draft on me, to *Charles Stevenfon*, or order, for —————— | 33 | 06 | 08
| Cafe 3d, Prob. 5th, Sect. 1ft, Chap. 1ft.

Reafon. As bills payable ftood credited by *James Thornton*, the 28th of *January*, to fhew that the faid bill remained unpaid, it is therefore reafonable now when you have paid it, that the faid accompt or bills payable fhould be charged Debtor, in order to fhew that it is paid, and cafh credited to inform you how you have difpofed of your money.

—————————18th.—————————

Sundries Dr. to *James Thornton* of *Wigan*, 144 *l.* 17 *s.* 6 *d.*

		l.	*s.*	*d.*

5 | Printed cottons, for 30 pieces, quantity 655 yards, at 2 *s.* 6 *d. per* yard — } | 81 | 17 | 6
11 | Ditto linens, for 20 ditto, quantity 420 yards, at 3 *s. per* yard —————— } | 63 | 0 | 0
6 | | | |
| | | 144 | 17 | 06

—————————20th.—————————

11 | *Devonfhire* planes Dr. to fundries, 135 *l.*
— |

		l.	*s.*	*d.*

1 | To cafh in part for 500 yards, at 5 *s.* 6 *d. per* yard —————— } | 66 | 15 | 0
7 | To bills receivable, for *Wilks's*, on *Maxwell* and *Co.* for —————— } | 68 | 5 | 0
| | | 135 | 00 | 00

Bought the above goods of *Jacob Ratcliff*, for which I paid him the faid cafh and draft.

Obfervation. Here you fee bills receivable is credited, the fame as if you had kept it in your own hands till it had become due and received the cafh for it, only in that cafe, cafh would have been the Debtor, whereas in the prefent cafe, *Devonfhire* planes is the Debtor; for whenever you part with any thing, it mutt be credited by fomething or other (viz. the thing you receive for it) to fhew that it has been difpofed of.

February

		l.	*s.*	*d.*

——————*February* 21 ft.——————

12 | Profit and lofs Dr. to bills receivable 60 *l.*
— | Loft out of my pocket book, a bill drawn by *James*
7 | *Fletcher* on *Richard Brecks*, for ——— | 60 00 00
| Cafe 1ft, Prob. 6th, Sect. 1ft, Chap. 1ft.

Reafon. As the accompt of bills receivable ftood formerly debited in your Ledger for the above bill, it is therefore evident (according to the general rule) that now when it is parted with, that the faid accompt of bills receivable muft be credited; but becaufe you receive nothing for it, from which you expect any returns, it therefore wants a correfpondent Debtor, for which you fubftitute profit and lofs.

3 | Velvets Dr. to *William Webfter* of *Manchefter*, 98 *l.*
— | Received from him 10 pieces, quantity 280 yards,
5 | at 7 *s.* per yard ——— | 98 00 00

2 | *Scots* lawns Dr. to *Thomas Burgis* of *Paifley*, 100 *l.*
12 | Received from him 20 pieces, at 5 *l.* per piece, as
| per my order, the 27th of *January* ——— | 100 00 00

——————22d.——————

6 | *John Martin* of *Kingfton* Dr. to fundries, 68 *l.* 3 *s.* 4 *d.*
| | *l.* | *s.* | *d.* |
5 | To printed cottons, for 5 pieces, quantity } 19 15 10
| 125 yards, at 3 *s.* 2 *d.* per yard — }
8 | To *Yorkfhire* planes, for 10 pieces, quan- } 48 7 6
| tity 215 yards, at 4 *s.* 6 *d.* per yard }
| | 68 03 04
| Sent him the above goods as *per* his order, the 10th inft.

——————23d.——————

| *James Wilks* of St. *Edmonds Bury* Dr. to fundries,
7 | 70 *l.* 7 *s.*
| | *l.* | *s.* | *d.* |
8 | To *Yorkfhire* planes, for 3 pieces, quantity } 18 4 0
| 78 yards, at 4 *s.* 8 *d.* per yard — }
9 | To hops, for 5 pockets, weight 4 *cwt.* 3 *qrs.* } 37 2 0
| 26 *lb.* at 1 *s.* 4 *d.* per *lb.* — }
11 | Printed linens, for 4 pieces, quantity 86 } 15 1 0
| yards, at 3 *s.* 6 *d.* per yard ——— }
| | 70 07 00
| Sent him the above goods as *per* his order, the 13th inft.

		L.	s.	d.
	————————February 24th.————			
7/9	Cash Dr. to *James Forster* of *Smithfield*, 12 *l.* 10 *s.* Received of him in full ——— ———	12	10	00
9	*James Forster* of *Smithfield* Dr. to sundries, 118 *l.* 18 *s.*			
		l.	*s.*	*d.*
11	To printed linens, for 10 pieces, quantity } 208 yards, at 3 *s.* 6 *d. per* yard —— } 36 8 6			
5	To printed cottons, for 15 pieces, quantity } 330 yards, at 3 *s.* 4 *d. per* yard —— } 55 0 0			
2	To *Scots* lawns, for 5 pieces, at 5 *l.* 10 *s.* } *per* piece ——— ——— } 27 10 0			
	Sold him the above goods to pay in 2 months.	118	18	00
1/6	Cash Dr. to sundries, 64 *l.* 5 *s.*			
		l.	*s.*	*d.*
	Rum, for 80 gallons, at 9 *s.* 6 *d. per* gallon 38 0 0			
11	Brandy, for 5 anchors, at 5 *l.* 5 *s. per* anchor 26 5 0			
	Sold the above goods for ready money.	64	05	00
	————————25th.————			
1/10	Cash Dr. to pickled pork, 38 *l.* Received for 10 barrels, (being a little damaged) at 3 *l.* 16 *s. per* barrel ———	38	00	00
	————————26th.————			
12/2	Suspence accompt Dr. to fustians, 21 *l.* Sent *James Gibson* of *Stilton*, 10 pieces of common fustians, desiring him to take them at 2 *l.* 2 *s. per* piece, if not, to return them at my expence ——	21	00	00

Reason. As the fustians were not positively sold, *James Gibson* could not properly be charged Debtor; but as the fustians (being gone from you) must be credited by something to shew what has become of them, there is nothing but suspence accompt can be charged Debtor, till we hear whether *Gibson* keeps or returns them.

		l.	s.	d.

————————February 26th.————————

13 | *John Kirkman* of *Richmond* Dr. to fundries, 100 *l.* 5 *s.* 4 *d.*

		L.	s.	d.
3	To velvets, for 6 pieces, quantity 168 yds. of fecond fort, at 8 *s.* 6 *d. per* yard —	71	8	0
5	To printed cottons, for 2 beft pieces, quantity 50 yards, at 3 *s.* 4 *d. per* yard —	8	6	8
8	To *Yorkfhire* planes, for 4 pieces, quantity 89 yards, at 4 *s.* 8 *d. per* yard ——	20	10	8

Sold him the above goods, to pay in 3 months. — 100 | 05 | 04

————————27th.————————

13 | *Robert Lamb* of *Yarmouth* Dr. to fundries, 55 *l.* 17 *s.* 8 *d.*

		l.	s.	d.
9	To hops, for 5 pockets, weight 5 *cwt.* 2 *qrs.* 26 *lb.* at 1 *s.* 4 *d. per lb.*	28	2	8
6	To rum, for 60 gallons, at 9 *s.* 3 *d. per* gallon	27	15	0

Sold him the above goods to pay in 2 months. — 55 | 17 | 08

————————28th.————————

Sundries Dr. to cafh, 220 *l.* 13 *s.* 4 *d.*

		l.	s.	d.
13	Jeans, for 50 pieces, quantity 1000 yds. at 2 *s.* 4 *d. per* yard ——	116	13	4
13	Shoes, for 400 pair of men's (leather) at 4 *s. per* pair ——	80	0	0
13 / 1	Thread hofe, for 20 dozen pair, (men's) at 1 *l.* 4 *s. per* dozen ——	24	0	0

Bought the above goods with ready money. — 220 | 13 | 04

14 | *Cuthbert Euftage* of *Stamford* Dr. to fundries, 78 *l.* 17 *s.*

		l.	s.	d.
10	To *Norwich* crapes, for 5 pieces, quantity 104 yards, at 2 *s.* 9 *d. per* yard —	13	17	0
11	*Devonfhire* planes, for 200 yards, at 6 *s.* 6 *d. per* yard ——	65	0	0

Sold him the above goods, to pay in 4 months. — 78 | 17 | 00

February

		L	s	d

———— *February* 28th.————

Sundries Dr. to *John Martin* of *Kingston*, 68 *l*. 3 *s*. 4 *d*.

                                       l. *s*. *d*.

1 | Cash for the compofition received, at 15 *s*. } 51 2 6
     per pound ———— }

12 | Profit and lofs for the fum abated ——17 0 10

6 | 68 03 04

John Martin having failed I have compounded with
            as above.

Obfervation. Here you fee *John Martin* is credited for
the whole fum he owed, the fame as if he had paid you the
whole debt, for as you have agreed to take the compofition
in full of all demands, you thereby relinquifh all future
claims upon him, and therefore his accompt muft ftand fully
difcharged. The cafh is made Dr. to fhew you what the
faid accompt is increafed, and the profit and lofs accompt
Dr. to fhew that you have loft fo much money.

Note. The Wafte-Book cafe of the above entry comprehends the payment of a debt and a lofs, and therefore the
Journal entry is a compound of the faid two cafes.

14 Charges on trade Dr. to cafh, 20 *l*.
——   Paid clerks wages, warehoufe rent, and other ex-
1 | pences on trade, fince the firft of *January* laft   20 00 00
   See Note 2d, Cafe 6th, Prob. 5th, Sect. 1ft, Chap. 1ft.

12 Profit and lofs Dr. to cafh, 8 *l*.
——   Paid my board, which together with pocket expen-
1 | ces, amounts to ————   8 00 00
   See Note 3d, Cafe 6th, Prob. 5th, Sect. 1ft, Chap. 1ft.

1 | Cafh Dr. to profit and lofs, 10000 *l*.
——   Given me by my father in order to extend my bufi-
12 | nefs ————   10000 00 00
       Cafe 6th, Prob. 4th, Sect. 1ft, Chap. 1ft.

Reafon. Here you fee (according to the general rule)
the thing received is ftill charged Debtor; but becaufe there
was no accompt in your Ledger which ftood debited for it
before, it therefore wants a correfpondent Creditor, as no
thing can be charged Debtor, but fome other accompt muft
at the fame be credited by it; we therefore having no returns to make for things of this kind, the profit and lofs
accompt muft of courfe be credited by the thing received.

LEDGER.

LEDGER.

o   ALPHA-

A		B		C	
	Fol.		*Fol.*		*Fol.*
		Bills receivable	7	Cash	1
		Bills payable	9	Cook (Ralph)	8
		Bradshaw (Daniel) Thames Street }	11	Charges on Trade	14
		Brandy	11		
		Burges (Thomas) of Paisley }	12		
		Ballance Accompt	14		

G		H		I & J	
	Fol.		*Fol.*		*Fol.*
Gray (James) of Leeds	4	Hats	7	Indigo	5
		Hops	9	Jeans	13

N		O		P	
	Fol.		*Fol.*		*Fol.*
Norwich Crapes	10			Printed Cottons	5
Ditto Stuffs	10			Pickled Pork	10
				Printed Linens	11
				Profit and Lofs	12

T		U & V		W	
	Fol.		*Fol.*		*Fol.*
Tomlinfon (James) of Hatfield }	3	Velvets	3	Wilkinfon (Samuel) of Bolton }	4
Thornton (James) of Wigan }	6			Webfter (William) of Manchefter }	5
Thread Hofe	13			Wilks (James) St. Edmond's Bury }	7

D	*Fol.*	E	*Fol.*	F	*Fol.*
Devonſhire Planes	11	Euſtage (Cuthbert)	14	Fuſtians	2
				Forſter (James) of } Smithfield	9

K	*Fol.*	L	*Fol.*	M	*Fol.*
Kirkman (John) of } Richmond	13	Lamb (Robert) of } Yarmouth	13	Martin (John) of } Barnet	3
				Martin (John) of } Kingſton	6

Q	*Fol.*	R	*Fol.*	S	*Fol.*
		Rum	6	Scots Lawns	2
		Rich (Samuel) of } Norwich	10	Silk Hoſe	2
				Stock	4
				Simpſon (Thomas) } of Mancheſter	8
				Shoes	13
				Suſpence Accompt	12

X	*Fol.*	Y	*Fol.*	Z	*Fol.*
		Yorkſh. Foreſt Cloths	1		
		Yorkſhire Planes	8		

Year and Month. 1777.	Cash,	Dr.	Fo	l.	s.	d.
Jan. 1	To stock, in the hands of my banker ———		4	500	00	00
10	To silk hose, for 6 dozen, at 7 l. per dozen ———		2	42	00	00
17	To velvets, in part for 15 pieces, 270 yards		3	60	00	00
26	To Scots lawns, in part for 10 pieces, 5l. 5s. per p.		2	20	00	00
28	To bills receivable received for Johnston on Ramsey		7	96	10	00
Feb. 3	To silk hose, in part for 8 dozen		2	18	00	00
5	To John Martin of Barnet, for the ball. of his acc.		3	2	07	06
	To sundries, as per Journal ———			76	16	00
12	To James Tomlinson, in part ———		3	20	00	00
14	To bills receivable, for Forster on Smith and Co.		7	20	00	00
24	To James Forster of Smithfield, in full ———		9	12	10	00
24	To sundries, as per Journal ———			64	05	00
25	To pickled pork, for 10 barrels		10	38	00	00
28	To J. Martin of Kingston, for composition recd.		6	51	02	06
	To profit and loss, given me by my father in order to extend my trade ———		12	100 00 00	00	
				1102	11	00

What debt and credit side of this accompt contains.
The debt side of this accompt shews you what cash you have received, and the credit side what you have paid, the difference between them is therefore the cash which remains in your hands.

	Yorkshire forest cloths,	Dr.	pieces.	yds.	Fo	l.	s.	d.
1777. Jan. 1	To stock, at 4s. 6d. per yard for		24	490	4	110	05	00
	To profit and loss, gained ———				12	15	11	00
			24	490		123	16	00

What the debt and credit side of this accompt contains.
The debt side of this (and every other accompt of goods) shews the quantity of the said goods bought, and at what price. The credit side of such accompt shews you what part of them are sold, and the price they were sold for, or how otherwise disposed off; the difference therefore of the two sides (if the goods are all sold) will be your neat gain or loss.

Year and Month.	Contra, Cr.	Fo	l.	s.	d.
1777,					
Jan. 3	By indigo, paid for 1 cwt. 2 qrs. at 3 s. per lb. —	5	25	04	00
20	By hats, in part for 20 dozen, at 6 l. per dozen	7	60	00	00
23	By Yorkshire planes, in part for 25 pieces, 525 yards, at 4 s. per yard	8	40	00	00
25	By Gray of Leeds, remitted. by T. Scott, wag.	4	35	10	00
26	By Samuel Wilkinson of Manchester, in full	4	55	00	00
Feb. 1	By William Webster of ditto, in part of his accompt	5	43	12	00
10	By Daniel Bradshaw, in part	11	60	00	00
15	By bills payable, paid Thornton's draft on me to Charles Stevenson, or order, for	9	33	06	08
20	By Devonshire planes, in part for 500 yards	11	66	15	00
28	By sundries, as per Journal		220	13	04
	By charges on trade, paid warehouse rent, clerk's wages, &c. since the 1st of January	14	20	00	00
	By profit and loss, for board, pocket expences. &c.	12	8	00	00
	By ballance, remaining in my hands	14	10353	10	00
			11021	11	00

How to ballance this accompt.
Cast first up the Debtor side, then next cast up the Creditor side upon a piece of waste-paper, and subtracting the one from the other, on the credit side, write, By ballance, &c. (as you see above) setting down the difference, which being all added up together, will be then even to the debt side.

N. B. The credit side of the accompt can never be heaviest, for this plain reason, viz. that you never can pay away more cash than you have.

Year and Month.	Contra, Cr.	pieces.	yds.	Fo	l.	s.	d.
1777.							
Jan. 15	By bills receivable, at 5 s. per yd. for	20	386	7	96	10	00
Feb. 5	By cash, at 5 s. 3 d. per yard, for	4	104	1	27	06	00
		24	490		123	16	00

How to ballance this accompt.
Having first added up the quantity columns of each side, I find that the goods are all sold; I next add up the money columns of the Creditor side, (it being heaviest) and subtracting the amount of the debt side from it, (upon a piece of waste-paper) the difference I find to be 12 l. 11 s. which is the sum I have gained by the said article: I therefore write on the debt side, (as you see) to profit and loss gained, inserting the said difference in the money columns, which being then cast up, will be exactly equal to the Creditor side, and to ballance the accompt.

Year and Month.		Fo	l.	s.	d.

Year and Month.	Scots lawns,	Dr.		Fo	l.	s.	d.
1777.		*pieces.*					
Jan. 1	To stock, at 4 l. 10 s. per piece, for —	15	4		67	10	00
Feb. 21	To Thomas Burges of Paisley, at 5 l. per piece, for ————	20	12		100	00	00
	To profit and loss, gained —		12		12	10	00
		35			180	00	00

Year and Month.	Fustians,	Dr.		Fo	l.	s.	d.
1777.		*pieces.*					
Jan. 1	To stock, at 2 l. 2 s. per piece, for —	30	4		63	00	00
	To ditto, at 2 l. 10 s. per piece, for —	20	4		50	00	00
	To profit and loss, gained —		12		16	10	00
		50			129	10	00

Year and Month.	Silk hose,	Dr.		Fo	l.	s.	d.
1777.		*dozen.*					
Jan. 1	To stock, at 6 l. 6 s. per dozen, for —	20	4		126	00	00
	To profit and loss, gained —		12		13	16	00
		20			139	16	00

Year and Month.		Fo	l.	s.	d.
	Contra, Cr.				
1777.		pieces.			
Jan. 26	By fundries as *per* Journal, at 5 *l.* 5 *s.* per piece, for — — — —	10	52	10	00
Feb. 5	By cafh, at 5 *l.* per piece, for —	5	1	25	00	00
24	By *James Forſter* of *Smithfield*, at 5 *l.* 10 *s.* per piece, for —— beſt	5	9	27	10	00
	By ballance, remaining unfold, at 5 *l.* per piece —— —— beſt	15	14	75	00	00
		35		180	00	00

How to ballance this accompt.

Having added up the quantity columns of each fide, I find that I have ſtill 15 pieces of my beſt lawns unfold : in order therefore to ſee what I have gained or loſt by what part of them is fold, I firſt credit the above ac-compt by ballance for the remaining 15 pieces unfold, at prime coſt, and then adding up both ſides, I find the credit ſide heavier then the debt ſide, by 11 *l.* 10 *s.*. which is the ſum gained ; wherefore I go to the debt ſide, and write, to profit and loſs gained for the ſaid difference, and the accompt is cloſed.

	Contra, Cr.				
1777.		pieces.			
Jan. 12	By *John Martin* of *Kingſton*, at 3 *l.* per piece, for —— beſt	20	6	60	00	00
Feb. 5	By cafh, at 2 *l.* 9 *s.* per piece, for com. fort	10	1	24	10	00
11	By *John Martin*, at 2 *l.* 8 *s.* per piece, for do.	10	3	24	00	00
26	By fufpence accompt, at 2 *l.* 2 *s.* per piece, fent *James Gibfon* of *Stilton* — ditto	10	12	21	00	00
		50		129	10	00

	Contra, Cr.				
1777.		dozen			
Jan. 10	By cafh, at 7 *l.* per dozen, for ——	6	1	42	00	00
Feb. 3	By fundries, as *per* Journal, at 7 *l.* 10 *s.* per dozen, delivered in barter ——	8		60	00	00
	By ball. remaining unfold, at 6 *l.* 6 *s.* per gal.	6	14	37	16	00
		20		139	16	00

Year & Month.	Velvets,	Dr.		pieces	yds.	Fo	l.	s.	d.
1777. Jan. 1	To ftock, at 8 s. per yard, for			25	450	4	180	00	00
Feb. 21	To William Webfter of Manchefter, at 7 s. per yard, for	}		10	280	5	98	00	00
	To profit and lofs, gained					12	50	17	00
				35	730		328	17	00

	John Martin of Barnet,	Dr.						
1777. Jan. 1	To ftock, due the 10th inftant			4	50	07	06
Feb. 11	To fundries, as per Journal, due in 4 months				114	00	00
					164	07	06

What the debt and credit fide of this accompt contains.
The debt fide of this, and every other perfonal accompt (if heavieft) fhews what debts the perfon has contracted with you, and the credit fide exhibits the payments which he has made, confequently the difference between them (if any) is the fum which remains due to you.

	James Tomlinfon of Hatfield,	Dr.						
1777. Jan. 1	To ftock, due on demand			4	28	04	00
Feb. 12	To fundries, as per Journal				55	15	00
					83	19	00

Year & Month.	Contra,	Cr.		Fo	l.	s.	d.
		pieces	*yds.*				
1777.							
Jan. 17	By fundries, as *per* Journal, at 9 *s.* 6 *d.* per yard, for ——— beſt ſort	15	270		128	05	00
Feb. 11	By *John Martin*, at 10 *d.* per yd. for ditto	10	180	3	90	00	00
26	By *John Kirkman* of *Richmond*, at 8 *s.* 6 *d. per* yard, for ſecond ſort	6	168	13	71	08	00
	By bal. remaining, at 7 *s.* per yd. ditto	4	112	14	39	04	00
		35	730		328	17	00

1777.	Contra,	Cr.					
Jan. 8	By rum, for my draft on him, payable to *Robert Smith* or order, at 3 days, for	6			48	00	00
Feb. 5	By caſh, in full, ———			1	2	07	06
	By ballance, due *April* 11th. ———			14	114	00	00
	How to ballance the above accompt.				164	7	6

The debt ſide being heavieſt caſt it up firſt, then caſting up alſo the payments on the credit ſide, ſubtract the ſum of the ſaid payments from the ſum on the debt ſide, and the difference is the ſum which remains due to you, for which difference, credit the accompt by ballance, and both ſides will then ſtand even.

1777.	Contra,	Cr.					
Jan. 23	By *Yorkſhire* planes for my draft on him at ſight, to *Ralph Cook*, ——— ——— ———	8			28	04	00
Feb. 12	By caſh in part, ——— ——— ———			1	20	00	00
	By ballance due to me, ——— ———			14	35	15	00
					83	19	00

P

Year & Month.		Fo.	L	s.	d.
	Stock, *Dr.*				
1777. Jan. 1	To *James Gray* of *Leeds*, due the 4th inst.	4	35	10	00
	To *Samuel Wilkinson* of *Manchester*, due 10th inst.	4	55	00	00
	To *William Webster* of *Manchester*, due the 1st } of *Feb.* next ― ―	5	73	00	00
	To ballance for the neat of my estate ―	14	11107	03	10
			11270	13	10
	What the debt and credit side of this accompt contains.				
	The debt side of this accompt contains a list of what debts you owe, and to whom. The credit side is an exact inventory of your effects, and the respective value of each article, together with the debts due to you. The difference therefore between the two sides (before you gave it credit by profit and loss) was your neat worth when you begun trade.				

	***James Gray* of *Leeds*,** *Dr.*				
1777. Jan. 25	To cash remitted him in full by the hands of *Thomas Scott*, waggoner ― . }	1	35	10	00

	***Samuel Wilkinson* of *Bolton*,** *Dr.*				
1777. Jan. 26	To cash in full ― ― ―	1	55	00	00

Year & Month.	Contra,	Cr.	Fo	l.	s.	d.
1777. Jan. 1	By cash in the hands of my banker, I. C.		1	500	00	00
	By Yorshire forest cloths for 24 pieces, qty. 490 yards, at 4s. 6d. per yard		1	110	05	00
	By Scots lawns for 15 pieces, at 4l. 10s. per piece		2	67	10	00
	By fustians for 30 pieces, at 2l. 2s. per piece		2	63	00	00
	By ditto for 20 ditto, at 2l. 10s. per piece		2	50	00	00
	By silk hose for 20 dozen, at 6l. 6s. per doz.		2	126	00	00
	By velvets for 25 pieces, qty. 450 yds. at 8s. per yd.		3	180	00	00
	By John Martin of Barnet, due the 10th inst.		3	50	0-	06
	By James Tomlinson of Hatfield, due on demand		3	28	04	00
	By profit and loss g ined since the 1st of Jan. last		12	10095	07	04
				11270	13	10

How to ballance this accompt.

Having first credited this accompt by profit and loss for the difference of that accompt, I next add up the said credit side, and subtracting the amount of the debt side from it, I write on the debt side *To Ballance, &c.* inserting the said difference in the money columns, which being then added up, closes the accompt.

Turn next to the ballance accompt.

Year & Month.	Contra,	Cr.	Fo	l.	s.	d.
1777. Jan. 1	By stock due the 4th instant		4	35	10	00

Year & Month.	Contra,	Cr.	Fo	l.	s.	d.
1777. Jan. 1	By stock due the 10th instant		4	55	00	00

Year & Month.	William *Webster* of *Manchester*, Dr.	Fo.	l.	s.	d.
1777. Feb. 1	To sundries as *per* Journal, in full ———		73	00	00
	By ballance due to him — ———	14	98	00	00
	What the debt and credit sides of this accompt contains.		171	00	00
	This, and all personal accompts (when the credit side is heaviest) shews on the said credit side the debts you have contracted with the person to whom the said accompt belongs; and the debt side shews what payments you have made him. The difference therefore between the two sides is the sum which remains due to him.				

	Indigo,				
		cwt *qrs.*			
1777. Jan. 3	To cash at 3s. per lb. for ——— 1 2	1	25	04	00
	To profit and loss gained — —	12	4	04	00
			29	08	00

	Printed Cottons, Dr.				
		pieces yds.			
1777. Jan. 5	To *James Thornton* at 2s. 8d. *per* yard for 10 250	6	33	06	08
Feb. 18	To ditto at 2s. 6d. *per* yard for — 30 655	6	81	17	06
	To profit and loss gained ———	12	22	18	0.
	40 905		138	02	0.

Year & Month.	Contra,	Cr.	Fo	l.	s.	d.
1777. Jan. 1	By ſtock, due the 1ſt of *February* next ———		4	73	00	00
Feb. 21	By velvets, for 10 pieces, quantity 280 yards, at 7*s.* per yard, as *per* my order ———		3	98	00	00
				171	00	00

How to ballance the above accompt.

The credit ſide here being heavieſt, add it up firſt, then find the difference between it and the debt ſide, which difference will be the money which remains due from you to the perſon whoſe accompt it is; go therefore to the debt ſide, and write To Ballance due to him, inſerting the ſaid difference in the money columns, and the accompt will then be cloſed, as you ſee.

	Contra,	Cr.		cwt.	qrs.	
1777. Feb. 1	By *William Webſter* at 3*s.* 6*d.* per lb. for	1	2	5	29	08	00

				29	08	00

	Contra,	Cr.		pieces	yds.				
1777. Feb. 12	By *James Tomlinſon* at 3*s.* per yard for beſt		8	200	3	30	00	00
22	By *John Martin* of *Kingſton* at 3*s.* 2*d.* per yard for —— 2d ſort	5	125	6	19	15	10
24	By *James Forſter* of *Smithfield*, at 3*s.* 4*d.* per yard for —— 2d ſort	15	330	9	55	00	00
26	By *John Kirkman* of *Richmond* at 3*s.* 4*d.* per yard for —— beſt	2	50	13	8	06	08
	By ballance remaining unſold at 2*s.* 6*d.* per yard —— 2d ſort	10	200	14	25	00	00
			40	905		138	02	06

Year & Month.		Fo	l.	s.	d.
	James Thornton of Wigan, Dr.				
1777.					
Jan. 28	To bills payable for his draft on me to *Charles Stevenson* or order, at 14 days — }	9	33	0	
	To ballance due to him — —	14	144		
			178		

		Fo	gal.	l.	s.	d.
	Rum, Dr.					
1777			gal.			
Jan. 8	To *John Martin, Barnet*, at 8s. 6d. per gal. for		120	3	48	00	00
Feb. 10	To *Daniel Bradshaw* at 8s. per gallon for		200	11	80	00	00
	To profit and loss gained —			12	21	15	00
			320		149	15	00

		Fo	l.	s.	d.
	John Martin of Kingston, Dr.				
1777.					
Jan. 12	To fustians, for 20 pieces (best) at 3l. per piece, due in 1 month }	2	60	00	00
Feb. 22	To sundries as per Journal, sent him as per his order the 10th instant — — }		68	03	04
			128	03	04

Year & Month		Fo	l.	s.	d.
	Contra, *Cr.*				
1777. Jan. 5	By printed cottons for 250 yards, at 2s. 8d. per yard, to be paid in fix weeks — }	5	33	06	08
Feb. 18	By fundries as *per* Journal for ——		14:	17	06
			178	04	02

			gal.		l.	s.	d.
	Contra, *Dr.*						
1777.							
Jan. 30	By hops delivered in barter at 10s. *per* gallon	120	9		60	00	00
Feb. 24	By cash received at 9s. 6d. per gallon for	80	1		38	00	00
27	By *Robert Lamb* of *Yarmouth* at 9s. 3d. per gal.	60	13		27	15	00
	By ballance remaining unfold at 8s. *per* gallon	60	14		24	00	00
		320			149	15	00

			l.	s.	d.
	Contra, *Cr.*				
1777.					
Feb. 12	By bills receivable for *Fletcher* on *Brooks*, due the 21st inftant for ——— —— }	7	60	00	00
29	By fundries as *per* Journal. (Compounded with him) See Journal. }		68	03	04
			128	03	04

Year & Month.		Fo	L.	s.	d.
	Bills Receivable, **Dr.**				
1777. Jan. 15	To *Yorkshire* forest cloths, for *David Johnston* on *Stephen Ramsay* at 10 days ———	1	96	10	00
26	To *Scots* lawns, for *Forster* on *Smith* and Co. at 15 days ———	2	20	00	00
Feb. 12	To *John Martin, Kingston,* for *Fletcher* on *Brooks,* due the 21st instant, for ———	6	60	00	00
14	To *James Wilks* of *St. Edmond's Bury,* for his draft on *Maxwell* and Co. for ———	7	68	05	00
	What the debt and credit side of this accompt contains. The debt side of this accompt exhibits a list of the several bills which you have taken in the course of trade; and the credit side shews you what part of them you have received cash for, or how otherwise disposed of. The difference therefore between the two sides (if any had been) would have shewn what part of them remain'd in your hands.		244	15	00
	James Wilks of St. Edmond's Bury, Dr.				
1777. Jan. 17	To velvets, in part for 15 pieces, quantity 270 yds. at 9s. 6d. per yard, due in one month ———	3	68	05	00
Feb. 23	To sundries as per Journal, sent him as per order the 10th instant		70	07	00
			138	12	00
	Hats, **Dr.**				
		doz.			
1777. Jan. 20	To sundries as per Journal at 6l. per dozen for	20	120	00	00

Year & Month.	Contra,	Cr.	Fo	l.	s.	d.
1777.						
Jan. 28	By cafh for *Johnston's* on *Ramfay*	—	1	96	10	00
Feb. 14	By cafh received for *Forfter's* on *Smith* and Co.	—	1	20	00	00
20	By *Devonfhire* planes, paid *Jacob Ratcliff Wilk's* draft on *Maxwell* and Co. for		11	68	05	00
21	By profit and lofs, loft *Fletcher's* draft on *Brooks* out of my pocket book		12	60	00	00
				244	15	00

How to ballance the above accompt.
The debt and credit fide of this accompt being equal, fhews that you have either received cafh for, or otherwife difpofed of, all your bills. Had the credit fide been lefs than the debt fide, (for it can never be heavier) then you muft have credited the accompt by ballance for the difference, which would have fhewn you what bills remain'd in your hands, and the amount of them.

1777.	Contra,	Cr.				
Feb. 14	By bills receivable, remitted me his draft on *Maxwell* and Co. for		7	68	05	00
	By ballance due to me	—	14	70	07	00
				138	12	00

	Contra,	Cr.		dcz.			
	By ballance remaining, at 6*l.* per dozen for,		20	14	120	00	00

N. B. As there were no part of the goods difpofed of, the accompt is neceffarily clofed by crediting it by ballance for the whole quantity at prime coft.

Q

Year & Month.		Fo	l.	s.	d.
1777.	*Thomas Simpson of Manchester,* Dr.				
	By ballance due to him the 20th of *Feb.* next ——	14	60	00	00

		pieces	yds		l.	s.	d.
	Yorkshire Planes, Dr.						
1777.							
Jan. 23	To sundries, as *per* Journal, 4s. *per* yd. for	25	525		105	00	00
	To profit and loss, gained ——			12	10	18	0:
		—	—		—	—	—
		25	525		115	18	0:

		Fo	l.	s.	d.
	Ralph Cook of Wakefield, Dr.				
	To ballance, due to him the 23d of *March* ——	14	36	16	00

Year & Month.		Fo	L.	s.	d.
	Contra,　　　　　　　　　　　　　　*Cr.*				
1777.					
Jan. 20	By hats, in part for 20 dozen, at 6*l. per dozen,* due } in 3 months ——— ———	7	60	00	00

	Contra,　　　　　　　　　　　　　　*Cr.*		pieces	yds				
1777.								
Feb. 22	By *John Martin, Kingston,* at 4*s.* 6*d. per* yd.	10	215	6	48	07	06
23	By *James Wilks* of *St. Edmond's Bury,* at } 4*s.* 8*d. per* yard for ———	3	78	7	18	04	00
26	By *J. Kirkman, Richmond,* at 4*s.* 8*d. per* yd.	4	88	13	20	10	08
	By ballance remaining, at 4*s. per* yard	8	144	14	28	16	00
		25	525		115	18	02

	Contra,　　　　　　　　　　　　　　*Cr.*				
1777.					
Jan. 23	By *Yorkshire* planes, in part for 25 pieces, 525 yds. } at 4*s. per* yard, due in 4 months ———	8	36	16	00

Year & Month.		Fo.	l.	s.	d.
	James Forster of Smithfield, Dr.				
1777.					
Jan. 26	To *Scots* lawns, in part for 10 pieces, at 5 *l.* 5 *s. per* } piece, due in 6 weeks ——— }	2	12	10	00
Feb. 24	To fundries, as *per* Journal, to pay in 2 months		118	18	00
			131	08	00

	Bills payable, Dr.				
1777.					
Feb. 15	To cafh, paid *Thornton's* draft on me to *Charles* } *Stevenfon,* or order ——— }	1	33	06	08

What the debt and credit fide of this accompt contains.
The credit fide of this accompt prefents to you an exact lift of what bills (drawn upon you) you have accepted, and the debt fide what part of them you have paid. The diffeŕ̵ence (if any had been) of the two fides, would have fhewn you what part of them remain'd unpaid.

		poc.	cwt.	qrs.	lb.				
	Hops, Dr.								
1777.									
Jan. 30	To rum recd. in barter, at 1 *s. per lb.*	10	10	2	24	6	60	00	00
	To profit and lofs, gained						5	04	08
		10	10	2	24		65	04	08

Year & Month.		Fo	l.	s.	d.
1777.	**Contra,** Cr.				
Feb. 24	By cash in full ——— ———	1	12	10	00
	By ballance due to me the 24th of Feb. ———	14	118	18	00
			131	08	00

1777.	**Contra,** Cr.				
Jan. 23	By James Thornton of Manchester, for his draft on me to Charles Stevenson or order, at 14 days }	6	33	06	08

How the above accompt is ballanced.

As the debt and credit sides of this accompt are already equal to each other, it therefore closes of itself. But had the debt side been less than the credit, (for it can never be greater) then you must have charged it Debtor to ballance for the difference, which would have closed the accompt, and shewn you what bills remained against you undischarged.

		poc.	cwt.	qrs.	lb.				
1777.	**Contra,** Cr.								
Feb. 23	By James Wilks of St. Edmond's Bury, at 1s. 4d. per lb. for }	5	4	3	26	7	37	02	00
27	By Robert Lamb of Yarmouth, at 1s. 4d. per lb. for ——— }	5	5	2	26	13	28	02	08
		10	10	2	24		65	04	08

Year & Month.		Fo	l.	s.	d.
	Pickled Pork,　　　　　　　*Dr.*				
1777. Fe. 3	To silk hose receiv'd in barter, at 4*l.* 4*s. per* bar.　bar.　10　2		42	00	00
	10		42	00	00
	Samuel Rich of Norwich,　　　　*Dr.*				
	To ballance due to him the 8th of *June* ———	14	44	06	08
	Norwich Crapes,　　　　　　*Dr.*				
1777. Feb. 8	To *Samuel Rich*, at 2*s. per* yard, for　pieces yds. To profit and lofs, gain'd ———　15 ｜ 310	10	31	00	00
	12		8	12	00
	15 ｜ 310		39	12	00
	Norwich Stuffs,　　　　　　*Dr.*				
1777. Feb. 8	To *Samuel Rich*, at 1*s.* 4*d. per* yard, for　pieces yds ｜ 10 ｜ 200	10	13	06	08

Year & Month		Fol	L.	s.	d.
	Contra, Cr.	bar.			
1777.					
Feb. 25	By cash at, 3l. 16s. per barrel for ———	10	1	38 00 00
	By profit and loss, lost ———			4 00 00
		10		42 00 00

	Contra, Cr.				
1777.					
Feb. 8	By sundries, as per Journal, due in 6 months			44 06 08

	Contra, Cr.	pieces	yds		
1777.					
Feb. 12	By *James Tomlinson*, at 2s. 6d. per yd. for	10	206	3	25 15 00
28	By *Cuthbert Eustage* of *Stamford*, at 2s. 9d. per yard for ———	5	104	14	13 17 00
		15	310		39 12 00

	Contra, Cr.	pieces	yds		
1777.	By ballance remaining, at 1s. 4d. per yard	10	200	14	13 06 08

Year & Month.		Fo	l.	s.	d.
	Daniel Bradſhaw, Thames-ſtreet, **Dr.**				
1777. Feb. 10	To caſh in part, for 200 gallons of rum, and 10 anchors of brandy ———	1	60	00	00
	To ballance due to him ———	14	65	00	00
			125	00	00
	Brandy,.. **Dr.**		anc.		
1777 Feb. 10	To *Daniel Bradſhaw*, at 4l. 10s. per anchor, for	10	11	45	00	00
	To profit and loſs, gained ———		12	3	15	00
		10		48	15	00
	Printed Linens, **Dr.**		pieces yds		
1777. Feb. 18	To *James Thornton*, at 3s. per yard, for	20	420	6	63	00	00
	To profit and loſs, gained ———				7	07	00
		20	420		70	07	00
	Devonſhire Planes, **Dr.**		yds.		
1777. Feb. 20	To ſundries, as per journal, at 5s. 6d. per yd. for	500		135	00	00
	To profit and loſs gained ———		12	12	10	00
		500		147	10	00

Year & Month.	Contra,	Cr.	Fol	l.	s.	d.
1777. Feb. 10	By sundries, as *per* Journal ——— ———			125	00	00

	Contra,	Cr.	anc.			
1777. Feb. 24	By cash, at 5 *l.* 5 *s. per.* anchor, for ———	5	1	26	05	00
	By ballance remaining, at 4 *l.* 10 *s. per* anchor	5	14	22	10	00
		10		48	15	00

	Contra,	Cr.	pieces	yds.		
1777. Feb. 23	By *James Wilks* of *St. Edmond's Bury*, at 3 *s.* 6 *d.* per yard, for ———	4	86	7	15	01	00
24	By *James Forster* in *Smithfield*, at 3 *s.* 6 *d.* *per* yard, for. ——— ———	10	208	9	36	08	00
	By ball. remaining unsold, at 3 *s. per* yd. for	6	126	14	18	18	00
		20	420		70	07	00

	Contra,	Cr.	yds.			
1777. Feb. 28	By *Cuthbert Eustage* of *Stamford*, at 6 *s.* 6 *d.* per yard, for ——— ———	200	14	65	00	00
	By ballance remaining, at 5 *s.* 6 *d. per* yard, for	300	14	82	10	00
		500		147	10	00

VOL. II.   **R**

Year & Month.	Profit and loss,	Dr.	Fo	l.	s.	d.
1777.						
Feb. 21	To bills receivable, loſt *Fletcher's* on *Brooks* out of my pocket book for ——— ———		7	60	00	00
Feb. 28	To *John Martin* of *Kingſton*, loſt by his compoſition		6	17	00	10
	To caſh, paid my board, which with pocket expences, &c. comes to ——— ———		1	8	00	00
	To pickled pork ——— ———		10	4	00	00
	To charges on trade ——— ———		14	20	00	00
	To ſtock, gained ſince the 1ſt of *Jan.* laſt ———		4	10095	07	04
	N. B. This accompt is firſt to be cloſed in the general ball.			10204	08	02

What the debt and credit ſide of this accompt contain.
The debt ſide of this accompt exhibits your loſſes, with
an account of the ſeveral things or articles by which thoſe
reſpective loſſes were ſuſtained. The credit ſide ſhews your
ſeveral gains, together with a liſt of the article or things
to which thoſe gains reſpectively belong; the difference
between the two ſides is your neat gain or loſs.

	Thomas Burges of *Paiſley,*	Dr.				
	To ballance due to him ——— ———		14	100	00	00

	Suſpence accompt,	Dr.				
1777.						
Feb. 26	To fuſtians, for 10 pieces, ſent *James Gibſon* of *Stilton,* at 2l. 2s. *per* piece ———		2	21	00	00

What the debt and credit ſide of this accompt contain.
This accompt is debited for all goods, &c. which you
have ſent to people without their particular order; it is
therefore credited by what of the ſaid goods are returned
to you, and by the perſons to whom ſent, for what part
of them they keep as ſoon as they adviſe you of it.

Year & Month.	Contra,　　　　　　　　　　　　　　Cr	Fo	l.	s.	d.
1777. Feb. 28	By cafh given me by my father to extend my trade	1	10000	00	00
	By *Yorkſhire* planes ———	1	13	11	00
	By *Scots* lawns ——— ———	2	12	10	00
	By fuſtians ——— ———	2	16	10	00
	By filk hoſe ——— ———	2	13	16	00
	By velvets ——— ———	3	50	17	00
	By indigo ———	5	4	04	00
	By printed cottons ——— ———	5	22	18	04
	By rum ——— ———	6	21	15	00
	By *Yorkſhire* planes ——— ———	8	10	18	02
	By hops ——— ——— ———	9	5	04	08
	By *Norwich* crapes ——— ———	10	8	12	00
	By brandy ——— ———	11	3	15	00
	By printed linens ——— ———	11	7	07	00
	By *Devonſhire* planes ———	11	12	10	00
			10204	08	02

How to ballance this accompt.
The credit fide of this accompt (if your affairs are in a good fituation) will always be heavieſt; you therefore debit it to ſtock for the difference, which cloſes the accompt. Turn now to your ſtock accompt.

	Contra,　　　　　　　　　　　　　　Cr				
1777. Feb. 21	By *Scots* lawns, for 20 pieces, at 5 l. per piece, per my order, the 27th of *Jan.* ——— }	2	100	00	00

	Contra,　　　　　　　　　　　　　　Cr.				
	By ballance, remaining, at 2 l. 2 s. per piece —	14	21	00	00

How to ballance the above accompt.
As you have neither received any part of the goods back again, or advice whether the perfon to whom they were fent keeps them at the price you fet upon them, it muſt therefore be credited by ballance for the whole a-mount, till further advice.

Year & Month		Fo	l.	s.	d.
	John Kirkman of Richmond, Dr.				
1777. Feb. 26	To fundries, as *per* journal, to pay in 3 months —		100	05	04
	Robert Lamb of Yarmouth, Dr.				
1777. Feb. 27	To fundries, as *per* journal, to pay in 2 months —		55	17	08
	Jeans, Dr.				
1777. Feb. 28	To cafh, at 2 s. 4 d. *per* yard, for —	*pieces. yards.* —	50	1000	1	116	13	04
	Shoes, Dr.				
1777. Feb. 28	To cafh, at 4 s. *per* pair, for — —	*pair.* 400	1	80	00	00
	Thread hose, Dr.				
1777. Feb. 28	To cafh, at 1 l. 4 s. *per* dozen, for —	*dozen.* 20	1	24	00	00

Year & Month.		Fo	l.	s.	d.
1777.	*Contra,* *Cr.*				
	By ballance, due to me the 26th of *May* ———	14	100	05	04
	Contra, *Cr.*				
	By ballance, due the 27th of *April* — — — —	12	55	17	08
	Contra, *Cr.*				
	pieces. yds.				
	By ballance remaining, at 2s. 4d. *per* yard |50|1000	14	116	13	04
	Contra, *Cr.*				
	pair.				
	By ballance remaining, at 4s. *per* pair — | 400	14	80	00	00
	Contra, *Cr.*				
	dozen.				
	By ballance remaining, at 1l. 4s. *per* dozen — | 20	14	24	00	00

Year & Month.		Fo	l.	s.	d.
1777. Feb. 28	**Cuthbert Euftage of Stamford,** *Dr*. To fundries, as *per* journal, to pay in 4 months — —		78	17	00

	Charges on trade, *Dr*.				
1777. Feb. 28	To cafh, paid clerk's wages, ware-houfe rent, and other ⎱ expences on trade, fince the 1ft of *Jan.* — —⎰	1	20	00	00

What the debt and credit fides of this accompt contain.
The debt fide of this accompt contains general charges on
trade, which as there can be expected no returns for, the
credit fide is therefore ballanced by profit and lofs.

	Ballance, *Dr*.				
	To cafh, remaining in my hands — — — —	1	10353	10	00
	To *Scots* lawns, for 15 pieces, at 5*l. per* piece — —	2	75	00	00
	To filk hofe, for 6 dozen, at 6*l.* 6*s. per* dozen —	2	37	16	00
	To cotton velvets, for 4 pieces, quantity 112 yds. at 7*s. p.* yd.	3	39	04	00
	To *John Martin* of *Barnet*, due the 11th of *June* —	3	114	00	00
	To *James Tomlinfon* of *Hotfield*, in part for goods fold ⎱ him the 12th of *Feb.* — — —⎰	3	35	15	00
	To printed cottons, for 10 pieces, quantity 200 yards, at ⎱ 2*s.* 6*d. per* yard —⎰	5	25	00	00
	To rum, for 60 gallons, at 8*s. per* gallon — —	6	24	00	00
	To *James Wilks* of St. *Edmond's Bury*, for goods fent ⎱ him the 23d of *Feb.* —⎰	7	70	07	00
	To hats, for 20 dozen, at 6*l. per* dozen — — —	7	120	00	00
	To *Yorkfhire* planes, for 8 pieces, quantity 144 yards, at ⎱ 4*s. per* yard — — —⎰	8	28	16	00
	To *James Forfter* of *Smithfield*, due the 24th of *Feb.* —	9	118	18	00
	To *Norwich* ftuffs, for 10 pieces, quantity 200 yards, at ⎱ 1*s.* 4*d. per* yard — — — —⎰	10	13	06	08
	To brandy, for 5 anchors, at 4*l.* 10*s. per* anchor —	11	22	10	00
	To printed linens, for 6 pieces, quantity 126 yds. at 3*s. p.* yd.	11	18	18	00
	To *Devonfhire* planes, for 300 yards, at 5*s.* 6*d. per* yard	11	82	10	00
	To fufpence accompt, for 10 pieces fuftians, fent *James* ⎱ *Gibfon* of *Stilton*, at 2*l.* 2*s. per* piece — —⎰	12	21	00	00
	To *John Kirkman* of *Richmond*, due the 26th of *March* —	13	100	05	04
	To *Robert Lamb* of *Yarmouth*, due the 27th of *Feb.* —	13	55	17	08
	To *Jeans*, for 50 pieces, quantity 1000 yds. at 2*s.* 4*d. per* yd.	13	116	13	04
	To fhoes, for 400 pair, at 4*s. per* pair — — —	13	80	00	00
	To thread hofe, for 20 dozen, at 1*l.* 4*s. per* dozen —	13	24	00	00
	To *Cuthbert Euftage* of *Stamford*, due the 28th of *June* —	14	78	17	00
			11656	04	00

What the debt and credit fides of this accompt contain.
The debt fide of this accompt contains a lift of what goods
you have remaining in hands unfold: What debts are due to
you, &c. &c. The credit fide fhews what debts you owe
to others, &c.

Year & Month.		Fol	l.	s.	d.
1777.	_Contra,_ _Cr._				
	By ballance, due to me the 28th of _June_ — — —	14	78	17	00
	Contra, _Cr._				
	By profit and loſs — — — — — —	12	20	00	00
	Contra, _Cr._				
	By _William Webſter_ of _Mancheſter_, for goods bought of him the 21ſt of _Feb._ — — — — —	5	98	00	00
	By _James Thornton_ of _Wigan_, for goods bought of him the 18th ditto — — — — — —	6	144	17	06
	By _Thomas Simpſon_ of _Mancheſter_, due the 20th of _April_ next — — — — — — —	8	60	00	00
	By _Ralph Cook_ of _Wakefield_, due the 23d of _May_ —	8	36	16	00
	By _Samuel Rich_ of _Norwich_, due the 8th of _Auguſt_ —	10	44	06	08
	By _Daniel Bradſhaw_, in part for goods bought of him the 10th of _Feb._ — — — — — —	11	65	00	00
	By _Thomas Burges_ of _Paiſley_, for goods bought of him the 21ſt ditto — — — — — —	12	100	00	00
	By ſtock for the neat of my eſtate — — —	4	11107	03	10
			11656	04	00

How to ballance this accompt.
Having credited this accompt by ſtock for the difference there, both ſides is, you ſee evened, which finiſhes the general ballance.

The learner has now feen how the general ballance is performed; but the reafon of thofe effects, perhaps, he do not yet clearly comprehend; this, however, will appear plain to him by reviewing thofe three principal accompts, viz. *Profit* and *Lofs*, *Stock*, and *Ballance*, and confidering what the difference between the debt and credit fides of each of them exhibited whilft they ftood unclofed. The difference of your ftock accompt was the neat of what you were worth at the opening of your books. The difference of your ballance accompt is your prefent worth. The difference, therefore, between what you was worth at opening of your books, and what you are worth now, muft neceffarily be equal to your neat gains, which is the difference between the credit and debt fides of your profit and lofs accompt. Now as the difference between the credit and debt fides of your ftock accompt (whilft it ftood open) was the neat of what you were worth at opening of your books, fo your neat gains being carried to the credit fide of your faid ftock accompt, the difference then muft be your prefent worth, and exactly equal to the difference between the debt and credit fides of your ballance accompt; which, as I before obferved, is alfo your prefent worth. Such difference being therefore placed to the deficient fide of each, viz. to the debt fide of your ftock, and to the credit fide of your ballance accompt, muft of confequence clofe both of them.

WASTE-BOOK.
No. II.

LONDON, *January* 1, 1777.

A N Inventory of the money, goods, and debts, belonging to me, A. B. also the debts due from me to others,
taken from ballance accompt of Ledger No. 1. as follows:

	£.	s.	d.
I have in ready money ———	10353	10	00
15 pieces of *Scots* lawns, at 5 *l.* per piece —	75	00	00
6 dozen of silk hose, at 6 *l.* 6 *s.* per dozen	37	16	00
4 pieces of cotton velvets, quantity 112 } yards, at 7 *s.* per yard ——— —}	39	04	00
John Martin of *Barnet*, owes me, due the } 11th of *April* }	114	00	00
James Tomlinson of *Hatfield*, in part for } goods sold him the 12th of *Decem.* last }	35	15	00
10 pieces printed cottons, quantity 200 } yards, at 2 *s.* 6 *d.* per yard ——— }	25	00	00
✓ 60 gallons of rum, at 8 *s.* per gallon ———	24	00	00
James Wilks of St. *Edmond's Bury*, for } goods sold him the 23d of *December* — }	70	07	00
20 dozen of hats, at 6 *l.* per dozen —	120	00	00
8 pieces *Yorkshire* planes, quantity 144 yards } at 4 *s.* per yard ——— }	28	16	00
James Forster, *Smithfield*, due the 24th of *Feb.*	118	18	00
10 pieces *Norwich* stuffs, quantity 200 yards, } at 1 *s.* 4 *d.* per yard ——— }	13	06	08
5 anchors of brandy, at 4 *l.* 10 *s.* per anchor	22	10	00
6 pieces printed linens, quantity 126 yds. at } 3 *s.* per yard — — }	18	18	00
300 yards *Devonshire* planes, at 5 *s.* 6 *d.* per yd.	82	10	00
Suspence accompt, for 10 pieces fustians to } *James Gibson* of *Stilton* ——— }	21	00	00
John Kirkman, *Richmond*, due 26th of *March*	100	05	04
Robert Lamb of *Yarmouth*, due 27th of *Feb.*	55	17	08
50 pieces jeans, qty. 1000 yds. at 2 *s.* 4 *d.* per yd.	115	13	04
400 pair of shoes, at 4 *s.* per pair	80	00	00
20 dozen thread hose, at 1 *l.* 4 *s.* per dozen	24	00	00
Cuthbert Eustage, *Stamford*, due 28th of *April*	78	17	00

11656 04 00

		l.	s.	d.	l.	s.	d.

———————— *January* 1ft.————————
I owe as follows:

	l.	s.	d.
To *William Webfter* of *Manchefter*, for goods bought the 21ft of *December*	98	0	0
To *James Thornton* of *Wigan*, for goods bought of him the 18th of *December*	144	17	6
To *Thomas Simpfon* of *Manchefter*, due the 20th of *Feb.*	60	0	0
✓ To *Ralph Cook* of *Wakefield*, due the 23d of *March*	36	16	0
To *Samuel Rich* of *Norwich*, due 8th of *June*	44	6	8
To *Daniel Bradfhaw*, in part for goods bought the 10th of *December*	65	0	0
To *Thomas Burges* of *Paifley*, for goods bought the 21ft ditto	100	0	0

549 | 00 | 02

———————— *January* 5th.————————

I. J.
No.
1
2
3

Sent as an adventure to *Virginia*, in the fhip *Happy Return*, Captain *Scott* mafter, confign'd to *James Johnfton*, the following goods, mark'd and numbered as *per margin*, viz.

	l.	s.	d.
8 pieces of *Yorkfhire* planes, quantity 144 yds. at 4s. per yard	28	16	0
✓ 300 yards *Devonfhire* planes, at 5s. 6d. per yd.	82	10	0
20 dozen pair thread hofe, at 1l. 4s. per doz.	24	0	0
Paid cuftom and other charges till on board	2	18	4

138 | 04 | 04

———————— 10th.————————

✓ **Sold** for ready money 15 pieces of *Scots* lawns, at 6l. per piece

90 | 00 | 00

———————— 14th.————————

✓ Ship'd for *James Bell* of *Berwick upon Tweed*, (on board the *London* packet, Captain *Wilkinfon* mafter) as *per* his order the 1ft inftant, the following goods, viz.

	l.	s.	d.
10 pieces printed cottons, quantity 200 yards, at 3s. per yard	30	0	0
60 gallons of rum, at 10s. per gallon	30	0	0
6 pieces of printed linens, quantity 126 yards, at 3s. 6d. per yard	22	1	0

82 | 01 | 00

Jan.

		l.	s.	d.

------———January 21ft.-------

W B Sent as an adventure to *Jamaica*, in the fhip *Hopewell*,
No. Captain *Gordon* mafter, confgned to *William Boyd*, the
1 following goods, mark'd and numbered as *per* margin, viz.
2

		l.	s.	d.
3	20 dozen of men's hats, at 6l. per dozen	120	0	0
✓	10 pieces *Norwich* ftuffs, quantity 200 yards, t 1s 4d per yard ——— }	13	6	8
	28 pieces of jeans, quantity 566 yards, at 2s. 4d. per yard }	66	0	8
	Paid charges till on board ———	14	11	4
	Paid alfo a premium to *Simon Smith* and Co. for infuring 200l. }	10	0	0

		223	18	08

------———— 27th.-------

✓ *James Watfon* of *Berwick upon Tweed*, advifes me that
he has bought and fhipped off *per* my order, on board the
fhip *Speedwell*, *George Gray* mafter, confgned to *James
Arnold* at *Dunkirk*, 1000 quarters of wheat at 30s. per
quarter. The amount of the whole, together with his com
miffion and other charges in fhipping, he has drawn on me
for payable to *Coats* and Co. due the 14th of *March*, being

		1535	10	00

------———— February 2d.-------

Lent *Charles Thompfon* on bond for 6 months, at 5l. per
cent. — — — —

		1000	00	00

------———7th.-------

✓ Received from *James Watfon* of *Berwick upon Tweed*,
a debenture bill, granted by the collectors of the cuftoms
there, for the bounty on my wheat exported to *Dunkirk*,
together with a certificate to the commiffioners of the cuftoms, fetting forth that he had not money in his hands fufficient to pay the faid bounty ; accordingly I have this day
prefented the faid debenture bill and certificate to the com
miffioners, who have caufed the fame to be indorfed, in or
der to be paid as foon as convenient. The bounty of 1000
quarters, at 5s. per quarter, is — —

		250	00	00

✓ Received of the collectors of excife, the draw back on my
200 yards of *Norwich* ftuffs, exported to *Jamaica*

		2	10	00

S 2   Feb.

		_l._	_s._	_d._

————————February 13th.————————

No 1
to 50
J. H
✓

Shipped on board the *Good Intent*, Captain *Richardson*
in her, for *Dublin*, configned to *Thomas Hervey* to fell for
my account, mark'd and numbered as *per* margin,
50 pockets of hops, wt. 42 cwt. 3 qrs. 14lb. at 4*l. per cwt.*

	_l._	_s._	_d._
Prefently bought of *George Gair*, to pay in 2 months	171	10	0
Paid charges till on board —	1	4	6

172 | 14 | 06

————————————— 20th. —————————————

✓ Paid *Thomas Simpfon* of *Manchefter* in full, as follows:

	_l._	_s._	_d._
In cafh ———	57	10	0
He has abated me —	2	10	0

60 | 00 | 00

————————————— 24th. —————————————

✓ Received of *James Forfter* in *Smithfield* in part — 100 | 00 | 00

✓ *James Gibfon* of *Stilton* has fent me back 5 pieces of my
fuftians, which I fent him,

	_l._	_s._	_d._
Valued at —	10	10	0
The other 5 pieces he has kept —	10	10	0

21 | 00 | 00

————————————— 27th. —————————————

✓ Drawn my bill on *Robert Lamb* of *Yarmouth* at 20 days
fter date, payable to *John Banks* or order, for which I
have received — — 55 | 17 | 08

✓ *John Martin* of *Barnet* has paid me in full, as follows:

	_l._	_s._	_d._
Given me in cafh —	112	0	0
I have abated him —	2	0	0

114 | 00 | 00

————————————— March 1ft. —————————————

Sent *Samuel Rick* of *Norwich* my 5 anchors of brandy,
as *per* his order the 25th of *February*, at 5*l.* 5*s. per* anchor 26 | 05 | 00

————————————— 7th. —————————————

✓ Difcounted *George Edgar* a bill for 1000*l.* drawn by
James Corrie in *Edinburgh*, on *Thomas Hamilton*, 30 days
to run.

	_l._	_s._	_d._
Paid him in cafh —	996	0	0
The difcount at 5*l. per cent.* is —	4	0	0

1000 | 00 | 00

March

	l.	s.	d.
——————March 10th.——————			
✓ Paid *Daniel Bradshaw* in full ———	65	00	00
——————14th.——————			
James Tomlinson of *Hatfield* has paid me in full —	35	15	00
——————18th——————			
Remitted *James Thornton* of *Wigan*, a bill drawn by *John Freeman* of *Glasgow* on *Campbell* and Co. at——— for which I gave ——— ———	100	00	00
——————24th.——————			
✓ The ship *Polly*, Captain *Todd* master, is this day arrived from *Berwick upon Tweed*, with 200 quarters of barley and 100 quarters of oats, consign'd to me by *James Green* there, to sell for his account.			
Freight, custom, and other charges which I have paid is	30	12	06
——————26th.——————			
✓ *Ralph Cook* of *Wakefield* has drawn his bill on me, payable to *James Wood* or order, due the 15th of *May*, which I have accepted, for ——— ——— ———	36	16	00
——————31st.——————			
✓ *John Kirkman* of *Richmond* has remitted me his bill on *John Dickson* in the *Strand*, which he having accepted, I have this day remitted the same to *Thomas Burges* of *Paisley*, in full of what I owed him, the bill being for	100	00	00
——————April 3d.——————			
✓ Paid *Watson's* bill on me to *Coats* and Co. —	1535	10	00
✓ Received of *James Wilks* of *St. Edmond's Bury* in full	70	07	00
——————6th.——————			
James Forster of *Smithfield* has paid me the ballance of his accompt in full, being ——— —	18	18	00
✓ Received for *George Edgar's* bill, drawn by *Corris* on *Hamilton* — ——— ——— —	1800	00	00
✓ *William Webster* of *Manchester* has drawn his bill on me, due the 16th of *May*, payable to *James Bardett* or order, which I have accepted, for ——— —	98	00	00
——————10th.——————			
✓ *James Thornton* of *Wigan* being in town, I have this day paid him the ballance of his accompt, being	44	17	06
✓ The receiver general of the customs has this day paid me the debenture of my wheat exported to *Dunkirk* —	250	00	00
——————13th.——————			
✓ Paid *George Gair* in full for hops ———	171	00	00

April

		£	s.	d.

———— *April* 16th. ————

James Arnold of *Dunkirk* advises me that the ship *Speed-well* arrived safe there the 10th of *February*, and that he has sold all my wheat for ready money, the neat proceeds of which (after paying freight and other charges, together with his commission at 2 ½ per cent.) amounts to 1650 *l.* 10s. 2d.

In return for which he shipp'd on board the *Eagle*, Captain *Davis* master, who arrived this day, the following goods, viz.

	l.	*s.*	*d*			
30 casks of brandy, containing 60 gallons each, at prime cost and charges there, comes to	540	0	0			
12 pipes of port wine, at prime cost and charges there	324	10	6			
Ballance remaining in his hands	785	19	8	1650	10	02

———— 17th. ————

	l.	*s.*	*d*			
Paid freight and duty on my brandy, with other charges of landing and bringing it into the warehouse	60	16	0			
Paid ditto on my 12 pipes of wine	50	13	0	111	09	00

———— 19th ————

Sold for ready money *James Green's* 100 quarters of oats, per the *Polly* from *Berwick*, at 16s. per quarter — | 80 | 00 | 00 |

———— 24th. ————

Thomas Harvey of *Dublin* advises me that he hath received my 50 pockets of hops per the *Good Intent*,

	l.	*s.*	*d.*			
25 pockets of which, weighing 22 cwt. he has sold for ready money, at 6l. 5s. per cwt. comes to	137	10	0			
The other 25 pockets he has put into his warehouse in hopes of a better market, which at prime cost and charges comes to	82	7	0	219	17	00

———— 28th. ————

Sold to *John Todd* of *Greenwich*, *James Green's* 200 quarters of barley, at 19s. per quarter, to pay in six weeks | 190 | 00 | 00 |

Paid waterage and other charges on *James Green's* barley, as per petty cash book — | 5 | 15 | 00 |

April

		l.	s.	d.
✓	———— April 28th. ———— My commiſſion on the *Polly's* cargo, amounting to 270 l. at 2 ½ per cent. is — —	6	15	00
✓	———— May 2 l. ———— bought in company with *John Ward*, each one half of the ſhip call'd the *Tyger*, of which we paid down our re- ſpective ſhares, the whole being — —	800	00	00
✓	———— 5th. ———— Received of *Cuthbert Euſtage* of *Stamford* in full —	78	17	00
✓	———— 8th. ———— *James Bell* of *Berwick upon Tweed*, has remitted me hi: bill on *Thomas Bailey*, due in 15 days, which *Bailey* ha: accepted, for	82	01	00
✓ J.G.	———— 12th. ———— Received from *James Green* of *Berwick upon Tweed*, per the *Nancy*, Capt. in *Nealſon*, the following goods to ſell for his account, mark'd as per margin. 200 kits of pickled ſalmon, and 10 cheſts of eggs. Paid freight, waterage, &c. on the above goods —	14	02	06
✓ W H	Received alſo at the ſame time, by the above veſſel, from *William Hogg*, the following goods to ſell for his account, mark'd as per margin, viz. 30 barrels of pickled pork, containing 3 cwt. each, and 50 firkins of butter.			
✓	———— 15th. ———— Paid freight, waterage, porterage, &c. on *William Hogg's* goods per the *Nancy* — —	6	03	06
✓	Paid *Ralph Cook's* draft on me to *James Wood* —	36	16	00
✓	———— 16th. ———— Paid alſo *William Webſter's* on me to *James Burdett*	98	00	00
✓	———— 20th. ———— Received advice from *James Johnſton* at *Virginia*, per the *Rover*, that the *Happy Return*, Captain *Scott*, arrived ſafe there the 15th of *February*, by which he received my goods as per invoice, the coſt and charges of which amounted to	138	04	04
✓	———— 23d. ———— Received for *James Bell's* draft on *Thomas Bailey*	82	01	00
✓	———— 28th. ———— *John Ward* has paid the carpenters, ſail makers, &c. for repairing and fitting out the *Tyger* ———	120	00	00

June

			L.	s.	d.

―――――――― *June* 2d. ――――――――

✓ Sold for ready money *James Green's* 200 kits of salmon, at 16*s. per* kitt

	l.	s.	d.			
Comes to — — —	160	0	0			
Also his 10 chests of eggs, at 3*l. per* chest	30	0	0			
				190	00	co

✓ Paid porterage on *James Green's* goods *per* the *Nancy* — | | 2 | 15 | co |

My commission at 5 *per cent.* on 190*l.* amounts to | | 9 | 10 | 00 |

――――――――― 5th. ―――――――――

Thomas James, John Wilson, and myself, have this day agreed to be equally concern'd in company in an adventure to *Jamaica,* for which they are to allow me as manager 2 ¼ *per cent.* commission ; and accordingly I have freighted the ship *Tyger* (belonging to *John Ward* and self) thither for 150*l.* to be paid on the safe arrival of the goods there.

――――――――― 7th. ―――――――――

✓ *Thomas Hervey* at *Dublin* advises me that he has bartered my other 50 pockets of hops for 60 pieces of *Irish* linens, quantity 1809 $\frac{7}{8}$ yards, at 19 ½ *d. per* yard *Irish*

	l.	s.	d			
Comes to in *English* money —	135	13	9			
And that he has also bought 27 pieces more, quantity 681 ⅔ yards, at 3*s.* 3*d. Irish,* comes to in *English* —	102	5	c			
				237	18	09

The whole of which he has shipp'd for me on board the *Delphin,* Captain *Grub,* who sailed from thence the 24th of *May* — — — —

✓ Freight, waterage, porterage, and warehouse room, which he has paid together with his commission on the cargo outward, at 2 ½ *per cent.*

	l.	s.	d			
Comes to — —	21	15	0			
Commission and charges on the cargo home is	13	10	c			
				35	05	00

――――――――― 8th. ―――――――――

✓ Remitted *Samuel Rich* of *Norwich, Cambell* and Co.'s note on demand, for which I gave — — | | 18 | 01 | 08 |

✓ Taken to victual the *Tyger* for a voyage to *Jamaica*

	l.	s.	d.			
5 casks of *William Hogg's* pork, at 4*l.* 4*s. per* barrel — — —	21	0	c			
3 firkins of ditto's butter, at 30*s. per* firkin	4	10	c			
				25	10	co

		l.	s.	d.

———————June 12th.————————

✓ *James Green* of *Berwick upon Tweed* has drawn his bill on me to *Thomas Stirling*, or order, due the 2d of *July*, which I have accepted for — — **36 17 06**

✓ The *Dolphin*, Captain *Grub*, is this day arrived from *Dublin*, by whom I have received my linen cloth, the value of which, as *per Thomas Hervey's* invoice to me, dated the 28th of *May*, together with his commission and charges in shipping,

	l.	s.	d.
Amounts to — —	251	8	9
I have paid freight, waterage, and other charges in bringing it into my warehouse — }	5	2	6

256 11 03

————————17th.————————

✓ Bought with ready money, bread, beef, beer, and other sea stores necessary for the *Tyger*, which comes to — **28 16 00**

Bought of *James Murray* and Co. for account of *Thomas James, John Wilson*, and self, to pay in 3 months

	l.	s.	d.
✓ 300 butts of porter, at 4l. 4s. *per* butt —	1260	0	0

We have also brought into company what goods each of us have proper for the voyage, viz.

	l.	s.	d.
Thomas James, 100 barrels of *Bristol* beer, at 36s. *per* barrel — }	180	0	0
John Wilson, 100 casks of shelled barley, containing 3 cwt. each, at 9s. 4d. *per* cwt. }	140	0	0
I have brought in 22 pieces jeans, quantity 434 yards, at 2s. 6d. *per* yard — }	54	5	0
Also 400 pair of shoes, at 4s. 6d. *per* pair	90	0	6
5 pieces of fustians, at 2l. 5s. *per* piece	12	5	0
87 pieces of *Irish* linens, of different sorts, quantity 2489 13/47 yards, valued at }	269	0	0
Bought also with ready money, various kinds of hardware, as *per* bill of parcels, to } 560 12 6			
I have paid charges till on board 25 0 0			
I have also paid *Jacob Wilkinson* and Co. for insuring 2000l. on our said adventure } 50 0 0			
	635	12	6

2641 03 00

		l.	*s.*	*d.*

————————————June 17th.————————————

W B Shipp'd the whole on board the *Tyger, James Bentick* master, consigned to *William Boyd* at *Kingston* in *Jamaica,* to sell for our account, mark'd as *per* margin

————————————18th.————————————

Received advice from *William Boyd* in *Jamaica,* that he hath received and sold my adventure *per* the *Hopewell,* the neat proceeds as *per* accompt of sales, amounting to 30*l.* 7*s. English.* In return for which he hath put on board the same ship sundry kinds of goods, which at prime cost and charges, as *per* invoice,

	l.	*s.*	*d.*
Amounts to ————	195	7	5
✓ Ballance in his hands, which he desires me to } draw for, is ———— ————	108	19	7

304|07|00

————————————20th.————————————

✓ Received of *John Todd* of *Greenwich,* in full for *Green's* barley   190|00|00

————————————24th.————————————

✓ Received the drawback for 400 pair of shoes, exported to *Jamaica,* in Co. with *Thomas James* and *John Wilson*   1|05|00

————————————27th.————————————

✓ I have paid Messrs. *Graves* and *Maxwell* for insuring 500 pounds, on our ship *Tyger* out and home ———— 45|00|00

✓ Paid clerk's wages, warehouse room, &c. from the first of *Jan.* to this day, with other expences on trade, as *per* petty cash-book ———— ———— ———— 95|00|00

✓ Paid also expences on house-keeping, viz. servants wages, house rent, &c. for the said time, as *per* petty cash-book   105|00|00

————————————*July* 2d.————————————

	l.	*s.*	*d.*
✓ Received f *Charles Thompson* for his bond	1000	0	0
Ditto for 6 months interest of the same ————	25	0	0

1025|00|00

✓ Paid *James Green's* bill on me to *Thomas Stirling* ———— 36|17|06

July,

		l.	*s.*	*d.*

───────── *July* 5th. ─────────

✓ Received advice from *James Johnston*, in *Virginia*, that he hath difposed of my adventure, fent him *per* the *Happy Return*, captain *Scott*, the neat proceeds of which, after freight, commiffion, and other charges were deducted, a-mounts to 178 *l.* 4 *s.* 4 *d.* In return for which he hath put on board the fame fhip which arrived this day

                         l.   *s.*   *d.*

47 hogds. of tobacco, weighing in the whole ⎫
175 *cwt.* 3 *qrs.* 22 *lb.* at 18 *s.* 8 *d. per cwt.* ⎬ 162   4   4
comes to ────── ⎭

His commiffion and other charges in fhipping, &c. is 16   0   0
                                 ───────   178   04   04

───────── 6th. ─────────

✓ Paid freight, duty, and other charges on landing my to-bacco, and putting it into my warehoufe   ──────   466   11   11

✓ Given my bond for the remaining part of the duties on my tobacco, payable in 18 months ── ── ──   82   02   02

───────── 9th. ─────────

✓ Ship *Hopewell* is this day arrived fafe with my goods from *Jamaica*, the feveral kinds of which, with their firft coft and charges there as *per* invoice, are as follows, viz.

                         l.   *s.*   *d.*

6 barrels of indigo, containing 126 *lb. per* bar- ⎫
rel, at 2 *s.* 2 *d. per lb.* with commiffion and ⎬ 86   12   6
charges, comes to ────── ⎭

5 hogfheads of pimento, containing in all 1535, ⎫
at 6 *d. per lb.* with charges, comes to ⎬ 42   17   6

5 hogfheads of fugar, containing 63 *cwt.* at ⎫
19 *s. per cwt.* and charges, is ────── ⎬ 65   17   5
                                 ───────   195   07   05

✓ Paid freight, duty, and other charges on my cargo *per* the *Hopewell*, as follows, viz.

                         l.   *s.*   *d.*

On my 6 barrels of indigo ──   33   1   6
On my 5 hogfheads of pimento ──   24   16   4½
On my 5 hogfheads of fugar ── ──   39   14   1½
                                     97   12   00

Note. The particular duties, and other expences, which the a-bove articles are chargeable with, are not juftly proportioned here, the indigo being much overcharged, the better to fhew the impro-priety of Mr. *Mair's* method of making the above two entries, and in order to agree with the obfervation made on the 5th and 6th cafes in problem 3d, fect. 2d, chap. 1ft.

                        T 2   *July*

		l.	s.	d.

——————————*July* 10th.——————————

Sold *John Dyer* my 6 barrels of indigo, at 4 s. 3 d. *per lb.*

		l.	s.	d.
Received in part	—	—	80	13	0
Rest due in 6 months	—	—	80	0	0

166 13 00

————————————15th.————————————

Sold for ready money, the remaining part of *William Hogg's* goods, *per* the *Nancy*, viz.

		l.	s.	d.
15 barrels of pork, at 4 l. 10 s. *per* barrel	—	67	10	0
47 firkins of butter, at 28 s. *per* firkin	—	65	16	0

133 06 00

Paid warehouse room, and other charges, on *William Hogg's* goods, as *per* petty cash-book ———

2 05 06

My commission on 166 l. 15 s. 8 d. at 2½ *per cent.* comes to ——— ———

4 03 4½

————————————22d.————————————

Sold *John Kirkman* of *Richmond* my 5 hogsheads of sugar, *per* the *Hopewell*, from *Jamaica*, weighing in the whole 63 cwt. at 28 s. 6 d. *per* cwt. to pay in 6 months, comes to ———

89 15 00

Note. Here, instead of shipping off my sugars, as Mr. *Mair* has done, at what he accounted their prime cost. viz. 59 l. 17 s. I have sold them at 50 *per cent.* advance; notwithstanding which, it will appear by the said accompt in the Ledger, that he loses (even at that rate) near 15 *per cent.* whereas, according to his method of making the several entries relative to that adventure, it will appear by his accompt of sugar, that he has gain'd 50 *per cent.*

————————————26th.————————————

Drawn my bill on *James Arnold* at *Dunkirk*, payable to *James Fordyce*, or order, at two months, so 3368 crowns, 1 livre and 10 sols exchange, at 4 s. 6 d. *per French* crown, for which I received ——— —

785 19 08

Received of *James Gibson* of *Stilton*, in full for 5 pieces of fustians, sent him the 24th of *February* last —

10 10 00

————————————28th.————————————

James Green of *Berwick-upon-Tweed*, has drawn his bill on me, payable to *John Stainton*, at 3 weeks, which I have accepted, for ——— ——— —

August

353 12 06

		l.	*s.*	*d.*

———————*August* 5th.———————

R.F. No. 1 2 — Ship'd on board the *Fly*, *William Davenport* mafter, conf2gned to *Robert Fergufon* merchant, in *Hamburg*, to fell for my account, the following goods, mark'd and number'd as *per* margin, viz.

	l.	*s.*	*d.*
My 4 pieces of cotton velvets, quantity 112 yards, at 7 *s. per* yard, comes to	39	4	0
12 fother of lead, immediately bought of *Hugh Shaw*, at 13 *l.* 5 *s. per* fother, due in 3 mths.	159	0	0
Paid cuftom and other charges	15	10	0

213 | 14 | 00

———————11th.———————

Henry Primrofe and myfelf having agreed to be equally concerned in an adventure to *Amfterdam*, (he to be manager) I have this day delivered to him my 47 hogfheads of tobacco, weighing in the whole 175 cwt. 3 qrs. 22 *lb.* each, ¼ valued at 3¼ *d. per lb.* comes to — — 285 | 16 | 08

———————14th.———————

Henry Primrofe having fhipped off our tobacco for *Amfterdam*, I have received of the collector of excife the drawback of duties paid on it at importation

	l.	*s.*	*d.*
Amounting to	451	11	11
I have alfo withdrawn my bond given for the remaining part at 18 months, for	82	2	2

533 | 14 | 01

———————17th.———————

Upon fettling accompts with *Thomas James*, and *John Willfon*, there appears due to me,

	l.	*s.*	*d.*
From *Thomas James*, together with intereft	281	2	8¼
From *John Wilfon*, with ditto	321	6	0¼
Which they have paid me, the whole being			

602 | 08 | 08¼

———————19th.———————

Upon fettling accompts with *John Ward*, there appears due to him, together with a ballance of intereft in his favour, which I have paid — — — 10 | 17 | 11½

———————22d.———————

Henry Primrofe has paid me for his ¼ of 47 hhds. of tobacco — — — — — 142 | 18 | 04

Auguft

		l.	*s.*	*d.*

————————*Auguſt* 25th.————————

T. B. Shipped on board the *Rover*, *James Corrie* maſter, by
No. 1 order, and for account of *Thomas Bell* merchant, in *Genoa*,
2 the following goods, marked and numbered as *per* margin.

	l.	*s.*	*d.*			
12 tun of lead, bought of *John Duke*, at 14 *l.* per tun, to pay in 2 months — — —	168	0	0			
8640 *lb.* of tanned leather, preſently bought for ready money, at 6 *d. per lb.* — —	216	0	0			
Paid cuſtom and other charges — —	12	5	0			
Paid to *Robert Smith*, for packing — — —	1	7	0			
My commiſſion, at 2 ½ *per cent.* — —	9	18	9			
Paid *George Reid* and *Co.* for inſuring 400 *l.* on the whole — — — —	12	0	0			
My commiſſion on ditto, at ½ *per cent.* — —	2	0	0			

		421	10	09

————————30th.————————

Sold for ready money my 5 hogſheads of pymento, quantity 1535 *lb.* for — — — — —   57 | 03 | 11

————————*September* 10th.————————

Received of the collectors of excife (for accompt of *Thomas Bell*, at *Genoa*) the drawback on 8640 *lb.* of tanned leather, ſhipped for him the 25th of *Auguſt*, which at one penny *per lb.* amounts to ————   36 | 00 | 00

————————17th.————————

Received from on board the *Good Intent*, *Chriſtopher Bains* maſter, the following goods, to ſell for account of *Herman Van Sanders*, merchant in *Amſterdam*, viz
36 *cwt.* of flax, and 30 butts of madder, each butt containing 12 *cwt.*
Paid cuſtom, freight, waterage, &c. — —   25 | 10 | 00

————————19th.————————

Paid *James Murray* for 30 butts of porter, ſhipp'd *per* the *Tyger*, for *Kingſton* in *Jamaica*, as follows, viz.

	l.	*s.*	*d.*
I have paid for myſelf and *Thomas James* —	840	0	0
John Wilſon has paid his ½ ſhare — —	420	0	0

		1260	00	00

————————23d.————————

Sold *Harman Van Sanders*'s 36 *cwt.* of flax, at 3 *l.* 5 *s. per cwt.* for ready money — — — —   117 | 00 | 00

————————28th.————————

Sold *Richard Croſby* in *Cannon-ſtreet*, *Harman Van Sanders*'s 30 butts of madder, at 2 *l.* 10 *s. per cwt.* to pay as follows, viz. ½ in 2 months, and the other half at 6 months ———— ————   900 | 00 | 00

		l.	*s.*	*d.*
————————————*September 28th.*————————				
✓	P id w rehoufe room and othe charges on *Harman Van Sanders* goods — — —	2	12	06
✓	My commiffion on 1048 *l.* 2 *s.* 6 *d.* at 2 ½ *per cent.* is —	26	04	00¼
	————————————*October 3d.*————————				
✓	Drawn by bill on *Thomas Bell*, in *Genoa*, for 1000 dollars, payable to *John Grayfon*, or order, for value here received, at 50 *d.* per dollar — — —	208	06	08
	————————————*8th.*————————				
V. S. *No. 1*	By order of *Harman Van Sanders*, I have shipped on board the *Wafp* floop, *James Dodds* mafter, bound for *Amfterdam*, the goods following, marked and numbered as per margin, viz.			

		l.	*s.*	*d.*			
✓	20 hogfheads of tobacco, prefently bought for ready money, qty. 122 *cwt.* at 2½ *d. per lb.*	188	3	4			
	Paid cuftom and other charges —	8	9	0			
	Due to *Benjamin Green*, for cooperage —	1	5	0			
	My commiffion on the whole, at 2½ *per cent.* is	4	18	11	202	16	03

	————————————*12th.*————————			
✓	Drawn my bill on *Harman Van Sanders*, at *Amfterdam*, payable to *Thomas Caftlehow*, or order, for 246 *l.* 6 *s.* 5 *d.* *Flemifh* exchange, a 35 *s.* 5 *d.* *Flemifh*, amounts to in fterling — — — —	143	02	09¼
	————————————*15th.*————————			
✓	Received advice from *Robert Ferguson* of *Hamburgh*, that he hath received and difpofed of my adventure, the neat proceeds as *per* accompt of fales, amounting to 462 *l.* 7 *s.* 10 *d.* *Flemifh* exchange, at 34 *s.* 5 *d.* makes fterling	268	14	00¼
	————————————*20th.*————————			
✓	*Henry Primrofe* has paid me my proportion of neat proceeds of an adventure to *Amfterdam*, as follows, viz.			

		l.	*s.*	*d.*			
	In cafh — — — —	42	18	4			
	By a draft on *James Snow*, at 30 days, for —	100	0	0	142	18	04

	————————————*25th.*————————			
✓	*John Ward* and felf refolving to trade further together, I have this day bought on our joint account, of *John Seby*, 100 *cwt.* of hops, at 3 *l. per cwt.* to pay in 3 months —	300	00	00
	————————————*28th.*————————			
✓	Delivered to *Henry Primrofe* my 6 dozen of filk hofe, to fell for our account, each ½ valued at 6 *l.* 16 *s. per doz.*	40	16	00

October

		l.	*s.*	*d.*
✓	————————*October* 31ft.————————			
	Robert Ferguſon hath remitted to me in full, exchange at 34 *s.* in bills on the following perſons, viz.			
	l. *s.* *d.*			
	One on *Peter Ycung,* for — — — 160 0 0			
	One on *William Harris,* for ——— — 111 19 10¾			
		271	19	10
✓	————————*November* 3d.————————			
	Sold for ready money 100 *cwt.* of hops, in Co. with *John Ward,* at 3 *l.* 8 *s. per cwt.* comes to ———	340	00	00
✓	————————————5th.———			
	Settled accompts with *John Ward,* and paid the ballance due to him, being — — — —	170	00	00
✓	————————————7th.———			
	Bought in company with *John Ward* 9 puncheons of rum, at 33 *l.* 6 *s.* 8 *d. per* puncheon, for which I paid —	300	00	00
✓	————————————-10th.———			
	Sold *Samuel Rich* of *Norwich* our 9 puncheons of rum, to pay in 3 months, for ——— ———	340	00	00
✓	———————————— 12th.———			
	John Ward has fettled accompts with me, and paid me the ballance, which is — — —	150	00	00
	Note. In the feveral tranſactions on account of *John Ward* and felf, between the 25th of *October* and the 10th of *November,* I have omitted charging commiſſion and other charges, both on buying and felling, in order that the ballances on either fide might exactly agree with my remarks on Mr. *Mair,* relative to his manner of making the Journal entries in the faid cafes.			
✓	—————————--16th.———			
	Received advice from *William Boyd,* at *Jamaica,* by the *Tyger,* that he hath received and fold our adventure *per* the faid ſhip, neat proceeds as *per* accompt of fales, amounting to 4228 *l. Jamaica* currency, making in *Engliſh* 3020 *l.* which he hath *per* our order advanced in purchaſing homeward cargo, for *George Gair* in the *Borrough* ———	3020	00	00
✓	*William Boyd* advifes us at the fame time, that he hath freighted our ſhip *Tyger* home with the faid goods, on account of *George Gair,* for — — —	140	00	00
✓	———————————-20th.———			
	Paid *Hugh Shaw* of *Cheſter,* in full for 12 fother of lead	159	00	00
✓	———————————- 25th.———			
	Paid *John Duke,* in full — —	168	00	00
✓	Received of *Richard Croſby* in *Cannon-ſtreet,* one half of 30 butts of madder ——— ———	450	00	00
	November			

		l.	s.	d.
——————— *November* 27th.———————				
	l. s. d.			
✓ *Henry Primrose* has paid me his ¼ share of 6 dozen of silk hose ——— ———	} 20 8 c			
He has also paid me my ¼ share of the sales of the whole, amounting to, ——— ———	} 23 16 c			
		44	04	00
——————— 30th.———————				
	l. s. d			
✓ Sold for ready money 15 casks of my brandy, *per* the *Eagle*, quantity 900 gallons, for	} 350 8 c			
Also 6 pipes of my port wine, *per* ditto, at 35 *l.* 10 *s. per* pipe ——— ———	} 213 0 0			
		563	68	00
——————— *December* 5th.———————				
✓ Received of *George Gair* in full, for what our factor (*William Boyd*) advanced for him ———		3020	0	00
✓ Received also of him freight of our ship *Tyger* home from *Jamaica* ——— ——— ———		140	00	00
——————— 10th.———————				
✓ Paid the seamen of the *Tyger* fix months wages ———		90	00	00
✓ Freight of our outward bound cargo to *Jamaica*, valued at ——— ——— ———		140	00	00
✓ My commission on 1108 *l.* 16 *s.* on account of the ship *Tyger*, at 2 ½ *per cent.* comes to ——— ———		27	1	04¼
——————— 12th.———————				
✓ Paid *John Ward* in full ——— ——— ———		81	0	09⅝
✓ My commission on 2781 *l.* 2 *s.* 6 *d.* at 2 ½ *per cent.* on accompt of voyage to *Jamaica* in Co. comes to ———		69	10	06¼
✓ Settled accompts with *Thomas James* and *John Willson*, and paid them as follows, viz.				
	l. s. d.			
To *Thomas James* in full ——— ———	512 18 10½			
To *John Willson* ditto ——— ———	937 15 5³			
		1450	14	04¼
——————— 16th.———————				
✓ Drawn my bill on *William Boyd*, at *Jamaica*, to *James Scott*, or order, for 152 *l.* 11 *s.* 5 *d. Jamaica* currency, for which I have received in *English* ——— ———		108	19	07
——————— 18th.———————				
✓ Received of *John Dyer* in full, for indigo ———		80	00	00

		l.	s.	d.
	——————————December 20th.———————			
✓	*William Hogg,* of *Berwick,* has drawn his bill upon me to *George Simpson,* or order, at 6 days, which I have paid	145	13	7½
✓	Drawn my bill on *Thomas Bell,* at *Genoa,* to *James Watts,* or order, for which I have received ————	177	04	01
	——————————28th.———————			
✓	Paid clerks wages, &c. since *July* 1st ————	104	16	00
	——— ——— ———30 th———————			
✓	Paid house rent, servants wages, &c. ————	120	00	00

J O U R N A L.

J O U R N A L.

No. II.

LONDON, January 1; 1777.

Sundries, Debtors to ſtock 2656 *l*. 4 *s*.

		l.	*s.*	*d.*	*l.*	*s.*	*d.*
1	Caſh in ready money ———— ————	10353	10	00			
2	*Scott* lawns for 15 pieces, at 5 *l.* per piece	7	00	00			
3	Silk hoſe for 6 dozen, at 6 *l.* 6 *s.* per dozen —	37	16	00			
3	Cotton velvets for 4 pieces, quantity 112 yds. at 7 *s.* per yard ———— —	39	04	00			
3	*John Martin* of *Barnet*, due the 11th of *Feb.*	114	00	00			
3	*James Tomlinſon* of *Hatfield*, in part for goods ſold the 12th of *Decem.* ————	35	15	00			
3	Printed cottons for 10 pieces, quantity 200 yards, at 2 *s.* 6 *d.* per yard ————	25	00	00			
3	Rum for 60 gallons, at 8 *s.* per gallon —	24	00	00			
3	*James Wilks* of St. *Edmond's Bury*, for goods ſold him the 23d of *Decem.* ————	70	07	00			
3	Hats for 20 dozen, at 6 *l.* per dozen ———	120	00	00			
3	*Yorkſhire* planes for 8 pieces, quantity 144 yards, at 4 *s.* per yard ————	28	16	00			
4	*James Forſter, Smithfield*, due the 24th of *Feb.*	118	18	00			
4	*Norwich* ſtuffs for 10 pieces, quantity 200 yards, at 1 *s.* 4 *d.* per yard — —	13	06	08			
4	Brandy for 10 anchors, at 4 *l.* 10 *s.* per anchor	22	10	00			
4	Printed linens for 6 pieces, quantity 126 yards, at 3 *s.* per yard ————	18	18	00			
4	*Devonſhire* planes for 300 yards, at 5 *s.* 6 *d.* per yard ———— ————	82	10	00			
4	Suſpence accompt for 10 pieces fuſtians ſent *James Gibſon* of *Stilton*, at 2 *l.* 2 *s.* p. piece	21	00	00			
4	*John Kirkman, Richmond*, due 26th of *March*	100	05	04			
4	*Robert Lamb* of *Yarmouth*, due the 27th of *Feb.*	55	17	08			
5	Jeans for 50 pieces, quantity 1000 yards, at 2 *s.* 4 *d.* per yard ———— ————	116	13	04			
5	Shoes for 400 pair, at 4 *s.* per pair —	80	00	00			
5	Thread hoſe for 20 dozen, at 1 *l.* 4 *s.* per dozen	24	00	00			
5	*Cuthbert Euſtage* of *Stamford*, due the 28th of *April* ———— ————	8	17	00			
					11656	00	00

——————January 1ft.——————

		l.	s.	d.

1| Stock, Debtor to fundries 549*l.* 00*s.* 2*d.*

			l.	s.	d.			
5	To *William Webfter* of *Manchefter*, for goods bought the 21ft of *December*		98	00	00			
5	To *James Thornton* of *Wigan*, for goods bought the 18th ditto		144	17	06			
5	To *Thomas Simpfon* of *Manchefter*, due the 20th of *February*		60	00	00			
5	To *Ralph Cook, Wakefield*, due the 23d of *March*		36	16	00			
6	To *Samuel Rich, Norwich*, due the 8th of *June*		44	06	08			
6	To *Daniel Bradfhaw* in part, for goods bought the 10th of *December*		65	00	00			
6	To *Thomas Burges* of *Paifley*, for goods bought the 21ft ditto		100	00	00			

549 | 00 | 02

——————5th.——————

6| Voyage to *Virginia*, Debtor to fundries 138*l.* 4*s.* 4*d.*

			l.	s.	d.			
3	To *Yorkfhire* planes for 8 pieces, quantity 144 yards, at 4*s. per* yard		28	16	00			
4	To *Devonfhire* planes for 300 yards, at 5*s.* 6*d. per* yard		82	10	00			
5	To thread hofe for 20 dozen, at 1*l.* 4*s. per* dozen		24	00	00			
2	To cafh, for cuftom and other charges		2	18	04			

138 | 04 | 04

Shipped the above goods on board the *Happy Return*, cap-tain *Scott*, mafter, configned to *James Johnfton* in *Virginia*, to fell for my account.

Cafe 1ft. Prob. 1ft. Sect. 2d, Chap. 1ft.

Reafon. As the above goods ftood formerly debited in your Ledger, it is evident, that now when you have parted with them, that they muft each of them be credited for their refpective values, for which the voyage muft be charged Debtor. For as the fafe arrival of them at *Virginia* is yet uncertain, fo there could nothing elfe (with any propriety) be charged till you hear whether they arrive fafe or not.

——————16th.——————

2| Cafh, Debtor to *Scots* lawns 90 *l.*
2| Received for 15 pieces, at 6 *l. per* piece

90 | 00 | 00

James

-----------*January* 14th.-----------

		l.	*s.*	*d.*

6 | *James Bell* of *Berwick upon Tweed*, Debtor to sundries
— 82 *l.* 1 *s.* 0 *d.*

		l.	*s.*	*d.*
3	To printed cottons, for 10 pieces, quantity 200 } yards, at 3 *s. per* yard	30	00	00
3	To rum, for 60 gallons, at 10 *s. per* gallon ———	30	00	00
4	To printed linens, for 6 pieces, quantity 126 } yards, at 3 *s.* 6 *d. per* yard ———	22	01	00

82 | 01 | 00

Shipped the above goods, as *per* his order, on board the *London Packet,* captain *Wilkinson,* matter, for *Berwick upon Tweed.*

Observation. Here you see, *James Bell* is immediately charged Debtor to the goods instead of voyage, for as he gave you an order for the goods, they therefore became his property the moment you shipped them; and consequently, (whether they arrive safe or are lost on the voyage) he is equally liable to you for the payment of them.

-----------21ſt.-----------

6 | Voyage to *Jamaica,* Debtor to sundries 223 *l.* 18 *s.* 8 *d.*

		l.	*s.*	*d.*
3	To hats, for 20 dozen, at 6 *l. per* dozen ——	120	00	00
4	To *Norwich* stuffs, for 10 pieces, quantity 200 } yards, at 1 *s.* 4 *d. per* yard ———	13	06	08
5	To jeans, for 28 pieces, quantity 566 yards, at } 2 *s.* 4 *d. per* yard	66	00	08
2	To cash, paid *Simon Smith* and Co. for insuring } 200 *l.* with other charges till on board ——	24	11	04

223 | 18 | 08

Shipped the above goods on board the ship *Hopewell,* captain *Gordon,* master, consigned to *William Boyd* to sell for my account.

-----------27th.-----------

6 | Voyage from *Berwick* to *Dunkirk,* Debtor to bills payable
— 1535 *l.* 10 s. 0 *d.*

7 | Received advice from *James Watson* of *Berwick,* that he has bought and shipped off for my account, on board the ship *Speedwell,* George *Grey,* master, for *Dunkirk,* consigned to *James Arnold* there, 1000 quarters of wheat, at 30 *s. per* quarter; the whole amount of which, together with his commission and all other charges he has drawn on me for, payable to *Coats* and Co. due the 14th of *March,* the sum is ——— 1535 | 10 | 00

Observation.

Obſervation. Had your factor at *Berwick* only adviſed you, that be had bought and ſhipped off the wheat with an account of the firſt coſt, together with his commiſſion and all other charges, without drawing upon you at the ſame time for the amount, then the voyage would have been Debtor to *James Watſon* your accompt current; but as you had no advice of it being ſhipped off, prior to his drawing up-on you, the circumſtances are the ſame as if you had bought the wheat yourſelf, and given the ſeller your note for the payment.

——————February 2d.——————

6/2 *Charles Thompſon*, Debtor to caſh 1000 *l.*
Lent him on bond, for 6 months, at 5 *l. per cent.*
Caſe 5th. Prob. 5th. Sect. 1ſt. Chap. 1ſt. | 1000 | 00 | 00

——————7th.——————

6/6 Cuſtom-houſe Debentures, Debtor to voyage to *Dunkirk*
250 *l.* 00 *s.* 0 *d.*
The collector of the cuſtoms at *Berwick* not having caſh in his hands ſufficient to pay the bounty on my wheat exported, he has granted me a debenture bill, with a certificate to the com-miſſioners in order to receive the ſame here, which at 5 *per* quarter is
See *Note* 2d. Prob. 1ſt. Sect. 2d. Chap. 1ſt. The reaſon of which is ſo clear, that it needs no further explanation. | 250 | 00 | 00

2/6 Caſh, Debtor to voyage to *Jamaica* 2 *l.* 10 *s.* 0 *d.*
Received of the collector of exciſe, the draw-back on my 200 yards *Norwich* ſtuffs exported to *Jamaica*, which at 3 *d.* per yard, is | 2 | 10 | 00

——————13th.——————

7 Voyage to *Dublin*, Debtor to ſundries 172 *l.* 14 *s.* 6 *d.*
                                          l.   s.   d.
7 To *George Gair* of the *Borough*, for 50 pockets } 171 10 0
of hops to pay in 2 months   }
2 To caſh, for cuſtom and other charges till on board 1 04 6 | 172 | 14 | 06

Shipped the above on board the *Good Intent*, captain *Rich-ardſon*, maſter, conſigned to *Thomas Hewy* to ſell for my account.
Caſe 3d. Prob. 1ſt. Sect. 2d. Chap. 1ſt.

——————20th.——————

5 *Thomas Simpſon* of *Mancheſter*, Debtor to ſundries 60 *l.*
                                          l.   s.   d.
2 To caſh   57 10 0
8 To profit and loſs, abated me   — 2 10 0 | 60 | 00 | 00
Paid him in full
Caſe 5th. Prob. 6th. Sect. 5ſt. Chap. 1ſt.
                                 Obſervation.

Observation. This Journal Entry is compounded of the two entries belonging to the 6th case in problem 4th, and the 1st case in problem 5th, both in section 1st, chapter 1st, for supposing the sum abated to be a present or legacy, payable by *Thomas Simpson,* it is then plain (according to the 1st note following the said case 6th, problem 4th, that *Thomas Simpson* should be charged Debtor to profit and loss for the value of the said present or legacy, which would then reduce the 60l. you owed him to 57 l. 10s. and it is equally evident, (according to case 1st, problem 5th) that when you pay him the afore-mentioned ballance of 57 l. 10s. that you ought then again to charge him Debtor to cash. For the reason of which two entries, see the 28th of *February,* and the 25th of *January,* 1777.

		l.	s.	d.
	────────February 24th.────────			
2/4	Cash, Debtor to *James Forster* 100 l. Received of him in part ──── ────	100	00	00

		l. s. d.	l.	s.	d.
	Sundries, Debtors to suspence accompt 21 l. 0s. 0d.				
8	*James Gibson* of *Stilton,* for 5 pieces which he has kept, at 2 l. 2s. *per* piece ──── } 10 10 0				
9	Fustians, for 5 pieces, at the same price returned 10 10 0				
4			21	00	00

Observation. As suspence accompt stood debited for the fustians when you sent them to *Gibson,* it is reasonable (now when you're resolved what part he keeps) that the said accompt should be discharged; *Gibson* is therefore charged Debtor to it, to shew he owes you for 5 pieces; and fustian Debtor to it for the very same reason as if you had bought 5 pieces.

		l.	s.	d.
	────────-27th.────────			
2/4	Cash, Debtor to *Robert Lamb* of *Yarmouth* 55 l. 17s. 8 d. Drawn my bill on him at 20 days to *John Banks,* or order, for which I have received ──── ────	55	17	08

Case 1st. Prob. 4th. Sect. 1st. Chap. 1st.

Note. The reason here is the same as if he had himself paid you in cash.

		l. s. d.	l.	s.	d.
	Sundries, Debtors to *John Martin* of *Barnet* 114 l.				
2	Cash for ──── ──── 112 00 0				
8	Profit and loss abated him ──── 2 00 0	114	00	00
3	Received of him in full ──── ────			

Case 6th. Prob. 6th. Sect. 1st. Chap. 1st.

Observation.

l. | s. | d.

Obfervation. Here it is evident, that as *John Martin* ftood for-merly debited in your Ledger for 114 *l.* that now when he has paid you (for you accept of 112 in full of it) he muft be credited for the whole fum, in order that his accompt may ftand difcharged: But as cafh cannot be debited for more than you realy received, there yet wants fomething to be made Debtor to him for the 2 *l.* abated, in order to correfpond with the credit of his accompt; we therefore (having no returns to expect for things of this kind) charge profit and lofs Debtor for the abatement.

Note. The circumftances of the above entry is comprehended in the 1ft and fixth cafes of problem 5th, and is exactly the reverfe of the Journal entry the 20th inftant.

——————————*March* 1ft.——————————

6			
4	*Samuel Rich* of *Norwich* Debtor to brandy, 26 *l.* 5 *s.* Sent him, *per* his order, 5 anchors, at 5 *l.* 5 *s. per* anchor	26	05	00

——————————7th.——————————

9 | Bills receivable Debtor to fundries, 1000 *l.*

l. | s. | d.

2 | To cafh — — — 996 0 0
8 | To profit and lofs for difcount at 5 *l. per cent.* 4 0 0

Difcounted *George Edgar* a bill, drawn by *James Corrie* of *Edinburgh* on *Thomas Hamilton*, 30 days to run, for — | 1000 | 00 | 00
Cafe 8th, Problem 6th, Sect. 1ft, Chap. 1ft.

Reafon. The bill is here confidered as any other article you deal in, with this difference only, that the inftant you buy it, the value and time of the return of your money being certain, your profit is confequently immediately determined, which in the cafe of goods bought, are both uncertain. The value of the bill therefore (as I before obferved) being certain, it could not be debited for lefs than the faid value; but a correfpondent credit being wanted, (which the cafh you paid for it not being equivalent to) it therefore becomes neceffary to credit profit and lofs for the difcount.

——————————10th.——————————

6			
7	*Daniel Bradfhaw* Debtor to cafh, 65 *l.* Paid him in full — — —	65	00	00

——————————14th.——————————

2			
3	Cafh Debtor to *James Tomlinfon* of *Hatfield*, 35 *l.* 15 *s.* Received of him in full — —	35	15	00

——————————18th.——————————

5			
2	*James Thornton* of *Wigan* Debtor to cafh, 100 *l.* Remitted him a bill, drawn by *John Freeman* of *Glafgow*, on *Campbell* and Co. for which I paid —	100	00	00

Cafe 1ft, Prob. 5th, Sect. 1ft, Chap. 1ft.

Reafon.

	l.	s.	d.

Reason. As you paid cash for the bill, and immediately remitted it to *Thornton*, without booking the said bill, it is therefore the very same thing, as if you had paid him directly in cash.

——————————*March* 24th.——————————

7 | *James Green* of *Berwick upon Tweed*, his accompt of goods
— | *per* the *Polly*, Debtor to cash, 30 *l.* 12 *s.* 6 *d.*
2 | Paid freight, custom, and other charges on 200 quarters of barley, and 100 of oats, consigned me *per* the *Polly*, captain *Todd*, master —   —   **30 | 12 | 06**

Reason. As you have no property in the above goods, but only have a commission for selling them, the cost or value of them is consequently no concern of yours, since you are only accountable to your employer for what you sell them for, after your commission and charges are deducted ; you therefore only charge him Debtor for such charges as above.

——————————26th.——————————

5 | *Ralph Cook* Debtor to bills payable, 36 *l.* 16 *s.*
7 | For his draft on me to *James Wood* or order, due the 15th of *May*, which I have accepted for   —   —   **36 | 16 | 00**

——————————31st.——————————

6 | *Thomas Burges* of *Paisley*, Debtor to *John Kirkman* of *Richmond*, 100 *l.*
4 | Remitted him *Kirkman*'s draft to me on *John Dickson* in the *Strand*   —   —   —   **100 | 00 | 00**

——————————*April* 3d.——————————

7 | Bills payable Debtor to cash, 1535 *l.* 10 *s.*
2 | Paid *Watson*'s on me to *Coats* and Co.   **1535 | 10 | 00**

2 | Cash Debtor to *James Wilks* of *St. Edmond's Bury*, 70 *l.* 7 *s.*
3 | Received of him in full —   —   —   **70 | 07 | 00**

——————————6th.——————————

2 | Cash Debtor to *James Forster* of *Smithfield*, 18 *l.* 18 *s.*
4 | Received the ballance of his accompt in full   —   **18 | 18 | 00**

2 | Cash Debtor to bills receivable, 1000 *l.*
9 | Received for *George Edgar*'s bill, drawn by *Corrie* on *Hamilton*   —   —   —   **1000 | 00 | 00**

5 | *William Webster* of *Manchester* Debtor to bills payable, 98 *l.*
7 | Drawn his bill on me to *James Burdett*, or order, due the 16th of *May*, which I have accepted for   —   **98 | 00 | 00**

——————————10th.——————————

5 | *James Thornton* of *Wiggan* Debtor to cash, 44 *l.* 17 *s.* 6 *d.*
2 | Paid him the ballance of his accompt in full   —   **44 | 17 | 06**

| | | *l.* | *s.* | *d.* |

-------------------*April* 10th.-------------------

2 | Cash Debtor to cuftom houfe debentures, 250*l.*
6 | Received of the receiver general of the cuftoms, the deben-
ture on my wheat exported to *Dunkirk* —— | 250 | 00 | 00

Obfervation. Cuftomhoufe debentures being charged Debtor to voyage to *Dunkirk*, when you received the debenture bill; it is therefore reafonable, that now when you have received cafh for the faid bill, that the accompt of cuftom houfe debentures fhould be credited, and cafh (being the thing received) made Debtor to it.

-------------------13th.-------------------

7 | *George Gair* Debtor to cafh, 171*l.* 10*s.*
2 | Paid him in full for hops — — — — | 171 | 10 | 00

-------------------16th.-------------------

Sundries Debtor to voyage from *Berwick* to *Dunkirk* Debtor, 1650*l.* 10*s.* 2*d.*

| | | *l.* | *s.* | *d.* |

9 | Brandy, for 30 cafks, quantity 60 gal. each | 540 | 0 | 0
9 | Port wine, for 12 pipes — — | 324 | 10 | 6
10 | *James Arnold* my accompt current, for ballance } 785 | 19 | 8
6 | in his hands — — — — }

1650 | 10 | 02

Received *per* the *Eagle*, captain *Davis*, advice from *James Arnold* of *Dunkirk*, that he has fold my wheat for ready money, and had fent me *per* the fame veffel in return, the above goods in part, defiring me to draw for the reft.

See the 3d variety of cafe 4th, with the note following it. Prob. 2d, Sect. 2d, Chap. 1ft.

Reafon. As voyage from *Berwick* to *Dunkirk* ftood debited the 27th of *January* laft, for the value of the outward bound cargo; the rifque of the feas being now over, it of courfe muft be difcharg-d. It is therefore evident that the goods received muft be charged Debtor to the faid voyage, for prime coft and charges paid by your factor abroad; and alfo that your factor (*James Arnold*) your accompt current muft be charged Debtor, for what money of yours remains in his hands.

-------------------17th.-------------------

Sundries Debtor to cafh, 111*l.* 9*s.*

| | | *l.* | *s.* | *d.* |

9 | Brandy, *per* the *Eagle*, capt. *Davis* from *Dun-* } 60 | 16 | 0
| kirk, for —— —— }
9 | Port wine, *per* ditto —— for | 50 | 13 | 0
2 |

Paid freight, duty, and other charges on the above goods. | 111 | 09 | 00

Cafh

		l.	s.	d.

——————————*April* 19th.——————————

2 | Cafh Debtor to *James Green* his accompt of goods *per the*
— | *Polly*, 80 *l.*
7 | Sold his 100 quarters of oats, for ready money, at 16 *s. per*
quarter ——————— ———— | 80 | 00 | 00

Cafe 1ft, Prob. 2d, Chap. 2d.
The reafon of this entry is evident.

——————————24th.——————————

Sundries Debtor to voyage to *Dublin*, 219 *l.* 17 *s.*

		l.	s.	d.

10 | *Thomas Hervey* my accompt current, for 25 ⎫ 137 | 10 | 0
pockets of hops fold ——————— ⎬
9 | Ditto my accompt of goods, for 25 ditto re- ⎫ 82 | 7 | 0
7 | maining in his hands —— ⎬ | 219 | 17 | 00

Cafes 1ft and 2d, Prob. 2d, Sect. 2d, Chap. 1ft.

Reafon. Voyage to *Dublin* is here difcharged for the fame reafon
as is given *April* 18. *Thomas Hervey*'s your accompt current is
charged Debtor for the money he has received for your goods, and
Thomas Hervey your accompt of goods Debtor to fhew the value of
the goods which ftill remains in his hands unfold. This Journal
entry is therefore compounded of the two entries belonging to the
two refpective cafes above referred to.

——————————28th.——————————

10 | *John Todd* of *Greenwich*, Debtor to *James Green* his accompt
— | of goods *per the Polly*, 190 *l.*
7 | Sold him 200 quarters of barley, at 19 *s.* per quarter, to pay
in fix weeks ——— | 190 | 00 | 00

Cafe 1ft, Prob. 2d, Chap. 2d.

Reafon. *John Todd* is here charged Debtor, the fame as if the
goods fold him had been your own, to fhew what he ftands indebted
to you, and *James Green*'s accompt of goods is credited to fhew what
part of them is difpofed of, and in what manner.

7 | *James Green*'s accompt of goods Debtor to cafh, 5 *l.* 15 *s.*
2 | Paid waterage, and other charges on them as per petty cafh-
book ——— | 5 | 15 | 00

Sent him at the fame time his accompt of fales.

7 | *James Green* his accompt of goods Debtor to commiffion ac-
— | count, 6 *l.* 15 *s.*
16 | For commiffion 270 *l.* at 2 ½ per cent. ——— | 6 | 15 | 00

X 2   Ship

		l.	s.	d.
	————————May 2d.————————			
11	Ship *Tyger* in company Debtor to sundries, 800 *l.*			

		l.	s.	d.
12	To *John Ward's* accompt in company, for his one half }	400	o	o
2	To cash for my half ——— ———	400	o	o

Bought the above ship in company with *John Ward*, each one half, for which we paid in the whole ——— ———   800|00|00
         Case 1st, Prob. 1st, Sect. 1st. Chap. 3d.

Reason. Ship *Tyger* in company is here charged Debtor for the same reason as any other article bought in proper domestic trade is, namely, to shew what the said ship cost. *John Ward's* accompt in company is credited, to shew what part of the said cost or charges belongs to him, according to the respective share he holds in company; and cash is credited for the money paid for your own share.

————————5th.————————
| 2 / 5 | Cash Debtor to *Cuthbert Eustage* of *Stamford*, 78 *l.* 17 *s.* Received of him in full ——— | 78 | 17 | 00 |

————————8th.————————
| 9 / 6 | Bills receivable Debtor to *James Bell* of *Berwick*, 82 *l.* 1 *s.* Remitted me his draft on *Thomas Bailey*, due in 15 days, which he has accepted for ——— ——— | 82 | 01 | 00 |

————————12th.————————
| 7 / 2 | *James Green* his accompt of goods *per* the *Nancy* Debtor to cash, 14 *l.* 2 *s.* 6 *d.* Paid freight, waterage, &c. on the above goods ——— | 14 | 02 | 06 |

————————15th.————————
| 12 / — 2 | *William Hogg* his accompt of goods *per* the *Nancy* Debtor to cash, 6 *l.* 3 *s.* 6 *d.* Paid freight, waterage, porterage, &c. ——— | 6 | 03 | 06 |

| 7 / 2 | Bills payable Debtor to cash, 36 *l.* 16 *s.* Paid *Ralph Cook's* draft on me to *James Wood* ——— | 36 | 16 | 00 |

————————16th.————————
| 7 / 2 | Bills payable Debtor to cash, 98 *l.* Paid *William Webster's* draft on me to *James Burdett* | 98 | 00 | 00 |

————————20th.————————
| 12 / — 6 | *James Johnston* my accompt of goods Debtor to voyage to *Virginia*, 138 *l.* 4 *s.* 4 *d.* Received advice from him *per* the *Rover*, that the *Happy Return*, captain *Scott*, arrived safe there the 15th of *Feb.* the value of my goods consigned him was ——— | 138 | 04 | 04 |
| | Case 1st, Prob. 2d, Sect. 2d, Chap. 1st. | | | |

The reason for this entry is the same as that given for debiting *Thomas Hervey* my accompt of goods, the 24th of *April.*

                               Cash

		l.	s.	d.
	————— *May* 23d. —————			
2	Cash Debtor to bills receivable, 82 *l.* 1 *s.*			
—	Received for *James Bell's* draft on *Thomas Bailey* —	82	01	00
9				
	—————————— 28th. ———————			
11	Ship *Tyger* in company Debtor to *John Ward* his accompt			
—	proper, 120 *l.*			
13	Ditto *Ward* has paid the carpenter, sail-maker, &c. for re-			
	pairing and fitting out the said ship ——	120	00	00
13	*John Ward* his accompt proper Debtor to ditto his accompt			
12	in company, for his one half of the above ——	60	00	00

Obſervation. After treating ſo fully of what a partner's accompt proper ſhould contain on the debt and credit ſides, I thought it unne-ceſſary to give a particular rule for making the above two entries. In the firſt entry it is plain that ſhip *Tyger* muſt be charged Debtor for the repairs, and as it was paid by your partner, it is equally evident that his accompt proper muſt be credited: But becauſe one half of the ſaid repairs belonged to himſelf, his accompt proper is again, by a ſecond entry, charged Debtor to his accompt in company for his ſaid half By this means the credit ſide of his company accompt will ſhew his ſhare of inputs, and the difference of his proper accompt (with reſ-peſt to that particular tranſaction) ſhew what he has advanced for you.

	————— *June* 2d. —————			
2	Caſh Debtor to *James Green's* accompt of goods. 190 *l.*			
—	Received for his 200 kitts of ſalmon, and 10 cheſts of eggs,			
7	*per* the *Nancy* —— —— ——	190	00	00
7	*James Green's* accompt of goods *per* the *Nancy* Debtor to			
—	caſh, 2 *l.* 15 *s.*			
2	Paid porterage, &c. on the above goods ——	2	15	00
7	*James Green's* accompt of goods *per* the *Nancy* Debtor to			
—	commiſſion accompt, 9 *l.* 10 *s.*			
10	For commiſſion on 190 *l.* at 5 *per cent.* ——	9	10	00

	——————— 7th. ———————			
13	Voyage from *Dublin* Debtor to ſundries, 237 *l.* 18 *s.* 9 *d.*			
		l.	*s.*	*d.*
9	To *Thomas Hervey* my accompt of goods, for 135	13	9	
10	To ditto my accompt current, for —— 102	5	0	
	Adviſes me that he has bartered my other 50 pockets of			
	hops, for 60 pieces of linens, quantity 1809 $\frac{7}{8}$ yards, at 19$\frac{1}{4}$ *d.*			
	Iriſh per yard which with 27 pieces more, quantity 681 $\frac{2}{3}$ yards			
	which he bought at 3 *s.* 3 *d. Iriſh per* yard amounts to in *Engliſh*			
	money	237	18	09

The whole of which he has ſhipp'd for me on board the *Dolphin*, capt. *Grub*, who ſail'd from thence the 24th of *May*.
See the general rule in all caſes of ſucceeding advices.
Prob. 2d, Sect. 2d, Chap. 1ſt.

Reaſon.

                                          l.   *s.*   *d.*

Reason. As *Thomas Hervey* my accompt current, and ditto my accompt of goods stood both debited to voyage to *Dublin* the 24th of *April*, they must therefore now (when he has made you returns) be both credited, viz. his accompt of goods for the value of returns made for them; and his accompt current, for what goods he bought and sent you. To both of which, voyage from *Dublin* must be charged Debtor.

─────── *June* 7th. ───────

Sundries Debtor to *Thomas Hervey* my accompt current, 35 *l.* 5 *s.*

                                       l.   *s.*   *d.*

7   Voyage to *Dublin* for his commission and charges } 21 15 0
    on the cargo out ────── ──────

13   Ditto from *Dublin* for ditto on the cargo home   13 10 0
10   35|05|00

Observation. As *Thomas Hervey* did not (in his first accompt of sales) charge freight, or other charges on your hops, nor commission for what part was then sold, his accompt current consequently stood charged for the whole amount of the 50 pockets disposed of, and his accompt of goods, Debtor for the whole value of the 50 pockets which remained unsold at prime cost. Now, as he has only made you returns equal to the neat proceeds, (after freight to *Dublin*, together with commission and other charges, both on the outward and homeward bound cargoes are deducted,) it is necessary that his accompt current should be credited for the whole of such charges, in order to discharge the same. Voyage to and from *Dublin* are therefore charged Debtors to his said accompt current, for their respective share of such charges, by which means you will see the real gain, or loss upon each.

─────── 8th. ───────

6   *Samuel Rich* Debtor to cash, 18 *l.* 1 *s.* 8 *d.*
─   Remited him *Campble* and Co's. note, for which I paid   18|01|08
2

11   Ship *Tyger* in company Debtor to *William Hogg's* accompt of goods, 25 *l.*

12   Taken 5 casks of his pork, and 3 firkins of his butter, for the use of the said ship ── ────── ──   25|00|00

13   *John Ward* his accompt proper Debtor to ditto his accompt
12   in company, for his one half share ── ──   12|10|00
       Case 2d, Prob. 1st, Sect. 1st, Chap. 3d.

Reason. As the above goods were immediately shipped on board the *Tyger*, the ship *Tyger* in company thereby becomes Debtor, instead of goods in company in the first entry; and, notwithstanding, you did not directly pay ready money for them, yet, as you are instantly accountable to your employer, for what goods of his you take to yourself at ready money price; so in the second entry, your partner's accompt proper is charged Debtor for his half.

                                              James

		l.	s.	d.

—————————— *June* 12th. ——————————

10 | *James Green* his accompt current Debtor to bills payable,
— | 36 *l.* 17 *s.* 6 *d.*
7 | Drawn his bill on me to *Thomas Stirling*, or order, which I have accepted for ———— ———— | 36 | 17 | 06

13 | *Irish* linens *per* the *Delphin* Debtor to sundries, 256 *l.* 11 *s.* 3 *d.*

| | | l. | s. | d. |

13 | To voyage from *Dublin*, for 60 pieces, quantity 1809 $\frac{7}{10}$ yards, at 1 *s.* 6 *d.* *English per* yard, and 27 pieces, quantity 681 $\frac{2}{3}$ yds. at 3 *s. per* yd. which with commission and charges, is } 251 | 8 | 9
2 | To cash for freight, waterage, porterage, &c. — 5 | 2 | 6
| | | 256 | 11 | 03

Case 5th, Prob. 3d, Sect. 2d, Chap. 1st.

Reason. As voyage from *Dublin* stood debited in your books the 7th inftant, upon receiving advice that the above goods were shipped for you; consequently, now (when the risque of the sea is over, and the goods safe arrived) voyage from *Dublin* must be credited, and the goods received, charged Debtor in its place, and also Debtor to cash for fresh charges paid here.

—————————— 17th. ——————————

11 | Ship *Tyger* in company Debtor to cash, 28 *l.* 16 *s.*
— | Paid for bread, beef, beer, and other sea stores necessary for
2 | a voyage to *Jamaica* ———— ———— | 28 | 16 | 00
13 | *John Ward* his accompt proper, Debtor to ditto his accompt
12 | in company, for his one half share — — | 14 | 08 | 00

14 | Voyage to *Jamaica*, in company with *Thomas James* and *John Wilson* Debtor to sundries, 2641 *l.* 2 *s.* 6 *d.*

| | | l. | s. | d. |

14 | To *James Murray*, for 300 buts of porter, at 4 *l.* 4 *s. per* but, to pay in three months } 1260 | 0 | 0
14 | To *Thomas James* his accompt proper, for 100 barrels of *Briftol* beer, at 36 *s. per* barrel } 180 | 0 | 0
15 | To *John Wilson*'s accompt proper, for 100 casks of shell'd barley, containing 3 *cwt.* each, at 9 *s.* 4 *d. per cwt.* } 140 | 0 | 0
5 | To jeans, for 22 pieces, quantity 434 yds. at 2 *s.* 6 *d. per* yard } 54 | 5 | 0
5 | To shoes, for 400 pair, at 4 *s.* 6 *d. per* pair — 90 | 0 | 0
13 | To *Irish* linens of different sorts, 87 pieces, quantity 2489 $\frac{7}{8}$ yards, valued at — } 269 | 0 | 0
9 | To fustians, for 5 pieces, at 2 *l.* 5 *s. per* piece — 12 | 5 | 0
2 | To cash, for sundry kinds of hardware, as *per* bills of parcels, with insurance and other charges till on board } 635 | 12 | 6
| | | 2641 | 02 | 06

Shipp'd

		l.	*s.*	*d.*

Shipp'd the above goods on board the *Tyger*, captain *James Beatic* master, configned to *William Boyd* in *Jamaica*, to fell for our accompt.

See the firft entries of Cafe 2d and 3d, Prob. 2d, Sect. 1ft, Chap. 3d.

Reafon. The voyage is here charged Debtor for the very fame reafon as it is in proper foreign trade, but as the goods brought into company by your partners are not equal to their proportion of the whole, their accompts proper are therefore credited for the value of goods each brought in, the fame as if they had been neutral perfons, which makes the following fecond entries neceffary.

Note. The above entry is compofed of the two cafes above quoted, except that the goods brought in by you and partners being fuppofed to be at ready money price; inftead of crediting your partners accompts on time for the value of their refpective fhares brought in, (according to cafe third, where it was fuppofed the goods bought of them was on credit) you credit their accompts proper, the fame as if they had paid fo much cafh in part.

———————*June* 17th.———————

Sundries Debtor to *Thomas James* his accompt in company, 880*l.* 7*s.* 6*d.*

		l.	*s.*	*d.*
14	*Thomas James* his accompt proper, for his ¼ fhare of goods bought for ready money, and brought in by partners, and charges	460	7	6
15 / 14	Ditto his accompt on time, for his ¼ fhare bought on credit	420	0	0
		880	07	06

Sundries Debtors to *John Wilfon* his accompt in company, 880*l.* 7*s.* 6*d.*

		l.	*s.*	*d.*
15	*John Wilfon's* accompt proper, for his ¼ fhare of goods bought for ready money, and brought in by partners and charges	460	7	6
15 / 15	Ditto his accompt on time, for his ¼ fhare on credit	420	0	0
		880	07	06

See the fecond entries of Cafe 2d and 3d, Prob. 2d, Sect. 1ft, Chap. 3d.

Reafon. Your partners accompts proper being credited in the firft entry, for the value of what goods they brought into company, and in the fecond entries above, being debited for their refpective fhares of the whole brought in both by you and them, together with their fhares

		l.	s.	d.

fhares bought for ready money and all charges, their proper accompts will now fhew what is due to each of them by the company, or from the company to them. Their accompts on time will fhew what part of the goods bought on credit they ftand indebted for, and when due; and their accompts in company being credited by for their whole fhare of both, will exhibit each partner's concern in company.

——————*June* 18th.——————

Sundries Debtors to voyage to *Jamaica* 304 *l.* 7 *s.*

                                         l.   *s.*   *d.*

15 | Voyage from *Jamaica* for goods returned and charges } 195 07 05

15 | *William Boyd* my accompt current, for ballance in his hands } 108 19 07

6 | 304 07 00

See the 3d variety of Cafe 4th, Prob. 2d, Sect. 2d, Chap. 1ft.

Reafon. This being the firft advice from your factor fince you fhipped off the goods for him, *January* 21, when voyage to *Jamaica* was charged Debtor for the value of the outward bound cargo, confequently, the faid voyage ftands yet undifcharged; we therefore now difcharge it, by making voyage from *Jamaica* Debtor to it, for prime coft and charges of the homeward bound cargo; and alfo *William Boyd* my accompt current, Debtor to it for what cafh remains in his hands.

——————20th.——————

2 | Cafh Debtor to *John Todd* 190 *l.*

10 | Received of him in full, for *James Green's* barley ——— 190 00 00

12 | *James Green's* accompt on time, Debtor to ditto his accompt current

Cafe 5th, Prob. 2d, Chap. 2d.   190 00 00

10 |

Reafon. As you have now received payment, confequently you are immediately accountable to your employer for the fum received, and therefore, his accompt on time muft be debited to his accompt current.

——————24th.——————

2 | Cafh Debtor to voyage to *Jamaica* in company 1 *l.* 5 *s.*

_ | Received the drawback on 400 pair of fhoes exported thither

14 | *Thomas James* his accompt in company, Debtor to ditto his

14 | accompt proper for his ⅓ fhare of it ——— 1 05 00

15 | *John Willfon's* accompt in company, Debtor to ditto his ac-

15 | compt proper for his ¼ ——— 08 04

15 | 08 00

Reafon. As your partners accompts in company ftands credited for their fhares of all cofts and charges, fo of courfe it muft be debited for their fhares of all fales or abatements; and confequently, their proper accompts muft be credited to fhew what money you have received on their account.

		l.	s.	d.
	——————*June* 27th.———————			
11	Ship *Tyger* in company Debtor to cash 45 l.			
2	Paid messrs. *Graves* and *Maxwell*, for insuring 500 l. on her out and home	45	00	00
13	*John Ward* his accompt proper Debtor to ditto his accompt in company, for his ¼	22	10	00
12	Case 2d, Prob. 2d, Sect. 1st, Chap. 3d.			

Reason. In the first entry, it is plain, ship *Tyger* must be charged Debtor to cash for what you paid for insurance; and it is equally evident, that your partner's accompt proper, must be charged Debtor to his accompt in company for his half share of it, by which means his accompt proper will shew what he stands indebted to you, and his accompt in company, his share of inputs.

		l.	s.	d.
	——————*July* 1st.———————			
15	Charges on merchandize Debtor to cash 95 l.			
2	Paid clerk's wages, &c. from the 1st of *January* to this day, with other expences on trade, as *per* petty cash-Book	95	00	00
16	Household expences Debtor to cash 105 l.			
17	Paid house rent, servants wages, provisions, &c. &c. for the same time	105	00	00
	——————2d.———————			
17	Cash Debtor to sundries 1025 l.			

		l.	s.	d.
6	To *Charles Thompson*, for his bond	1000	0	0
8	To profit and loss, for 6 months Interest of the same, at 5 *per cent.*	25	0	0

		l.	s.	d.
		1025	00	00

Case 1st and 6th, Prob. 4th, Sect. 1st, Chap. 1st.

		l.	s.	d.
7	Bills payable Debtor to cash 36 l. 17 s. 6 d.			
17	Paid *James Green*'s on me to *Thomas Stirling*, or order	36	17	06
	——————5th.———————			
16	Tobacco Debtor to *James Johnston*, at *Virginia*, my accompt of goods 178 l. 4 s. 4 d.			
12	Received 47 hogsheads, *per* the *Happy Return*, weighing in the whole, 175 cwt. 3 qrs. 22 lb. first cost, together with commission and charges, as *per* invoice, is	178	04	04

See Case 6th, with the 2d Note after it in Prob. 3d, Sect. 2d, Chap. 1st.

Reason. As *James Johnston*, my accompt of goods, stood debited on his receipt of them the 20th of *May*, for prime cost and charges here, it is but reasonable, that now when he has made you returns for them, that the said accompt should be discharged; and as your tobacco is safe arrived, and the risk of the seas over, it of course becomes Debtor.

Tobacco,

		l.	s.	d.
	────────── *July* 6th. ──────────			
16	Tobacco Debtor to cash 466 *l.* 11 *s.* 11 *d.*			
17	Paid freight, duty, and other charges, on landing and putting it into my ware-house ━━━ ━━━	466	11	11
16	Tobacco Debtor to bonded duties 82 *l.* 2 *s.* 2 *d.*			
16	Given my bond for the remaining part of the duty, payable in 18 months ━━━ ━━━	82	02	02

────────── 9th. ──────────

Sundries Debtors to voyage from *Jamaica* 195 *l.* 7 *s.* 5 *d.*

		l.	s.	d.			
16	Indigo, for 6 barrels, containing in all 756 *lb.* at prime, with commission and charges there, comes to	86	12	6			
16	Pymento, for 5 hogsheads, quantity 1535 *lb.* cost and charges, amounts to	42	17	6			
16	Sugar, for 5 ditto, containing 63 *cwt.* cost and charges, is	65	17	5			
15					195	07	05

See Case 5th, with the 1st Note following Case 9th, in Prob. 3d, Sect. 2d, Chap. 1st.

Reason. As on the 18th of *June*, voyage from *Jamaica* stood debited for the value of goods shipped by your factor, and which were then at sea, the risk of the seas now being over, and the goods safe arrived, voyage from *Jamaica* must now be discharged, by making the several kinds of goods Debtors to it for their respective share of cost and charges.

Sundries Debtors to cash 97 *l.* 12 *s.*

		l.	s.	d.			
16	Indigo, for freight, duty, and other charges, which I have paid here	33	1	6			
16	Pymento, for ditto ━━━	24	16	4½			
16	Sugar, for ditto ━━━ ━━━	39	14	1½	97	12	00
17	See the Case and Note above referred to.						

────────── 10th. ──────────

Sundries Debtors to indigo 160 *l.* 13 *s.*

		l.	s.	d.			
17	Cash, received in part, for 6 barrels, containing 756 *lb.* at 4 *s.* 3 *d.* per *lb.*	80	13	0			
16	*John Dyer*, for the rest, due in 6 months ━━━	80	0	0	160	13	00

────────── 15th. ──────────

		l.	s.	d.
16	Cash Debtor to *William Hogg* his accompt of goods, per the *Nancy* 133 *l.* 6 *s.*			
17	Sold his 15 barrels of pork, at 4 *l.* 10 *s.* per barrel, and 47 firkins of butter, at 28 *s.* per firkin, for ready money, amounting together, to ━━━	133	06	00
12				

Y 2   *William*

		L.	s.	d.

------------------July 15th.------------------

12 *William Hogg* his accompt of goods Debtor to cash 2 l. 5 s. 6 d.

17 Paid ware-house room, and other charges on them, as per petty cash-book ————— ————— | 2 | 05 | 06

16 *William Hogg*, his accompt of goods, Debtor to commission accompt 4 l. 3 s. 4¼ d. which at 2½ per cent. on 166 l. 15 s.

15 8 d. comes to ————— ————— | 4 | 03 | 04¼

----------------22d.----------------

4/**16** *John Kirkman* of *Richmond* Debtor to sugar 89 l. 15 s. 6d. Sold him my 5 hogsheads, per the *Hopewell*, weighing 63 cwt. at 28 s. 6 d. per cwt. to pay in 6 months — | 89 | 15 | 06

----------------26th.----------------

17 Cash Debtor to *James Arnold* at *Dunkirk* my accompt current 785 l. 19 s. 8 d.

10 Drawn my bill on him to *James Fordyce*, or order, at 2 months, for 3368 crowns 1 livre and 10 sols, exchange at 4 s. 6 d. sterling, per *French* crown, amounts to — Case 1st, Prob. 3d, Sect. 2d, Chap. 1st, | 785 | 19 | 08

Reason. As *James Arnold*, my accompt current, stood debited for the above sum, the 16th of *April*, now when you have drawn upon him, the said accompt must be discharged, by making cash (which you received for your draft) Debtor to it.

17/**8** Cash Debtor to *James Gibson* 10 l. 10 s. Received of him in full, for 5 pieces of fustians ——— | 10 | 10 | 00

----------------28th.----------------

10 *James Green* his accompt current Debtor to bills payable 353 l. 12 s. 6 d.

7 Drawn his bill on me to *John Stanton*, at 3 weeks, which I have accepted for ————— ————— | 353 | 12 | 06

----------------*August* 5th.----------------

17 Voyage to *Hamburg* Debtor to sundries 213 l. 14 s.

| | | l. | s. | d. |

3 To cotton velvets, for 4 pieces, quantity 112 yards, at 7 s. per yard ————— } 39 04 0

18 To *Hugh Shaw*, 12 fother of lead, at 13 l. 5 s. per fother, to pay in 3 months ————— } 159 0 0

17 To cash, for custom and other charges ——— 15 10 0 | 213 | 14 | 00

Shipped the above goods on board the *Fly, William Devonport*, master, consigned to *Robert Ferguson*, to sell for my account.

Sundries,

————————*August* 11th.————————

Sundries Debtors to tobacco 285 *l.* 16 *s.* 8 *d.*

		l.	*s.*	*d.*
18	*Henry Primrose*, my accompt in company, for my half	142	18	04
19	*Henry Primrose*, my accompt proper, for his half	142	18	04

285	16	08

16   Delivered to him my 47 hogsheads, weight 175 *cwt.* 3 *qrs.* 22 *lb.* to sell for our account, each one half, valued at 3¼ *d.* per *lb.*

Reason. As you found both your own share, and your partner's of goods, so of course there must be two accompts made Debtor to the tobacco, viz. *Henry Primrose*, my accompt in company, to shew your share of the concern, and *Henry Primrose*, my accompt proper, for his share bought of you; the returns for the former, depends upon the success of the adventure; but that of the latter is a positive debt, the goods being absolutely sold to him, and consequently is liable for it, if he never makes a penny of them.

————————14th.————————

Sundries Debtors to tobacco 533 *l.* 14 *s.* 1 *d.*

		l.	*s.*	*d.*
17	Cash, received the drawback of duties paid at importation	451	11	11
16	Bonded duties, for my bond withdrawn	82	02	02

533	14	01

Henry Primrose having shipped off our tobacco for *Amster-dam*, I have received back my bond to the custom-house, and also received the drawback of duty paid.

Observation. As the price you delivered your tobacco to your partner at, was but a small advance upon prime cost, exclusive of duty and all charges, consequently you reserved the drawback at exportation to yourself, which he is not intitled to any share of; tobacco is therefore credited for value of the said bond and drawback.

————————17th.————————

17   Cash Debtor to sundries 602 *l.* 8 *s.* 8½ *d.*

		l.	*s.*	*d.*
14	To *Thomas James* his accompt proper	281	02	08¼
15	To *John Willson*, ditto	321	06	0¼

602	08	08½

Received the ballance of their accompts with interest.

Observation. Your partner's accompts proper, being the same as any other personal accompt, so they must of course be charged and discharged in the same manner; cash therefore being the thing received, it is plain, it must be made Debtor to each partner's accompt proper.

                              John

		l.	*s.*	*d.*
	────*August* 19th.────			
13 / 17	*John Ward*'s accompt proper Debtor to cash 10*l.* 17*s.* 11¼. Settled accompts with him, and paid him the ballance, together with a ballance of interest in his favour, the whole being	10	17	11¼
	────22d.────			
17 / —	Cash Debtor to *Henry Primrose,* my accompt proper 142 *l.* 18 *s.* 4 *d.*			
19	Received of him for his half share of 47 hogsheads of tobacco	142	18	04
	────25th.────			
18	*Thomas Bell* at *Genoa* his accompt current, Debtor to sundries 421 *l.* 10 *s.* 9 *d.*			

		l.	*s.*	*d.*				
18	To *John Duke,* for 12 ton of lead, at 14*s. per* ton, to pay in 3 months	168	0	0				
17	To cash, for 8640 *lb.* of tanned leather, at 6 *d. per lb.* with custom, insurance, &c.	241	12	0				
	To commission accompt	11	18	9				
10					421	10	09

Shipped the above goods, *per* his order, on board the *Rover, James Corrie,* master, for *Genoa.*

Observation. This entry is the same as in domestick trade, where you ship off goods of your own to your correspondent by his order; only in this case, you charge commission, (notwithstanding part or all of the goods be your own) and instead of charging your correspondent Debtor simply by his name, you here charge the person, his accompt current, Debtor.

		l.	*s.*	*d.*
	────30th.────			
17	Cash Debtor to pymento 57 *l.* 3 *s.* 11 *d.*			
16	Sold my 5 hogsheads, quantity 1535 *lb.* for ready money	57	03	11
	────*September* 10th.────			
17 / —	Cash Debtor to *Thomas Bell* at *Genoa* his accompt current 36 *l.*			
18	Received the drawback on 8640 *lb.* of tanned leather, shipped for him the 25th of *August*	36	00	00

Reason. As *Thomas Bell*'s accompt current stood charged for the whole price of the leather at shipping, the said accompt must now be credited by cash, as the money you received is his property.

		l.	*s.*	*d.*
	────17th.────			
18 / —	*Herman Van Sanders* his accompt of goods Debtor to cash 28 *l.* 10 *s.*			
17	Paid custom, freight, and other charges on them	28	10	00

James

		l.	*s.*	*d.*
	──────────September 19th.──────			
14	*James Murray* Debtor to sundries 1260 *l.*			
		l.	*s.*	*d.*
17	To cash, for myself and *Thomas James* ── 840	0	0	
15	To *John Willson*, his accompt on time, for his ⅓ } 420	0	0	
	share ────── ──────			
		1260	00	00

See Note 1st and 2d, after Case 3d. Prob. 2d, Sect. 1st, Chap. 3d.

Reason. Here (according to note first) *James Murray*, who was the seller, is made Debtor to cash for your own share, and *Thomas James*'s is advanced by you; and according to note second, he is made Debtor to *John Willson*'s accompt on time, for his one third share which he paid himself; for as his accompt on time stood debited when the goods were bought, so of course it must be credited when he pays them.

14	*Thomas James* his accompt proper Debtor to ditto, his			
──	accompt on time, for his ⅓, which I paid ──────	420	00	00
15	See 2d Entry in Note 2d.			

Reason. As the goods are now paid for, consequently, *Thomas James* (whose share you advanced for him) is intitled to no longer credit; his accompt on time is therefore discharged, by making his accompt proper, Debtor to it, which shews that his said share is immediately due to you, and bears interest from the time you advanced it, till the time he pays you.

	────────23d.──────			
17	Cash Debtor to *Herman Van Sanders* his accompt of			
──	goods 117 *l.*			
18	Received for his 36 cwt. of flax, at 3 *l.* 5 *s.* per cwt. ──	117	00	00

	────────28th.──────			
18	*Richard Crosby* in *Cannon Street*, Debtor to *Herman Van*			
──	*Sanders*, his accompt of goods 900 *l.*			
18	Sold him 30 butts of madder, at 2 *l.* 10 *s.* per cwt. half to be			
	paid in 2 months, and half at 6 months. ──────	900	00	00

18	*Herman Van Sanders* his accompt of goods Debtor to cash			
──	2 *l.* 12 *s.* 6 *d.*			
17	Paid ware-house room, and other charges on them ──────	2	12	06

18	*Herman Van Sanders* his accompt of goods, Debtor to			
──	commission accompt 26 *l.* 4 *s.* 0¾ *d.*			
10	For my commission, 2½ per cent. on 1048 *l.* 2 *s.* 6 *d.* ──	26	04	00¾

cash,

		l.	s.	d.

————————*October* 3d.————————

1' Cash Debtor to *Thomas Bell* at *Genoa*, his accompt cur-
— rent 208 *l.* 6 *s.* 8 *d,*

18 Drawn my bill on him to *John Greyson*, or order, for 1000
dollars exchange, at 50 *d. per* dollar, for which I have
received | | 208 | 06 | 08 |

————————8th.————————

19 *Herman Van Sanders* his accompt current, Debtor to fundries 202 *l.* 16 *s.* 3 *d.*

		l.	s.	d.
17	To cash, for 20 hogsheads of tobacco, at 2 ½ *d.* } *per lb.* with custom and other charges ——	196	12	4
19	To *Benjamin Green*, for cooperage ——	1	5	0
10	To commission accompt, at 2 ½ *per cent.* ——	4	18	11

| | | 202 | 16 | 03 |

. Shipped the above goods, *per* his order, on board the *Wasp*
Sloop, captain *Dods,* master, bound for *Amsterdam.*
Case 1st, Prob. 3d, Chap. 2d.

Reason. As your employer's accompt current is credited for neat
proceeds of all sales, it therefore of course must be debited for all returns you make him, whether in goods, bills, or cash.

————————12th.————————

17 Cash Debtor to *Herman Van Sanders* his accompt current
— 143 *l.* 2 *s.* 9 ¾ *d.*

19 Drawn my bill on him to *Thomas Castlehow,* or order, for
246 *l.* 6 *s.* 5 *d.* Flemish exchange at 35 *s.* 5 *d.* amounts to
in sterling ———————— —— | 143 | 02 | 09¾ |

Case 2d, Prob. 3d, Chap. 2d.
Reason. As your employer's accompt current is debited for all
goods you send him by his order, or for what cash or bills you pay
on his account, so it must be also credited for what remittances he
makes you, or for what bills you draw upon him.

————————15th.————————

19 *Robert Ferguson* my accompt current Debtor to voyage to
— *Hamburg* 268 *l.* 14 *s.* 0 ½ *d.*

17 Received advice, that he hath received and sold my goods, the
neat proceeds amounting to 462 *l.* 7 *s.* 10 *d.* Flemish, ex-
change at 34 *s.* 5 *d.* makes sterling ———— | 268 | 14 | 00½ |

Case 2d, Prob. 2d, Sect. 2d, Chap. 1st.

Reason. This being the first advice, and the goods being all sold,
and no returns made, R. F. my accompt current, is immediately
charged Debtor to voyage to *Hamburg*, in order that the said voyage
may be discharged, and R. F.'s, my accompt current, will then shew
what he stands indebted to you.

Sundries,

						l.	*s.*	*d.*

——————————*October* 20th.——————————

Sundries Debtors to *Henry Primrose,* my accompt in company, 142 *l.* 18 *s.* 4 *d.*

					l.	*s.*	*d.*			

17 | Cash ———— ———— ———— 42 18 4

9 | Bills receivable, for one on *James Snow,* for 100 0 0

19 | 142 18 04

Received of him my ⅛ proportion of an adventure to *Amsterdam*

Observation. As *Henry Primrose,* my accompt in company, stood debited the 11th of *August* for my half share of the above adventure, it is therefore reasonable, (now when he has paid me my half share of returns) that the said accompt should be credited by what I have received, viz. by cash and bills receivable.

——————————25th.——————————

19 | Hops, in company with *John Ward,* Debtor to *John Selby,* 300 *l.*

19 | Bought 100 *cwt.* of him, at 3 *l. per cwt.* to pay in 3 months 300 00 00

20 12 | *John Ward* his accompt on time Debtor to ditto his accompt in company, for ———— 150 00 00

Observation. In the second Journal entry here, *John Ward's* accompt in company is credited to shew his share of inputs; but instead of making his accompt proper Debtor to it, as Mr. *Mair* and others have done, I have debited his accompt on time, as you have no right to receive payment from him, till you pay *Selby* for the goods; whereas, according to their method, it would appear by your partner's accompt proper, that he stood immediately indebted to you, 150 *d.*

See this case journalized and posted according to Mr. *Mair,* at the latter end of your Ledger.

——————————28th.——————————

Sundries Debtors to silk hose, 40 *l.* 16 *s.*   *l. s. d.*

18 | *Henry Primrose,* my accompt in company, for my ⅛ share ———— } 20 8 0

19 | Ditto, my accompt proper, for his ⅛ share 20 8 0

    40 16 00

3 | Delivered to him my 6 dozen of silk hose at 6 *l.* 16 *s. per* dozen, to sell for our account.

——————————31st.——————————

9 | Bills receivable Debtor to *Robert Fergason* my accompt current, 271 *l.* 19 *s.* 10¼ *d.*

19 | Remitted to me in full of 462 *l.* 7 *s.* 10 *d.* exchange at 34 *s.* in bills, viz.

	l. s. d.

One on *Peter Young* for ———— 160 0 0

One on *William Harrison* for ———— 111 19 10¼

    271 19 10¼

Case 1st, Prob. 3d, Sect. 2d, Chap. 1st.

	l.	s.	d.

Reason. As *Robert Ferguson*, my accompt current, stood charged Debtor the 15th instant, upon his advising you that he had sold your goods for ready money, it therefore is proper (now when he has remitted you) that the said accompt should be discharged, by making bills receivable Debtor to it.

————*November* 3d.————

17 / 19   Cash Debtor to hops in company with *John Ward*, 340 *l.* Sold for ready money 100 *cwt.* at 3*l.* 8*s. per cwt.* comes to — 340 00 00

12 / 13   *John Ward's* accompt in company Debtor to ditto his accompt proper for his half share of the above ——— 170 00 00

Observation. Here the hops being sold for ready money by a second Journal Entry, *John Ward*, his accompt in company is charged Debtor to ditto his accompt proper, for his half share of the sales, by which means, the debt side of the former will shew his share of returns, and the credit side of the latter, that you owe your said partner for his half of the sales, notwithstanding the goods remain yet unpaid for by you and partner, so that when this is posted to your Ledger, it will then appear by your partner's accompt proper, that you stand indebted to him 170*l.* whereas, according to Mr. *Mair's* method, there would only appear a ballance of 20*l.* in his favour.

See the case also journalized and posted according to Mr. *Mair.*

————5th.————

13 / 17   *John Ward* his accompt proper Debtor to cash, 170 *l.* Settled accompts with him, and paid him the ballance, being 170 00 00

————7th.————

20 / 17   Rum in company with *John Ward* Debtor to cash, 300 *l.* Paid for 9 puncheons, at 33*l.* 6*s.* 8*d. per* puncheon — 300 00 00

13 / 12   *John Ward* his accompt proper Debtor to ditto his accompt in company for his half share of the above ——— 150 00 00

Observation. The second entry here, is the same as Mr. *Mair's*, for as the rum was bought for ready money, which you paid entirely yourself, it is therefore reasonable, that your partner's accompt proper should be immediately debited for his half share, because it is instantly due to you; and his accompt in company credited, to shew his share of inputs.

————10th.————

6 / 20   *Samuel Rich* of *Norwich* Debtor to rum in company, 340 *l.* Sold him our 9 puncheons, to pay in 3 months ——— 340 00 00

12 / 20   *John Ward* his accompt in company Debtor to ditto his accompt on time for his half share of the above ——— 170 00 00

Observation. Notwithstanding the rum was sold on credit, it is nevertheless necessary that your partner's accompt in company, should be debited for his share of the sales; but his accompt proper could not, with any propriety, be credited, as you are not accountable for the cash till you have received it from *Samuel Rich*; but as his said

		l.	s.	d.

said accompt in company muſt have a correſpondent ceedit, we therefore make his accompt in company Debtor to ditto his accompt on time, which accompt ſhews that you will owe your partner ſo much money when you receive it from Rirb, ſo that when this is poſted to your Ledger, it will ſtill appear, that your partner owes you for the whole of his ſhare of the purchaſe, viz. 150 l. whereas, according to Mr. Mair's method, you would owe him a ballance of 20 l.

See this caſe likewiſe journalized and poſted according to Mr. Mair.

——————— November 12th. ———————

17/13   Caſh Debtor to John Ward his accompt proper 150 l. | 150 | 00 | 00 |
Received in full, for his half ſhare of 9 puncheons of rum

Note. When this is poſted, your partner's accompt proper will then be evened as it ought to be, but, according to Mr. Mair, there will be a wide difference, notwithſtanding he would make the ballance to be the ſame, but by what means he diſcovers the ballance to be ſo I cannot conceive, ſince your partner's accompt proper, (which ought to exhibit truly how matters ſtands between you) according to him, makes a ballance of 20 pounds in the oppoſite ſide.

See this likewiſe according to Mr. Mair.

——————— 16th. ———————

7/14   George Gair of the Borough Debtor to voyage to Jamaica in company, 3020 l. | 3020 | 00 | 00 |
Received advice from William Boyd, per the Tyger, that he hath received and ſold our adventure, neat proceeds, as per accompt of ſales, amounting to 4228 l. Jamaica currency, which he has, per our order, advanced in purchaſing a homeward cargo for George Gair, and adviſed him of the ſame, value in Engliſh money

Obſervation. Had the homeward bound cargo been on your own and partner's accompts, then voyage from Jamaica in company have would been Debtor; but as the amount of the outward bound cargo was advanced on account of George Gair, and by his order, he of courſe becomes Debtor immediately, and muſt have been accountable to you for the ſum advanced, whether the ſhip had arrived ſafe or not.

7/11   George Gair Debtor to ſhip Tyger in company 140 l. | 140 | 00 | 00 |
William Boyd likewiſe adviſes us, that he had freighted the ſaid ſhip home for Mr. Gair, for

——————— 20th. ———————

18/37   Hugh Shaw Debtor to caſh 159 l. | 159 | 00 | 00 |
Paid him in full

		l.	s.	d.
	————————*November* 25th.————————			
18 / 17	*John Duke* Debtor to cash, 168 *l.* Paid him in full ——— ——— ———	168	00	00
17 / 18	. Cash Debtor to *Richard Crosby,* 450 *l.* Received of him in part ——— ——— —	450	00	00
	————————27th.————————			
17	Cash Debtor to Sundries, 44 *l.* 4 *s.*			
19	To *Henry Primrose* my accompt proper — 20 8 0			
18	To ditto my accompt in company — 23 16 0	44	04	00
	Received of him for his half share of 6 dozen of silk hose, and also for my half share of sales of the whole.			
	————————30th.————————			
17	Cash Debtor to sundries, 563 *l.* 8 *s.*			
9	To brandy, *per* the *Eagle,* for 15 casks, quantity 900 gallons ——— ——— } 350 8 0			
9	To port wine, *per* ditto, for 6 pipes, at 35 *l.* 10 *s. per* pipe ——— } 213 0 0	563	08	00
	Sold the above for ready money — — —			
	————————*December* 5th.———			
17 / 7	Cash Debtor to *George Gair,* 3020 *l.* Received of him in full for what our factor, *William Boyd,* advanced for him ———————	3020	00	00
14 / 14	*Thomas James* his accompt in company Debtor to ditto his accompt proper for his ½ — — —	1006	13	04
15 / 14	*John Willson's* ditto ditto for his ½	1006	13	04
17 / 7	Cash Debtor to *George Gair,* 140 *l.* Received of him in full for freight of ship *Tyger* —	140	00	00
12 / 13	*John Ward's* accompt in company Debtor to ditto his accompt proper for his half — — —	70	00	00

Observation. The second entry of the above two, might have been made under the two Journal entries of *November* the 16th, which, according to Mr. *Mair,* would have been the very same as here, and consequently rendered them in this place unnecessary : But as I have in my cases and rules proved the impropriety of crediting your partner's accompt proper before you had value actually in your own hands, so had I made the second Journal entries under those of the 16th of *November,* your partners accompts of time (instead of their accompts proper) would have been credited, which would have varied the second Journal entries

<table>
<tr><td align="right"></td><td></td><td align="right">l.</td><td>s.</td><td>d.</td></tr>
</table>

		l.	s.	d.

tries of *December* 5th, for it would then have been each partner's accompt of time Debtor to ditto their accompt proper: But as we meant to take the first opportunity of settling accompts with Mr. *Gair*, I therefore postponed the second entries of the 16th of *November*, by which I saved the said second Journal entries, and the partners accompts in company and accompts proper will now stand the same, as they would have done had I made the above-mentioned second entries both on the 16th of *November* and 5th of *December*.

—————————*December* 10th.—————————

11	Ship *Tyger* in company Debtor to cash, 90 *l.*			
17	Paid the seamen six months wages — —	90	00	00
13	*John Ward*'s accompt proper Debtor to ditto his accompt in			
12	company for his ½ of the above	45	00	00

14	Voyage to *Jamaica* in company Debtor to ship *Tyger* in			
—	company, 140 *l.*			
11	For freight of outward bound cargo, in company with *Tho-*			
	mas James and *John Wilson* — ——	140	00	00
14				
14	*Thomas James*'s accompt proper Debtor to ditto his accompt			
	in company for his ⅓ share of the above —	46	13	04
15	*John Wilson*'s ditto ditto for his ⅓ — —	46	13	04
15	*John Ward*'s accompt in company Debtor to ditto his ac-			
12	compt proper for his ½ of freight of ship *Tyger* —	70	00	00
13				

Observation. In the last Journal entry of this date, you see three second Journal entries were necessary; for as you were concerned with *Thomas James* and *John Wilson* in the voyage to *Jamaica*, and with *John Ward* in the ship *Tyger*, so the first two relates to your partners in the voyage, and the last to your partner in the ship.

11	Ship *Tyger* in company Debtor to commission accompt for			
10	my commission on 1108 *l.* 16 *s.* at 2½ *per cent.* —	27	14	04¼
13	*John Ward*'s accompt proper Debtor to ditto his accompt in			
12	company for ½ of the above — —	13	17	02⅛

—————————12th.—————————

| 13 | *John Ward* his accompt proper Debtor to cash, 81 *l.* 2 *s.* 9¼ *d.* | | | |
| 17 | Paid him in full — — — | 81 | 02 | 09¼ |

| 14 | Voyage to *Jamaica* in company Debtor to commission ac- | | | |
| 10 | compt — — — | 69 | 10 | 06¾ |

14				
14	*Thomas James*'s accompt proper Debtor to ditto his accompt			
	in company for his ⅓ of the above —	23	03	06¼
15	*John Wilson*'s ditto ditto for his ⅓ —	23	03	06¼
15				

December

		l.	s.	d.
	———————*December* 12th.———————			
	Sundries Debtors to cash, 1450 *l.* 14 *s.* 4¼ *d.*			
		l.	*s.*	*d.*
14	*Thomas James's* accompt proper —	512	18	10½
15	To *John Wilson's* ditto — —	937	15	5¾
17	r'd them in full			
		1450	14	4¼
	———————16th.———————			
17	Cash Debtor to *William Boyd* my accompt current, 108 *l.*			
—	19 *s.* 7 *d.*			
15	Drawn my bill on him to *James Scott* or order, for 152 *l.* 11 *s.*			
	5 *d. Jamaica* currency, for which I have received in *English*	108	19	7
	———————18th.———————			
17	Cash Debtor to *John Dyer,* 80 *l.*			
16	Received of him in full for indigo — —	80	00	0
	———————20th.———————			
17	*William Hegg's* accompt current Debtor to cash, 145 *l.*			
—	13 *s.* 7½ *d.*			
17	Drawn his bill on me to *George Simpson* or order, at six days			
	after date, which I have paid —	145	13	7½
17	Cash Debtor to *Thomas Bell* (at *Genoa*) his accompt cur-			
—	rent, 177 *l.* 4 *s.* 1 *d.*			
18	Drawn my bill on him to *James Watts* or order, for the above			
	sum, which I have received in cash —	177	04	1
	———————28th.———————			
15	Charges on merchandize Debtor to cash, 104 *l.* 16 *s.*			
17	Paid clerk's wages, warehouse-room. &c. since 1st of *July*	104	16	0
	———————30th.———————			
16	Houshold expences Debtor to cash, 120 *l.*			
17	Paid house rent, servants wages, &c. since 1st of *July* —	120	00	0

L E D G E R.

L E D G E R.

(No. II.)

A	Fo	B	Fo	C	Fo
Arnold (James) my accompt current	10	Brandy	4	Cash	2 17
		Bradshaw (Daniel)	6	Cotton velvets	3
		Burgis (Tho.) Paisley	6	Cook (R.) Wakefield	5
		Bell (James) Berwick	6	Custom-house debentrs.	6
		Bills payable	7	Commission accompt	10
		Bills receivable	9	Charges on merchand.	15
		Brandy, per the Eagle, from Dunkirk	9	Crosby (Richard) Cannon-street	18
		Boyd (Wm.) my accompt current	15		
		Bonded duties	15	**I**	**Fo**
		Bell (Tho.) Genoa, his accompt current	17	Jeans	5
				Johnston (James) at Virginia, my accompt of goods	12
G	**Fo**	**H**	**Fo**	Irish linens	13
Gair (Geo.) Borough	7	Hats	3	James (Tho.) his accompt in company	14
Green (James) Berwick his ac. of goods	7	Hervey (Tho.) my accompt current	10	Ditto his ac. proper	14
Gibson (James) Stilton	8	Ditto my accompt of goods	9	Ditto his ac. on time	15
Green (James) his accompt current	10	Hogg (Wm.) Berwick, his accompt of goods	12	Indigo	16
Ditto his ac. on time	12	Household expences	16	**P**	**Fo**
				Printed cottons	3
N	**Fo**	**O**	**Fo**	Printed linens	4
Norwich stuffs	4			Profit and loss	8
				Port wine per the Eagle	9
				Pymento	16
				Primrose (Henry) my ac. company	18
				Ditto my ac. proper	19
				V	**Fo**
				Voyage to Virginia	6
				Voyage to Jamaica	6
				Voyage from Berwick to Dunkirk	6
T	**Fo**	**U**	**Fo**	Voyage to Dublin	7
Tomlinson (James) Hatfield	3			Ditto from Dublin	13
Thread hose	5			Voyage to Jamaica in co. wit T. James and John Wilson	14
Thornton (Jam.) Wigan	5			Voyage from Jamaica	15
Thompson (Charles)	6			Voyage to Hamburg	17
Todd (John) Greenwich	10			Van Sanders his accompt of goods	18
Tobacco	16			Ditto his ac. on time	18
				Ditto his ac. current	19

D	Fo	E	Fo	F	Fo
Devonfhire Planes	4	Euftage (Cuthbert) } Stamford	5	Forfter (J.) Smith- } field	4
D er (John)	16			Fuftians	9
Duke (John)	18				

K	Fo	L	Fo	M	Fo
Kirkman (John) } Richmond	4	Lamb(Robert) Yar- } mouth	4	Martin(John)ofBarnet	3
				Murray (James)	14

Q	Fo	R	Fo	S	Fo
		Rum	3	Stock	1
		Rich (Samuel) of } Norwich	6	Scots lawns	2
				Silk hofe	3
				Sufpence accompt	4
				Shoes	5
				Simpfon(T.)Manchefter	5
				Ship *Tyger* in co.	
				Sugar	16
				Snaw (Hugh)	18

W	Fo	X	Fo	Y	Fo
Wilks (James) St } Edmond's Bury	3			Yorkfhire Planes	3
Webfter (William) } Manchefter	5				
Ward(John) his ac- } compt in company	12				
Ditto his ac. proper	13				
Wilfon (John) his } accompt proper	15				
Do. his ac. in company	15				
Ditto his ac. on time	15				

A 2

Year & Month	Stock,	Dr	Fo	l.	s.	d.
1777. Jan. 1	To *William Webster* of *Manchester*	—	5	98	00	0
	To *James Thornie* of *Wigan*	—	5	114	17	6
	To *Thomas Simpson* of *Manchester*	—	5	60	00	0
	To *Ralph Cook* of *Wakefield*	—	5	36	16	0
	To *Samuel Rich* of *Norwich*	—	6	44	06	8
	To *Daniel Bradshaw*	—	6	65	00	0
	To *Thomas Burgis* of *Paisley*	—	6	100	00	0
	To ballance for the neat of my estate	—	20	11911	02	4¼
				12430	02	6⅝

Year & Month.	Contra,	Cr.	F.	£	s.	d.
1777.						
Jan. 1	By cash in ready money	——	2	1033	10	00
	By Scots lawns, for 5 pieces, at 5 l. per piece	——	2	75	00	00
	By silk hose, for 6 dozen, at 6 l. 6 s. per dozen		3	37	16	0d
	By cotton velvets, for 4 pieces, quantity 112 yards, at 7 s. per yard		3	39	04	00
	By John Martin of Barnet	——	3	114	00	00
	By James Tomlinson of Hatfield	——	3	35	15	00
	By printed cottons, for 10 pieces, quantity 200 yards, at 2 s. 6 d. per yard		3	25	00	00
	By rum, for 60 gallons, at 8 s. per gallon	——	3	24	00	00
	By James Wills of St. Edmond's Bury	——	3	70	07	00
	By hats, for 20 dozen, at 6 l. per dozen	——	3	120	00	00
	By Yorkshire planes, for 8 pieces, quantity 144 yards, at 4 s. per yard		3	28	16	00
	By James Forster of Smithfield, for	——	4	118	18	00
	By Norwich stuffs, for 10 pieces, quantity 260 yards, at 1 s. 4 d. per yard		4	15	05	08
	By Brandy, for 5 ankers, at 4 l. 10 s. per anker	——	4	22	10	00
	By printed linens, for 6 pieces, quantity 156 yards, at 3 s. per yard		4	18	18	00
	By Devonshire planes, for 300 yards, at 5 s. 6 d. per yard		4	82	10	00
	By suspence accompt	——	4	21	00	00
	By John Kirkman of Richmond	——	4	100	05	04
	By Robert Lamb of Yarmouth	——	4	55	17	08
	By jeans, for 50 pieces, quantity 1000 yards, at 2 s. 4 d. per yard		5	116	13	04
	By shoes, for 400 pair, at 4 s. per pair	——	5	80	00	00
	By thread hose, for 20 dozen. at 1 l. 4 s. per dozen		5	24	00	00
	By Cuthbert Eustage of Stamford	——	5	76	17	00
	By profit and loss, gained	——	5	773	18	6¼
				12430	02	6¼

A 2

Year & Month.	Cash,	Dr	Fo	l.	s.	d.
1777.						
Jan. 1	To stock in ready money ————		1	10353	10	00
10	To Scots lwns, for 15 pieces, at 6 l. per piece		2	90	00	00
Feb. 7	To voyage to Jamaica, for the drawback on 200 yards of Norwick stuffs ————		6	2	10	00
24	To James Forster, in part ————		4	100	00	00
27	To Robert Lamb, in full ————		4	55	17	08
	To John Martin, in full ————		3	112	10	00
Mar 14	To James Tomlinson, in full ————		3	35	15	00
April 3	To James Wilks, in full ————		3	70	07	00
6	To James Forster, for the ballance of his accompt		4	18	18	00
	To bills receivable, for Corrie's on Hamilton —		9	1000	00	00
	To custom-house debentures, received for my debenture bill ————		6	250	00	00
19	To James Green his accompt of goods, for 100 quarters of barley sold — ————		7	80	00	00
May 5	To Cuthbert Eustage, of Stamford, in full ———		5	78	1	00
23	To bills receivable, for Bell's on Bailey ———		9	82	0	00
June 2	To James Green's accompt of goods, per the Nancy		7	190	00	00
20	To John Todd, received of him in full, for Green barley		10	190	00	00
24	To voyage to Jamaica in company, for the drawback on 400 pair of shoes exported —		14		05	00
				12711	00	08

	Scots Lawns,	Dr.	pieces.		l.	s.	d.
1777.							
Jan. 1	To stock, at 5 l. per piece ————		15	1	75	00	00
	To profit and loss, gained ———			8	15	00	00
			15		90	00	00

Year & Month.	Contra, Cr.	Fo	l.	s.	d.
1777.					
Jan. 5	By voyage to *Virginia*, for cuftom and other charges	6	2	18	04
21	By voy. to *Jamaica*, for infurance and other charges	6	24	11	04
27	By *Charles Thompfon*, lent him on bond for 6 months	6	1000	00	00
Feb. 13	By voyage to *Dublin*, for cuftom and other charges	7	1	04	06
20	By *Thomas Simpfon*, in full	5	57	10	00
Mar. 7	By bills receivable, difcounted *George Edgar* a bill of a thoufand pounds, for which I paid	9	996	00	00
10	By *Daniel Bradfhaw*, in full ———	6	65	00	00
18	By *J. Thornton*, paid for a bill which I remitted him	5	100	00	00
24	By *James Green*'s acc. of goods per the *Polly*, for freight, &c.	7	30	12	06
April 3	By bills payable, for *Watfon* s on me to *Coats* and co.	7	1535	10	00
10	By *J. Thornton*, paid him the ball. of his acc. in full	5	44	17	00
13	By *George Gair*, paid him in full for hops —	7	17	10	00
17	By fundries, as per Journal ———	7	111	09	00
28	By *James Green*'s acc. of goods, for waterage, &c.	7	5	15	00
May 2	By fhip *Tyger* in company, for my ⅓ fhare of coft	11	400	00	00
12	By *James Green* s accompt of goods per the *Nancy*	7	1	02	06
15	By *William Hogg*'s accompt of goods per ditto	12	6	03	06
	By bills payable, for *Ralph Cook*'s on me to *James Wood*	7	38	16	00
16	By ditto, for *William Webfter*'s to *James Burdett*	7	98	00	00
June 2	By *James Green*'s accompt of goods per the *Nancy*, for porterage, &c. ———	7	2	15	00
8	By *Samuel Rich*, in full for the ball nce of his acc.	6	18	01	08
12	By *Irifh* linens, paid freight, waterage, and other charges in bringing them into my wareh ufe	13	5	02	06
17	By fhip *Tyger* in company, paid for beef, bread beer, &c.	11	28	16	00
	By voyage to *Jamaica* in company, for ———	14	635	1	06
27	By fhip *Tyger* in company, paid for infurance —	11	45	00	00
July 1	By charges on merchandize, paid clerks wages, &c. fince the rft of *Jan.* ———	15	95	00	00
	By the new accompt of cafh ———	17	178	12	10
			12711	00	08

	Contra, Cr.		pieces.		l.	s.	d.
1777.							
Jan. 1	By cafh, at 6 l. per piece, for ———	15	2		9	00	00
		15			90	00	00

Year & Month.		Fo	l.	s.	d.
	Silk Hose, Dr.				
	dozen.				
1777. Jan. 1	To Stock, at 6l. 6s. per dozen, for —— 6	1	73	16	00
	To profit and loss, gained ——	8	3	00	00
	6		40	16	00
	Cotton Velvets, Dr.				
	pieces yds.				
1777. Jan. 1	To stock, at 7s. per yard, for — 4 112	1	39	04	00
1777. Jan. 1	**John Martin of Barnet,** Dr. To stock, due the 11th of Feb. next ——	1	114	00	00
1777. Jan. 1	**James Tomlinson of Hatfield,** Dr. To stock in part, for goods sold him the 12th December last ——	1	35	15	00
	Printed Cottons, Dr				
	pieces yds.				
1777. Jan. 1	To stock, at 2s. 6d. per yard, for — 10 200	1	25	00	00
	To profit and loss, gained —	8	5	00	00
	10 200		30	00	00
	Rum, Dr				
	gall.				
1777. Jan. 1	To stock, at 8s. per gallon, for —— 60	1	24	00	00
	To profit and loss, gained ——	8	6	00	00
	60		30	00	00
1777. Jan. 1	**James Wilks, St. Edmond's Bury,** Dr. To stock, for goods sold him the 23d December —	1	70	07	00
	Hats, Dr				
	doz.				
1777. Jan. 1	To stock, at 6l. per dozen, for —— 20	1	120	00	00
	Yorkshire Planes, Dr.				
	pieces yds.				
1777. Jan. 1	To stock, at 4s. per yard, for — 8 144	1	28	16	00

Year & Month.		Fo.	L.	s.	d.
	Contra, Cr.				
	doz.				
1777. Oct. 28	By fundries, as _per_ Journal, at 6l. 16s. per dozen, for 6		40	16	00
	6		40	16	00
	Contra, Cr				
	pieces yds.				
1777. Aug 5	By voyage to _Hamburg,_ at 7s. per yd. for 4 112	17	39	04	00
	Contra, Cr.				
1777. Feb. 27	By fundries, as _per_ Journal		114	00	00
	Contra, Cr.				
1777. May 14	By cafh, in full	2	35	15	00
	Contra, Cr.				
	pieces yds.				
1777. Jan.14	By _James Bell,_ at 3s. per yard, for 10 200	6	30	00	00
	10 200		30	00	00
	Contra, Cr.				
	gall.				
1777. Jan.14	By _James Bull,_ at 10s. per gallon, for 60	6	30	00	00
	60		30	00	00
	Contra, Cr.				
1777. April 3	By cafh, in full	2	70	07	00
	Contra, Cr				
	doz.				
1777. Jan.12	By voyage to _Jamaica,_ at 6l. per dozen, for 20	6	120	00	00
	Contra, Cr.				
	pieces yds.				
1777. Jan. 5	By voyage to _Virginia,_ at 4s. per yard, for 8 144	6	28	16	00

Year & Month		Fo	l.	s.	d.
	James Forster of Smithfield, Dr.				
1777. Jan. 1	To flock, due the 24th of February next —	1	118	18	00
			118	18	00
	Norwich Stuffs, Dr.				
			pieces	yds	
1777. Jan. 1	To flock, at 1s. 4d. per yard, for —	10	200	1	13	06	08
	Brandy, Dr.				
			ankers		
1777. Jan. 1	To flock, at 4l. 10s. per anker, for —	5	1	22	10	00
	To profit and lofs, gained — —		8	3	15	00
		5	26	05	00
	Printed Linens, Dr.				
			pieces	yds	
1777 Jan.	To flock, at 3s. per yard, for —	6	126	1	18	18	00
	To profit and lofs, gained — —		8	3	03	00
		6	126	22	01	00
	Devonshire Planes, Dr				
			yds	
1777. Jan. 1	To flock, at 5s. 6d. per yard, for —	300	1	82	10	00
1777. Jan. 1	Suspence Accompt, Dr				
	To flock, for 10 pieces fuftians, sent James Gibfon of Stilton, at 2l. 2s. per piece — }	1	21	00	00
	John Kirkman of Richmond, Dr.				
1777. Jan. 1	To flock, due the 26th of March ——	1	100	05	04
July 22	To fugar, for 5 hhds. containing 63 cwt. at 28s. 6d. per cwt. due in 6 months —— }	16	89	15	06
			190	00	10
	Robert Lamb of Yarmouth, Dr.				
1777. Jan. 1	To flock, due the 27th of February next —	1	55	17	08

Year & Month.		Fo	l.	s.	d.
	Contra, *Cr.*				
1777. Feb. 24	By cash, in part ——— ———	2	100	00	00
April 6	By cash, in full ——— ——— —	2	18	18	00
			118	18	00

			pieces	yds.				
	Contra, *Cr.*							
1777. Jan. 21	By voyage to *Jamaica*, at 1s. 4d. per yard, for ——— ——— }	10	200	6	13	06	08

			ankers.			
	Contra, *C-*					
1777. Mar. 1	By *Samuel Rich*, at 5l. 5s. per anker, for		5	6	26	05	00
			5		26	05	00

			pieces	yds.				
	Contra, *Cr.*							
1777. Jan. 14	By *James Bell*, at 3s. 6d. per yard for	6	126	6	22	01	00
		6	126		22	01	00

			yds.				
	Contra, *Cr.*						
1777. Jan. 5	By voyage to *Virginia*, at 5s. 6d. per yard, for	300	6	82	0	08

	Contra, *Cr.*					
1777. Feb. 24	By sundries, as *per* Journal ———		21	00	00

	Contra, *Cr.*					
1777. Mar. 31	By *Thomas Burgis*, for his draft to me on *John Dickson*, remitted him ——— }	6	100	00	00
	By ballance, due *January* 22d ——— —	20	90	00	10
			190	00	10

	Contra, *Cr.*					
1777. Feb. 27	By cash recd. for my bill on him to *J. Banks*, or order	2	55	17	08

Year & Months		Fo	l.	s.	d.
17 7. Mar. 1 June 8 Nov. 10	**Samuel Rich of Norwich,** Dr To brandy, for 5 ankers, at 5*l* 5*s* per anker — To cash, in full, remitted him Campble and co's note, for which I paid ——— To rum, in company with John Ward for 9 puncheons, due in 3 months ———	 4 2 20	 26 18 340	 00 01 0	 00 08 00
			384	06	08
1777. Mar 10	**Daniel Bradshaw, Thames-street,** Dr To cash, in full ——	 2	 65	 00	 00
1777. Mar 31	**Thomas Burgis of Paisley,** Dr To John Kirkman, remitted him said Kirkman draft to me on John Dickson ———	 4	 100	 0	 00
1777. Jan. 5	**Voyage to Virginia,** Dr To sundries, as per Journal ——		 138	 04	 04
1777. Jan.14	**James Bell of Berwick-upon-Tweed,** Dr. To sundries, as per Journal, sent him per the London Packet, as per his order ———		 82	 01	 00
1777. Jan.21	**Voyage to Jamaica,** Dr To sundries, as per Journal —— To profit and loss, gained	 8	 223 8.	 18 18	 08 04
			306	17	00
1777. Jan.27	**Voyage from Berwick to Dunkirk,** Dr To bills payable, for James Watson's on me to Coats and company, for To profit and loss, gained —— —	 7 8	 1535 65	 10 00	 00 02
			1900	10	02
1777. Feb. 2	**Charles Thompson Parliament street,** Dr. To cash, lent him on bond for 6 months, at 5 p. ct. p. an.	 2	 1000	 00	 00
1777. Feb. 7	**Custom-house Debentures,** Dr. To voyage from Berwick to Dunkirk, for bounty on my wheat exported ———	 6	 250	 00	 00

Year & Month.		Fo	L	s.	d.
1777.	*Contra,* Cr.				
Jan. 1	By ftock, due the 8th of *June* — —	1	44	06	08
	By ballance, due *February* 3d — —	20	340	00	00
			384	06	08
1777.	*Contra,* Cr				
Jan. 1	By ftock, for goods bought the 10th of *Decem.* laft	1	65	00	00
1777.	*Contra,* Cr.				
Jan. 1	by ftock, for goods bought the 21ft of *December* laft	1	100	00	00
1777.	*Contra,* Cr.				
May 20	By *James Johnfon* my accompt of goods —	12	138	04	04
1777.	*Contra,* Cr.				
May 8	By bills receivable, for his draft on *Thomas Bailey*	9	82	01	00
1777.	*Contra,* Cr.				
Feb. 7	By cafh, for the drawback on 200 yards *Norwick* ⎫ ftuff exported — — — ⎬	2	2	10	00
June 18	By fundries, as *per* Journal —		304	07	00
			306	17	00
1777.	*Contra,* Cr				
Feb. 7	By cuftom-houfe debentures, for the bounty on ⎫ 1000 quarters wheat, at 5s *per* quarter — ⎬	6	250	00	00
Apr. 16	By fundries, as *per* Journal —		1650	10	02
			1900	10	02
1777.	*Contra,* Cr.				
July 2	By cafh, in full, for his bond —	17	1000	00	00
1777.	*Contra,* Cr.				
Feb. 7	By cafh, received for my debenture bill, for wheat ⎫ exported to *Dunkirk* — — ⎬	2	250	00	00

Year & Month.		Fo	l.	s.	d.
1777.	*Voyage to Dublin,* Dr				
Feb. 13	To sundries, as *per* Journal — —		172	14	06
June 7	To *Thomas Harvey* my accompt current, for freight commission, and other charges — —	10	21	15	00
	To profit and loss, gained — —	8	25	07	06
			219	17	00
1777.	*George Gair in the Borough,* Dr.				
Apr. 18	To cash, in full, for hops —————	2	171	10	00
Nov. 16	To voy. to *Jamaica* in co. advanced him by *W. Boyd*	14	3020	00	00
	To ship *Tyger* in co. for freight of said ship from *Jama.*	11	140	00	00
			3331	10	00
1777.	*James Green of Berwick-upon- Tweed, his accompt of goods per the Polly,* Dr				
Mar 24	To cash, paid freight, and other char. on the *Polly* scar	2	30	12	06
Apr. 28	To do. paid waterage and other char. as p. petty cash-bk	2	5	15	00
	To commission accompt, at 2½ per cent. — —	10	6	15	00
	To *James Green's* acc. on time, due from *John Todd*	12	190	00	00
	To ditto his accompt current, for ball. in my hands	10	36	17	06
			270	00	00
	Per the Nancy.				
May 12	To cash, for freight, waterage, &c. — —	2	14	02	06
June 2	To ditto, for porterage —————	2	2	15	00
	To commission accompt, at 5*l.* per cent. on 190*l.* —	10	9	10	00
	To *James Green's* accompt current for neat proceeds	10	163	12	06
			190	00	00
1777.	*Bills Payable,* Dr.				
April 3	To cash, paid *Watson's* bill on me to *Coats* and co.	2	1535	10	00
May 15	To cash, paid *Ralph Cook's* draft on me to *J. Wood*	2	36	16	00
16	To ditto, paid *William Webster's* on me to *J. Burdett*	2	98	00	00
July 2	To ditto paid *James Green's* on me to *Thos. Stirling*	17	36	17	06
	To ball. for *James Green's* on me, not yet presented	20	353	12	06
			2060	16	00

Date & Month.	Contra, Cr.	Fo.	L	s	d
1777. Apr. 24	By sundries, as per Journal		219	17	00
			219	17	00

1777.	Contra, Cr.				
Feb. 13	By voy. to Dublin, for 50 pockets hops; to pay in 2 m.	7	171	10	00
Dec. 5	By cash, in full, advanced by W. Boyd, per our order	17	3020	00	00
	By ditto, in full, for freight of our ship Tyger home	17	140	00	00
			3331	10	00

1777.	Contra, Cr.				
Apr. 19	By cash, received for 100 quarters of oats, at 16s. per quarter	2	80	00	00
28	By John Todd, for 200 quarters of barley, at 19s. per quarter	10	190	00	00
			270	00	00

June 2	By cash, received for his 200 kitts, of salmon, and 10 chests of eggs	2	190	00	00
			190	00	00

1777.	Contra, Cr.				
Jan. 27	By voyage from Berwick to Dunkirk, for Watson's on me o Coats and co. due the 14th of March	6	1535	10	00
Mar 16	By Ralpl Cook, for his draft on me to James Wood, due the 15th of May	5	36	16	00
April 6	By William Webster, for his bill on me to James Burdett, or order, due the 16th of May	5	98	00	00
June 12	By James G en's accompt current, for his bill on me to Thomas Stirling, due the 2d of July	10	36	17	06
July 18	By do. for his bill on me to J. Sesson, due the 24th Aug.	10	353	12	06
			2060	16	00

Year & Month.	Profit and Loss, Dr	Fo	l.	s.	d.
1777. Feb. 27	To *John Martin* of *Barnet*, abated him —	3	2	00	00
Aug. 19	To *John Ward* his accompt proper, for ballance } of interest ———	12		05	11¼
Dec. 12	To *John Wilson*'s accompt proper, for interest in } his favour ———	15		19	00
	To charges on merchandize ———	15	199	16	00
	To houfehold expences — ———	16	225	00	00
	To pymento ———	16	10	09	11¼
	To fugar — — — ———	16	15	16	00¼
	To ftock, gain'd ———	1	773	18	0¼
			1228	05	05¼

	James Gibfon of *Stilton*, Dr.				
1777. Feb. 24	To fufpence accompt, for 5 pieces of fuftians, at } 2l. 2s. per piece ———	4	10	10	00

Year &c Month.	Contra, *Cr.*	Fo	L	s.	d.
1777.					
Feb. 20	By *Thomas Simpson*, abated me	5	2	10	00
Mar. 7	By bills receivable, for discount of a bill	9	4	00	00
July 2	By cash, for fix months interest of 1000*l.* lent } Charles *Thompson*	17	25	00	00
Aug. 17	By *Thomas James* his accompt proper, for interest	14	1	03	6¼
	By *John Wilson's* ditto, for ditto	15	1	06	10¾
Dec. 12	By *Thomas James* his accompt proper, for interest } in my favour	14	3	17	07¾
	By *Scots* lawns	2	15	00	00
	By filk hose	3	3	00	00
	By printed cottons	3	5	00	00
	By rum	3	6	00	00
	By brandy	4	3	15	00
	By printed linens	4	3	03	00
	By shoes	5	10	00	00
	By jeans	5	3	12	04
	By voyage to *Jamaica*	6	82	18	04
	By voyage from *Berwick* to *Dunkirk*	6	365	00	02
	By voyage to *Dublin*	7	25	07	06
	By fustians	9	1	15	00
	By *Thomas Hervey* my accompt of goods	9	53	06	09
	By brandy, *per the Eagle*, from *Dunkirk*	9	50	00	00
	By port wine, from ditto	9	25	08	03¼
	By commission accompt	10	160	15	00¼
	By ship *Tyger* and company	11	31	14	9½
	By *James Johnston*, at *Virginia*, my acc. of goods	12	40	00	00
	By *Irish* linens, *per the Dolphin*	13	12	08	09
	By voyage to *Jamaica* in company	14	56	17	03¼
	By tobacco	16	92	12	04
	By indigo	16	40	19	00
	By voyage to *Hamburg*	17	55	00	00¼
	By *Henry Primrose* my accompt in company	18	3	08	00
	By *Robert Ferguson*, at *Hamburg*, my accompt } current	19	3	05	10¾
	By hops, in company with *John Ward*	19	20	00	00
	By rum, in company with *John Ward*	20	20	00	00
			1228	05	05¾

Year &c Month.	Contra, *Cr.*		L	s.	d.
1777.					
July 26	By cash, in full	17	16	10	00

VOL. II.   C c

Year & Month.		Fo	l.	s.	d.

Fuſtians,   *Dr.*

pieces.

1777.

Feb. 24	To ſuſpence acc. returned by *James Gibſon* of *Stilton*, at 2l. 2s. per piece —— 5	4	10	10	00
	To proſit and loſs, gained ——	8	1	15	00
	5		12	05	00

Bills Receivable,   *Dr.*

1777.

Mar. 7	To ſundries, as per Journal ——		1000	00	00
May 8	To *James Bell*, for his draft on *Thomas Bailey*, due in 15 days, for ——	6	82	01	00
Oct. 20	To *Henry Primroſe* my accompt in company, for one on *James Snow* ——	18	100	00	00
31	To *Robert Ferguſon* my acc. current, for one on *Peter Young* —	19	160	00	00
	for one on *William Harriſon*		111	19	10¼
			1454	00	10¼

Thomas Hervey, at Dublin, my accompt of goods,   *Dr.*

1777.

Apr. 24	To voyage to *Dublin*, for 25 pockets of hops, remaining unſold ——	7	82	07	00
	To profit and loſs ——	8	53	06	09
			135	13	09

Brandy, per the Eagle, from Dunkirk,   *Dr.*

1777.

caſks.   gall.

Apr. 16	To voy. from *Berwick* to *Dunkirk*, for	30	1800	6	540	00	00
17	To caſh, for freight, duty, & other char.			2	60	16	00
	To profit and loſs, gained			8	50	00	00
		30	1800		650	16	00

Port Wine, per the Eagle, from Dunkirk,   *Dr.*

1777.

pipes

Apr. 16	To voyage from *Berwick* to *Dunkirk*, for	12	6	324	10	06
17	To caſh, paid freight, duty, and other charges		2	50	13	00
	To profit and loſs ——		8	25	08	03¼
		12		400	11	09¼

Year & Month.		Fo	l.	s.	d.
	Contra, **Cr.** pieces.				
1777. June 17	By voyage to *Jamaica* in company, at 2 *l.* 5 *s.* per piece, for ——— } 5	14	12	05	00
			12	05	00
	Contra, **Cr**				
1777. Apr. 6	By cash, received for *Corrie's* on *Hamilton* —	2	1000	00	00
May 23	By ditto, received for *Bell's* on *Bailey* —	2	82	01	00
	l. *s.* *d.*				
	{ for one on *James Snow* 100 0 0 }				
	By ball. { for one on *Peter Young* 160 0 0 } 20				
	{ for one on *Wm. Harrison* 111 19 10¾ }				
			371	19	10¾
			1454	00	10¾
	Contra, **Cr.**				
1777. June 7	By voyage from *Dublin*, for returns per the *Dolphin*	13	135	13	09
			135	13	09
	Contra, **Cr.** casks. Galls.				
1777. Nov. 30	By cash, in full for ——— 15 900	17	350	08	00
	By ballance unsold ——— 15 900	20	300	08	00
	30 1800		650	16	00
	Contra, **Cr.** pipes				
1777. Nov. 30	By cash, at 35 *l.* 10 *s.* per pipe, for — 6	17	213	00	00
	By ballance, at 31 *l.* 5 *s.* 3¼ *d.* per pipe, for 6	20	187	11	09¾
	C c 2 12		400	11	09¾

Year & Month.		Fo	l.	s.	d.
	James Arnold, at Dunkirk, } **Dr.** *my accompt current,* }				
1777.					
Apr. 16	To voyage from *Berwick* to *Dunkirk*, for ballance } in his hands	6	785	19	08
	Thomas Hervey, at Dublin, } **Dr** *my accompt current,* }				
1777.					
Apr. 24	To voyage to *Dublin*, for 25 pockets of my hops, } sold for ready money	7	137	10	00
			137	10	00
	John Todd of Greenwich, **Dr.**				
1777.					
Apr. 28	To *James Green's* accompt of goods, for 200 qrs. } barley, at 19s. per qr. due in 6 weeks	7	190	00	00
	Commiſſion accompt, **Dr**				
	To profit and loſs	8	160	15	00¼
			160	15	00¼
	James Green of Berwick, } **Dr.** *his accompt current,* }				
1777.					
June 12	To bills payable, for his draft on me to *Thomas* } *Stirling*, or order, for	7	36	17	06
July 28	To ditto for his draft on me to *John Stanton*, at } 3 weeks	7	353	12	06
			390	10	00

Year & Month.		Fo	l.	s.	d.
	Contra, *Cr.*				
1777.					
July 26	By cash, for my bill on him to *James Fordyce*, or order, at 2 months — }	17	785	19	08
	Contra, *Cr.*				
1777.					
June 7	By voyage from *Dublin*, for returns *per* the *Dolphin*	13	102	05	00
	By sundries, as *per* Journal, for commission and charges of the cargo, out and home — }		35	05	00
			137	10	00
	Contra, *Cr.*				
1777.					
June 20	By cash, in full —— —	2	190	00	00
1777.	*Contra,* *Cr.*				
Apr. 28	By *James Green*'s accompt of goods *per* the *Polly*, at 2 ¼ *per cent.* — }	7	6	15	00
June 2	By ditto *per* the *Nancy*, at 5 *per cent.* —	7	9	10	00
July 16	By *William Hogg* his accompt of goods, at 2 ½ *per cent.* }	12	4	03	04½
Aug. 25	By *Thomas Bell*'s accompt current, at *Genoa*, at 2 ½ *per cent* }	17	11	18	09
Sep. 28	By *Harman Van Sanders* his accompt of goods, at 2 ¼ *per cent.* }	18	26	04	00¼
Oct. 8	By ditto his accompt current, for my commission on goods sent him *per* the *Wasp* }	19	4	18	11
Dec. 10	By ship *Tyger* and company, on 1108 *l.* 16*s.* at 2 ½ *per cent.* }	11	27	14	04½
12	By voyage to *Jamaica* in company, no 2781*l.* 2*s.* 6*d.* at 2 ½ ditto }	6	69	10	06¾
			160	15	00¼
1777.	*Contra,* *Cr*				
Apr. 28	By *James Green*'s accompt of goods, ballance in in my hands — }	7	36	17	06
June 2	By ditto, for neat proceeds of the *Nancy*'s cargo	7	163	12	06
20	By ditto his accompt on time, received of *John Todd* for his barley — }	12	190	00	00
			390	10	00

Year & Month.	Ship *Tyger* in company with *John Ward*, Dr.	Fo	l.	s.	d.
1777.					
May 2	To sundries, as *per* Journal, for first cost —		800	00	00
28	To *John Ward's* accompt proper, paid carpenter, sail-maker, &c.	13	120	00	00
June 8	To *William Hogg's* accompt of goods, taken for the use of the ship *Tyger*	12	25	00	00
17	To cash, paid for bread, beef, beer, &c. —	2	28	16	00
27	To ditto, paid for insuring 500 *l.* on her out and home	2	45	00	00
Dec. 10	To cash, paid seamen's wages, for 6 months —	17	90	00	00
	To commission accompt, at 2½ *per cent.* on the whole	10	27	14	04¾
	To *John Ward's* accompt in company, for his half gained	12	31	14	9¹⁹⁄₁₆
	To profit and loss, for my half gained —	8	31	14	9¹⁹⁄₁₆
			1200	00	00

Year & Month.	Contra,	Cr.	Fo	L	s.	d.
Nov. 16	By *George Gair*, for freight from *Jamaica*	—	7	140	00	00
Dec. 10	By voy. to *Jamaica*, in co. for freight, our cargo out		14	140	00	00
	By *J. Ward's* accompt in co. for ¼ remaining unfold		12	460	00	00
	By ballance, for my ½	—	20	460	00	00
				1200	00	00

Note. As this is the only company accompt in the Ledger, where the goods or article remains ſtill diſpoſed of at the time of ballancing my books; and as I am concerned in two other articles, in company with the ſame perſon, viz. *John Ward*, I have ballanced this accompt, and conſequently, my partner's accompt in company, according to Mr. *Mair's* method, in order the more clearly to ſhew the impropriety of it in this and ſimilar circumſtances. Whenever it happens indeed, that the partnerſhip is diſſolved, (whether before or at the time you generally ballance your books) and there ſhould at that period remain a part or all of the goods or article unfold; and thoſe goods, or that article, is capable of being divided, and your partner receives his ſhare of it into his own poſſeſſion, then the above method is right, but cannot, in the preſent or ſuch likecaſes, for the following reaſons.

1ſt. By this method, your partner's accompt in company ſtands finally cloſed, and conſequently, will not appear in your new books to ſhew he has any property in your hands. And

2dly. Incloſing this accompt, by giving it credit by ballance for your own half only, the accompt of ſhip *Tyger* in company will ſtand in your new books, Debtor to ſtock for your own half only, which ought to have ſtood Debtor for the whole; and your partner's accompt in company, ſhould have ſtood credited for one half, which accompt (as I obſerved before) will not appear at all in your new books.

The beſt method therefore, to cloſe this accompt, and your partner's accompt in company, and all others of the ſame kind, viz. where all, or part of the goods remains unfold at the time you ballance your books, is by a double ballance, for inſtance, in ſhip *Tyger* in company.

Omit the laſt two lines in both debt and credit ſide, and caſt them both up upon a piece of paper; then on the debt ſide, write, *To Ballance*, and inſert the ſum of the credit ſide in the columns of the debt ſide; and on the credit ſide, ſay, *To Ballance*, and inſert in the columns, the ſum of the debt ſide, by this means, the accompt will ſtand evened, and the ſame accompt will ſtand opened in your new books, and exhibit the ſame on both debt and credit ſide as it did in your old one, and then proceed in the ſame manner with your partner's accompt in company, which will then likewiſe appear in your new books the ſame as it ſtood in your old one.

Year & Month.		Fo	l.	s.	d.
	John Ward's accompt in company, Dr.				
1777.					
Nov. 3	To ditto, his accompt proper, for half of 100 cwt. of hops, at 3l. 8s. per cwt.	13	170	00	00
10	To ditto, his accompt on time, for half sale of 9 puncheons of rum	20	170	00	00
Dec. 5	To ditto, his accompt proper, for half freight of ship *Tyger* home	13	70	00	00
10	To ditto, for his half freight out to *Jamaica*	13	70	00	00
	To ship *Tyger* in company, for his half remaining unfold	11	460	00	00
			940	00	00
	William Hogg of Berwick, his accompt of goods, per the Nancy, Dr.				
1777.					
May 15	To cash, for freight, waterage, porterage, &c.	2	6	03	06
July 15	To ditto, for ware-house room, and other charges	17	2	05	06
16	To commission accompt, at 2½ per cent.	10	4	03	04¼
	To *Wm. Hogg's* accompt current, for neat proceeds	17	145	13	07½
			158	06	00
	James Green of Berwick, his accompt on time, Dr.				
1777.					
June 20	To ditto, his accompt current, received of *John Todd*, for his barley	10	190	00	00
	James Johnston at Virginia, my accompt of goods, Dr.				
1777.					
May 20	To voyage to *Virginia*, for value of my goods configned him	6	138	04	04
	To profit and loss, gained	8	40	00	00
			178	04	04

Year & Month.		Fo	l.	s.	d.
1777.	Contra, Cr				
May 2	By ship *Tyger* in company, for half share of cost	11	400	00	00
28	By *John Ward's* accompt proper, for his half of repairing the ship *Tyger*	13	60	00	00
June 8	By ditto, for his one half of 5 casks of pork, and 3 firkins of butter, for the use of ship *Tyger*	13	12	10	00
17	By ditto, for ditto of bread, beef, beer, &c. for the use of ship *Tyger*	13	14	08	00
27	By ditto, for half of insurance on ship *Tyger*	13	22	10	00
Oct. 25	By ditto his ac. on time, for ¼ of 100 cwt. of hops	20	150	00	00
Nov. 7	By ditto, his accompt proper, for his half of 9 puncheons of rum	13	150	00	00
Dec. 10	By ditto, for his half of seamens wages, for 6 months, *per* the *Tyger*	13	45	00	00
	By ditto, for his half commission on accompt of ship	13	13	17	02¼
	By ship *Tyger*, for his half profit	11	31	11	9¾
	By hops, in company, for his half profit	19	20	00	00
	By rum, in company, for his half profit	20	20	00	00
			940	00	00
1777.	Contra, Cr.				
June 8	By ship *Tyger*, in company, taken for the use of said ship, 5 casks of pork, and 3 firkins of butter	11	25	00	00
July 15	By cash, received for 15 barrels of pork, and 15 firkins of butter	17	133	06	00
			158	06	00
1777.	Contra, Cr				
Apr. 28	By *James Green's* accompt of goods, due from *John Todd*	7	190	00	00¼
1777.	Contra, Cr				
July 5	By tobacco, for 47 hogsheads, *per* the *Happy-Return*	16	178	04	04
			178	04	04

VOL. II.   Dd

Year & Month		Fo	l.	s.	d.
	John Ward's accompt proper, Dr.				
1777					
May 28	To ditto his accompt in company, for his half of repairing the ship Tyger	12	60	00	00
June 8	To ditto for half of 5 casks of pork, and 3 firkins of butter, for the use of ship Tyger	12	12	10	00
17	To ditto for half of bread, beef, beer, &c. for the use of ship Tyger	12	14	08	00
27	To ditto for half of insurance on ship Tyger	12	22	10	00
Aug. 19	To cash, for the ballance of this accompt	17	10	17	11¼
Nov. 5	To cash, paid him his half share of sales of hops	17	170	00	00
7	To ditto his accompt in company, for his half of 9 puncheons of rum	12	150	00	00
Dec. 10	To ditto for his half of 6 months wages, paid the seamen of the ship Tyger	12	45	00	00
	To ditto for his half commission on the ship Tyger's accompt	12	13	17	02¼
12	To cash, paid him the ballance	17	81	02	09¾
			580	05	11¼

	Voyage from Dublin, Dr.				
1777.					
June 7	To sundries, as per Journal, for returns from Thomas Hervey		237	18	09
	To Thomas Hervey my accompt current, for commission and charges	10	13	10	00
			251	08	09

	Irish linens per the Dolphin, Dr.	pieces	yards		l.	s.	d.
1777.							
June 12	To sundries, as per Journal, at 1s. 6d. per yd. and charges for	60	1809 7/16		256	11	03
	And at 3s. per yd. and ditto for	27	680¾				
	To profit and loss, gained			8	12	08	09
		87	2489 5/8		269	00	00

Year &		Fo	l.	s.	d.
Month. **Contra,** Cr.					

1777.

		Fo	l.	s.	d.
May 28	By ship *Tyger* in company, paid carpenter, sail-maker, &c.	11	120	00	00
Aug. 19	By profit and lofs, for the ballance of interest in his favour	8		05	11¼
Nov. 3	By *John Ward's* accompt in company, for his half fales of 100 cwt. of hops	12	170	00	00
12	By cash, received in full, for his half coft of 9 puncheons of rum	17	150	00	00
Dec. 5	By *John Ward's* accompt in company, for half freight of the *Tyger* home	12	70	00	00
10	By ditto for half freight out to *Jamaica*	12	7	00	00
			580	05	11¼

Contra, Cr.

1777.

		Fo	l.	s.	d.
June 12	By *Irish linens*, received as *per* Invoice	13	251	08	09
			251	08	09

Contra, Cr.

1777.

		pieces	yards	Fo	l.	s.	d.
June 17	By Voyage to *Jamaica* in company, for	8	2489⅜	14	269	00	00
					269	00	00
		87	2489⅜				

Dd 2

Year & Month.		Fo	l.	s.	d.
1777.	*Voyage to Jamaica, in company with Thomas James and John Willison.* Dr				
June 17	To sundries, as *per* Journal, — —		2641	02	06
Dec. 10	To ship *Tyger* in co. for freight of our goods to *Jamaica* — — —	11	140	00	00
12	To commission accompt, at 2½ *per cent.* on 2781 *l.* 2 *s.* 6 *d.* — —	10	69	10	06¾
	To *Thomas James*'s accompt in co. for his ⅓ profit	14	56	17	03¾
	To *John Wilson*'s ditto, for his ⅓ ditto —	15	56	17	03¾
	To profit and loss, for my ⅓ gained — —	8	56	17	03¾
			3021	05	00
1777.	*James Murray, Knaves-Acre,* Dr.				
Sep. 19	To sundries, as *per* Journal — —		1260	00	00
1777.	*Thomas James's accompt proper,* Dr.				
June 17	To ditto his accompt in company, for —	14	460	07	06
Aug. 17	To profit and loss, for 1 month's interest of 280*l* 7*s* 8*d*	8	1	03	06¼
Sep. 19	To ditto his accompt on time — —	15	420	00	00
Dec. 10	To *Thomas James* his accompt in company, for his ⅓ of freight to *Jamaica* — —	14	46	13	04
12	To *Thomas James* his accompt in company, for his ⅓ commission on voyage to *Jamaica*	14	23	03	06¼
	To profit and loss, for bal. of interest in my favour	8	3	17	07¼
	To cash, in full — — —	17	512	18	10½
			1468	04	04¼
1777.	*Thomas James his accompt in company,* Dr.				
June 24	To ditto his accompt proper, for ⅓ of the draw-back on 400 pair of shoes —	14		08	04
Dec. 5	To ditto for his ⅓ of 3020 *l.* advanced *George Gair* by *William Boyd* — —	14	1006	13	04
			1007	01	08

Year & Month.		Fo	l.	s.	d.
	Contra, *Cr.*				
1777.					
June 24	By cash, for the drawback on 400 pair of shoes exported thither	2	1	05	00
Nov. 16	By *George Gair*, for the amount of the cargo advanced him by *William Boyd*	7	3020	00	00
			3021	05	00

	Contra, *Cr*				
1777.					
June 17	By voyage to *Jamaica* in company, for 300 butts of porter, due in 3 months	14	1260	00	00

	Contra, *Cr*				
1777.					
June 17	By voyage to *Jamaica* in company, for 300 butts of porter	14	180	00	00
24	By his accompt in company, for ⅓ of the drawback on 400 pair of shoes	14		08	04
Aug. 17	By cash, for the ballance of this accompt	17	281	02	08½
Dec. 5	By *Thomas James*'s accompt in company, for ⅓ of 3020 *l.* advanced by *William Boyd*	14	1006		04
			1468	0	04½

	Contra, *C.*				
1777.					
June 1	By sundries, as per Journal, for his ⅓ share of an adventure to *Jamaica*		88c		06
Dec. 10	By *Thomas James*'s accompt proper, for his ⅓ freight to *Jamaica*	14	4	3	04
12	By ditto his accompt proper, for his ⅓ commission on voyage to *Jamaica*	14	23	03	05½
	By voyage to *Jamaica* in company, for his ⅓ gained	14	56	17	03½
			1007	01	08

Year & Month.		Fo	l.	s.	d.
	John Willson's accompt proper, Dr.				
1777.					
June 17	To ditto his accompt in company, for —	15	460	07	06
Aug. 17	To profit and loss, for 1 month's interest of 320*l.* 7*s.* 8*d.* — —	8	1	06	10½
Dec. 10	To *John Willson's* accompt in company, for his ½ of freight to *Jamaica* —	15	46	13	04
12	To ditto ditto for his ½ commission on voyage to *Jamaica* — — —	15	2½	03	06
	To cash, in full — — —	17	937	15	03½
			1469	06	08½
1777.	*John Willson's accompt in company* Dr.				
June 24	To ditto his accompt proper, for his ½ of the drawback on 400 pair of shoes —	15		08	04
Dec. 5	To ditto for his ½ of 3020*l.* advanced by *William Boyd* to *George Gair* — — —	15	1006	13	04
			1007	01	08
1777.	*Thomas James's accompt on time,* Dr				
June 17	To ditto his accompt in company, due in 3 months	14	420	00	00
1777.	*John Willson's accompt on time,* Dr				
June 17	To ditto his accompt in company, due in 3 months	15	420	00	00
1777.	*Voyage from Jamaica,* Dr.				
June 18	To voyage to *Jamaica,* for returns and charges —	6	195	07	05
1777.	*William Boyd, at Jamaica,* } *my accompt current,* } Dr.				
June 18	To voyage to *Jamaica,* for ballance in his hands	6	108	19	07
1777.	*Charges on merchandize,* Dr.				
July 1	To cash, paid clerks wages, &c. since the 1st of *Jan.*	2	95	00	00
Dec. 28	To cash, paid ditto since the 1st of *July* —	17	104	16	00
			199	16	00

Year & Month.		Fo	l.	s.	d.
1777.	*Contra*, *Cr*				
June 17	By voyage to *Jamaica* in company, for 100 casks of shelled barley — —	14	140	00	00
24	By his accompt in company, for ⅓ of the draw-back on 400 pair of shoes —	15		08	04
Aug. 17	By cash, in full, for the ballance of this accompt	17	321	06	00¼
Dec. 5	By *John Williams* accompt in company, for his ⅓ of what *Boyd* advanced for *George Gair* —	15	1006	13	04
12	By profit and loss, for interest in his favour —	8	1	9	00
			1469	06	08¼

1777.	*Contra*, *Cr*.				
June 17	By sundries, as *per* Journal, for his ⅓ of an adventure to *Jamaica* — —		880	07	06
Dec. 10	By *John Williams's* accompt proper, for his ⅓ freight to *Jamaica* — —	15	46	13	04
12	By ditto for his ⅓ commission on voyage to *Jamaica*	15	2	03	06¼
	By voyage to *Jamaica* in company, for his ⅓ gained	14	56	17	04¼
			1007	01	08

1777.	*Contra*, *Cr*.				
Sep. 19	By ditto his accompt proper — —	14	420	00	00

1777.	*Contra*, *Cr*.				
Sep. 19	By *James Murray*, for his ⅓ of 300 butts of porter sent to *Jamaica* — —	14	420	00	00

1777	*Contra*, *Cr*				
July 9	By sundries, as *per* Journal — —		195	07	08

1777.	*Contra*, *Cr*				
Dec. 16	By cash, for my bill on him to *James Scott*, or order	17	108	19	07

	Contra, *Cr*				
	By profit and loss — — —	8	199	16	00
			199	16	00

Year & Month.		Fo	L.	s.	d.
	Houſehold expences, Dr.				
July 1	To caſh, paid houſe rent, ſervants wages, &c. ſince the 1ſt of January — —	17	105	00	00
Dec. 30	To ditto paid ditto ſince the 1ſt of July —	17	120	00	00
			225	00	00

	Tobacco, Dr	Hhds.	cwt.	qrs.	lb.	Fo	L.	s.	d.
1777.									
July 5	To James Johnſton, my accompt of goods, for —	47	175	3	22	12	178	04	04
6	To caſh, for freight, duty, and other charges paid here					17	466	11	11
	To bonded duties payable in 18 months —					16	82	02	02
	To profit and loſs gain'd					8	92	12	04
		47	175	3	22		819	10	09

	Bonded Duties, Dr.				
1777. Aug. 14	To tobacco for my bond withdrawn —	16	82	02	02

	Indigo, Dr	bar.	lb.	Fo	L.	s.	d.
1777.							
July 9	To voyage from Jamaica for —	6	756	15	86	12	06
	To caſh, for freight, duty, and other charges —			17	33	01	06
	To profit and loſs gain'd —			8	40	19	00
		6	756		160	13	00

	Pymento, Dr.	Hhds.	lb.	Fo	L.	s.	d.
1777.							
July 9	To voyage from Jamaica for	5	1535	15	42	17	06
	To caſh for freight, duty, & other charges			17	24	16	04¼
		5	1535		67	13	10½

	Sugar, Dr.	Hhds.	cwt.	Fo	L.	s.	d.
1777.							
July 9	To voyage from Jamaica for —	5	63	15	65	17	05
	To caſh, for freight, duty, and other charges			17	39	14	01¼
		5	63		105	11	06½

	John Dyer, Dr	Fo	L.	s.	d.
1777. July 10	To indigo in part for 6 barrels, quantity 756 lb. at 4 s. 3 d. per lb. — —	16	80	00	00

Year & Month		Fo	l.	s.	d.
	Contra,　　　　　　　*Cr.*				
	By profit and lofs　—　　—		225	00	00
			225	00	00

		Hhds.	cwt.	qrs.	lb.	Fo	l.	s.	d.
1777.	*Contra*,　　　　*Cr.*								
Aug. 11	By fundries, as *per* Journal, delivered *Henry Primrofe*, at 3½ d. per lb.　—	47	175	3	22	18	285	16	08
14	By fundries, as *per* Journal, for drawback　—						533	14	01
		47	175	3	22		819	10	09

		Fo	l.	s.	d.
1777.	*Contra*,　　　　　　　　　*Cr.*				
July 6	By tobacco for my bond, due in 18 months　—	16	82	02	02

		bar.	lb.	l.	s.	d.
1777.	*Contra*,　　　　　*Cr*					
July 10	By fundries, as *per* Journal　—	6	756	160	13	00
		6	756	160	13	00

		Hhds.	lb.	Fo	l.	s.	d.
1777.	*Contra*,　　　　*Cr*						
Aug. 30	By cafh, for　　———	5	1535	17	57	03	11
	By profit and lofs　　———				10	09	11½
		5	1535		67	13	10½

		Hhds.	cwt.	Fo	l.	s.	d.
1777.	*Contra*,　　　　*Cr.*						
July 22	By *John Kirkman*, at 28 s. 6 d. per cwt.	5	63	4	89	15	06
	By profit and lofs　　———				15	16	00¼
		5	63		105	11	06½

		Fo	l.	s.	d.
1777.	*Contra*,　　　　　　　*Cr.*				
Dec. 18	By cafh in full　　———	17	80	00	00

E e

Year:	Fo	l.	s.	d.

Month		Fo	l.	s.	d.
1777.	**Cash,** _Dr._				
	To the old accompt of cash —	2	7178	12	10
July 2	To sundries, as _per_ Journal — —		1025	00	00
10	To indigo, in part for 6 barrels —	16	80	13	00
15	To _Wm. Hegg_ his accompt of goods _per_ the _Nancy_	12	133	06	00
26	To _James Arnold_ my ac. current for my bill on him	10	785	19	08
26	To _James Gibson_ in full for 5 pieces fustians	8	10	10	00
Au. 14	To tobacco, for the drawback on 175 cwt. 2 qrs. 22 lb. delivered _Henry Primrose_, exported — }	16	451	11	11
17	To sundries, as _per_ Journal — —		602	08	08½
30	To pimento, for my 5 hogsheads —	16	57	03	11
22	To _Henry Primrose_ my accompt proper, for his ¼ of 47 hogsheads of tobacco — }	18	142	18	04
Sep.10	To _Thomas Bell_ (at _Genoa_) his accompt current, for drawback on leather — — }	17	36	00	00
23	To _Herman Van Sanders_ his accompt of goods, received for 36 cwt. of flax — }	19	117	00	00
Oct. 3	To _Thomas Bell_ (at _Genoa_) for my draft on him to _John Grayson_ for — }	18	208	06	08
12	To _Herman Van Sanders_ his accompt current	19	143	02	09½
20	To _Henry Primrose_ my accompt in company —	18	42	18	04
Nov. 3	To hops in company with _John Ward_ —	19	340	00	00
12	To _John Ward_ his accompt proper, received his ¼ cost of 9 puncheons of rum — }	13	150	00	00
25	To _Richard Crosby_ in part — —	18	450	00	00
27	To sundries, as _per_ Journal —		44	04	00
30	To ditto as _per_ ditto — —		563	08	00
Dec. 5	To _George Gair_ in full for what _Wm. Boyd_ advanced for him }	7	3020	00	00
	To ditto in full for freight of our ship _Tygar_ home	7	140	00	00
16	To _Wm. Boyd_ my ac. current, for my bill on him	15	108	19	07
18	To _John Dyer_ in full —	16	80	00	00
20	To _Thomas Bell_ (at _Genoa_) his accompt current, for my bill on him }	17	177	04	01
			16089	07	10¼

		Fo	l.	s.	d.
1777.	**_William Hogg of Berwick_, my accompt current,** } _Dr._				
Dec.20	To cash, paid his bill on me to _Geo. Simpson_	17	145	13	07½

		Fo	l.	s.	d.
1777.	**_Voyage to Hamburg_,** _Dr._				
Aug.5	To sundries, as _per_ Journal — —		213	14	00
	To profit and loss gain'd —	8	55	00	00½
			268	14	00¼

Year Month	Contra, Cr.	Fo	l.	s.	d.
1777. July 1	By houfhold expences, fince the 1ft of January	16	105	00	00
2	By bills payable, for James Green's on me to Thomas Stirling	7	36	17	06
6	By tobacco, paid freight, duty, and other charges, on 47 hogfheads from Virginia	16	466	11	11
9	By fundries, as per Journ 1		97	12	00
15	By W. Hogg's ac. of goods, for warehoufe room, &c.	12	2	05	06
Aug. 5	By voyage to Hamburg for cuftom and other charges	17	15	10	00
19	By John Ward his ac. proper, for ball. of faid acc.	13	10	17	11¼
25	By T. Bell his ac. current, (at Genoa) for leather, &c.	17	241	12	00
Sep. 17	By Herman Van Sanders's ac. of goods, for charges	18	28	10	00
10	By James Murray of Knaves-Acre	14	840	00	00
28	By Herman Van Sanders's accompt of goods	18	2	12	06
Oct. 8	By ditto his accompt current, for goods fent him	19	196	12	04
Nov. 5	By John Ward his accompt proper, paid him his ¼ fhare of fales of hops	13	170	00	00
7	By rum in company with John Ward, for 9 puncheons	20	300	00	00
20	By Hugh Shaw in full	18	159	00	00
25	By John Duke in full	18	168	00	00
Dec 10	By fhip Tyger, paid the feamen 6 months wages	11	90	00	00
12	By John Ward's accompt proper, paid him the ballance in full	13	81	02	09¼
	By fundries, as per Journal		1450	14	04¼
20	By Wm. Hogg's accompt current, for his bill on me		145	13	07¼
28	By charges on merchandize, for clerks wages, &c.	15	104	16	00
30	By houfhold expences for rent, &c.	6	120	00	00
	By ballance remaining in my hands	20	11285	19	04¼
			16089	07	10¼

1777.	Contra, Cr.				
Jul 16	By his ac. of goods per the Nancy, for neat proceeds	12	145	13	07¼

1777.	Contra, Cr.				
Oct 15	By Robert Fergufon my accompt current, for neat proceeds	19	268	14	00¼
			268	14	00¼

Year & Month.		Fo	l.	s.	d.
	Hugh Shaw at Chester, Dr.				
1777 Nov. 20	To cash, received of him in full ——	17	159	00	00
1777. Aug. 11	*Henry Primrose my accompt in Co.* Dr. To tobacco, for my ½ of 175 cwt. 3 qrs. 22 lb. at 3¼ d. per lb. —— ——	16	142	18	04
Oct. 28	To silk hose, for my ⅓ of 6 doz. at 6 s. 6 d. per doz.	3	20	08	00
	To profit and loss gain'd ——	8	3	08	00
			166	14	04
1777. Aug. 25	*Thomas Bell (at Genoa) his ac- compt current,* } Dr. By sundries, as per Journal ——		421	10	09
			421	10	09
1777. Nov. 25	*John Duke, Newcastle upon Tyne,* Dr. To cash in full —— —— ——	17	168	00	00
1777. Sep. 17	*Herman Van Sanders (at Amster- dam) his accompt of goods,* } Dr. To cash, for freight, custom, and other charges —	17	28	10	00
28	To ditto, for warehouse-room, and other charges	17	2	12	06
	To commission accompt, for ditto on 1048 l. 2 s. 6 d. at 2½ per cent. ——	10	26	04	00¾
	To Herman Van Sanders his accompt on time, due by Richard Crosby —— }	18	900	00	00
	To ditto his ac. current, for ballance in my hands	19	59	13	05¼
			1017	00	00
1777. Sep. 28	*Richard Crosby, Cannon Street,* Dr. To Herman Van Sanders his ac. of goods, for 30 butts of madder, to pay ½ in 2, and ½ in 6 months }	18	900	00	00
			900	00	00
1777. Nov. 25	*Herman Van Sanders's ac. on time,* Dr. To ditto his ac. current, received of Richard Crosby	19	450	00	00
	To ballance —— ——		450	00	00
			900	00	00

Year & Month.		Fo	l.	s.	d.
1777. Aug. 5	*Contra,* *Cr.* By voyage to *Hambnrg,* for 12 fother of lead, at 13 *l.* 5 . *per* fother, due in 3 months —	17	159	00	00
1777. Oct. 20	*Contra,* *Cr.* By fundries, for my ½ fhare of an adventure to *Amfterdam* — — —		142	18	04
Nov. 27	By cafh in full, for my ½ fhare of fales of 6 dozen of hofe	17	23	16	00
			166	14	04
1777. Sep. 10	*Contra,* *Cr.* By cafh, for the drawback on 8640 *lb.* of tanned leather fent him	17	36	00	00
Oct. 3	By ditto, for my draft on him to *John Grayfon* or order, for 1000 dollars, exchange at 50 *d.*	17	208	06	08
Dec. 20	By cafh, for my bill on him —	17	177	04	01
			421	10	09
1777. Aug. 25	*Contra,* *Cr.* By *Thomas Bell* (at *Genoa*) his accompt current, for 12 tons of lead, due in 3 months —	17	168	00	00
1777. Sep. 23	*Contra,* *Cr.* By cafh, rec. for his 36 *cwt.* flax, at 3*l.* 5*s. per cwt.*	17	117	00	00
28	By *Richard Crofby,* for 30 butts of madder, at 2*l.* 10*s. per* butt, due ½ in 2, and ½ in 6 months	18	900	00	00
			1017	00	00
1777. Nov. 25	*Contra,* *Cr.* By cafh in part — —	17	450	00	00
	By ballance, due the 28th of *March* next —	20	450	00	00
			900	00	00
1777. Sep. 28	*Contra,* *Cr.* By ditto his accompt of goods, due by *Richard Crofby,* ½ in 3, and ½ in 6 months —	18	900	00	00
			900	00	00

Year & Month.		Fo	l.	s.	d.
	Herman Van Sanders (at Amster-dam) his accompt current, Dr.				
1777.					
Oct. 8	To sundries, as per Journal, sent him per the Wasp	2	202	16	03
	To ballance due to him ———		450	00	00
			652	16	03
	Benjamin Green (Cooper) in Thames-Street, Dr				
	To ballance due to him —— —	20	1 0	.	00
1777.	Henry Primrose my accompt proper, Dr				
Aug. 11	To tobacco, for his ½ share of 175 cwt. 3 qrs. 2 lb. delivered to him at 3½ d. per lb. —	6	142	18	04
Oct. 28	To silk hose, for his ½ share of 6 dozen, at 6 l. 16 s. per dozen — —	3	20	08	00
			163	06	04
	Robert Ferguson (at Hamburg) my accompt current, Dr. Flemish.				
1777.					
Oct. 15	To voyage to Hamburg, per the Fly, at 34 s. 5 d. exchange — 462 7 10	17	268	14	00¼
	To profit and loss gain'd by exchange —	8	3	05	10¼
			271	19	10½
	Hops in Co. with John Ward, Dr. cwt.				
1777.					
Oct. 25	To John Selby, at 3 l. per cwt. for — 100	19	300	00	00
	To John Ward's accompt in co. for ½ profit	12	20	00	00
	To profit and loss for my ½ gain'd —	8	20	00	00
	100		340	00	00
1777.	John Selby, Dr.				
Oct. 25	To hops in co. with John Ward, due in 3 months	19	300	00	00
	To ballance due to him — —		300	00	00
			600	00	00

Year & Month		Fo	l.	s.	d.
1777. *Contra,*	*Cr.*				
S p. 28 By ditto his ac. of goods, for ballance in my hands		18	59	13	05¼
Oct. 12 by cash, for my bill on him to *Thomas Castlehow* or order, for		17	143	02	09½
Nov. 25 By *Herman Van Sanders's* accompt on time, received f *Richard Crosby*		18	450	00	00
			652	16	03
1777. *Contra,*	*Cr.*				
Oct. 8 By *Herman Van Sanders* his accompt current, for cooperage		19	1	05	00
1777. *Contra,*	*Cr.*				
Aug 22 By cash in full		17	142	18	04
Nov. 27 By cash, received for his ½ of 6 dozen of silk hose delivered him		17	20	08	00
			163	06	04
1777. *Contra,*	*Cr* *Flemish.*				
Oct. 31 By bills receivable in full, exchange at 34 s. 462 7 10		9	271	19	10½
			271	19	10½
1777. *Contra,*	*Cr.* *cwt.*				
Nov. 3 By cash, at 3 l. 8 s. per cwt.	100	17	340	00	00
	100		340	00	00
1777. *Contra,*	*Cr.*				
Oct. 25 By error on the credit side of this accompt		19	300	00	00
By hops in co. with *John Ward,* due in 3 months		19	300	00	00
			600	00	00

Year Month		Fo	l.	s.	d.
1777 Oc. 25	*John Ward's accompt on time,* Dr.				
	To ditto his accompt in company, for his ⅓ share of 100 cwt. of hops, due in 3 months —	12	150	00	00
	To ballance, due the 10th of *March* next —		170	00	00
			320	00	00
	Rum in Co. with John Ward, Dr	punc.			
1777 Nov. 7	To cafh, at 33 *L.* 6 *s.* 8 *d.* per puncheon, for	9 17	300	00	00
	To *John Ward's* accompt in co. for his ⅓ profit	12	20	00	00
	To profit and lofs for my ⅓ gain'd —	8	20	00	00
		9	340	00	00
	Ballance, Dr.				
	To *John Kirkman* of *Richmond,* due 22d *Jan.* —	4	90	00	10
	To *Samuel Rich* of *Norwich,* due *February* 3d	6	340	00	00
	To bills receivable, for one on *James Snow* —	9	100	00	00
	Ditto for one on *Peter Young* —	9	160	00	00
	Ditto for one on *William Harrifon* —	9	111	19	10½
	To brandy, for 15 cafks, quantity 900 gallons ,	9	300	08	00
	To port wine, for 6 pipes, at 31 *l.* 5 *s.* 3½ *d.* per pipe	9	187	11	09¾
	To fhip *Tyger* in co, for my ⅓ remaining unfold	11	460	00	00
	To cafh remaining in my hands —	17	1285	19	04½
	To *Richard Crofby,* due 28th *March* next —	18	450	00	00
	To *John Ward's* ac. on time, due 25th *January*	20	150	00	00
			13635	19	10½

Year Month		Fo	l.	s.	d.
1777. No.10	*Contra,* Cr.				
	By *John Ward's* ac. in co. for his ¼ fales of 9 puncheons rum, at 3 months — }	12	170	00	00
	By ballance, due the 25th of *Jan.* next		150	00	00
			320	00	00
	Contra, Cr.		punc.		
1777. No.10	By *Samuel Rich,* for —	9	6	340	00	00
		9		340	00	00
	Contra, Cr.				
	By bills payable, for *James Green's,* not yet prefented — — }	7	353	12	06
	By *Herman Van Sanders's* accompt on time	18	450	00	00
	By ditto his accompt current —	19	450	00	00
	By *Benjamin Green* — — —	19	1	05	00
	By *John Selby* — — —	19	300	00	00
	By *John Ward's* accompt on time, due 10th *March* —————— }	20	170	00	00
	By ftock for the neat of my eftate —	1	11911	02	04¼
			13635	19	10¼

P f

Remarks on Mr. MAIR, *with respect to his method of managing a partner's accompt proper.*

YOUR partner's accompt proper (as I have often observed before) is debited for what cash or goods you immediately advance for him, and for the payments you make him for what he had formerly advanced for you : It is credited for what cash or good· he immediately advances for you, and for the payment he makes you for what you formerly advanced for him.

The ballance therefore, in whosoever's favour it happens to be, is immediately due to or from the partner, and therefore chargeable with lawful interest from the time advanced to the time of payment. Now whether or not your partner's accompt proper will exhibit a true state of affairs, as they really stand between you, (according to Mr. *Mair's* method of making his second Journal entries, for it is those only which can affect your partner's accompt proper) will best appear by proper examples.

Those which I have made choice of to illustrate this matter, are selected from my transactions in company with *John Ward,* of the 25th of *October,* the 3d, 5th, 7th, 10th, and 12th of *November;* in Waste-Book, No. II. and which were purposely contrived to correspond with my remarks made in the rules for journalizing the several cases in company accompts.

Now, notwithstanding I only differ from Mr. *Mair* in making my second Journal entries of the 25th of *October* and 10th of *November,* yet it is necessary to post the whole for cases, so far as they relate to my partner's accompt proper, and accompt on time ; and although the said second Journal entries of the 25th of *October* and 10th of *November* are journalized and posted in the Journal and Ledger, No. II, according to the rules given for making such entries, yet as *John Ward's* accompt proper in the said Ledger contains other company transactions between us, I shall also post the whole afresh, independent of any other concerns ; so that by comparing the two Ledger accompts together, you will then clearly perceive the propriety of the one, and the impropriety of the other.

Here follow the two second Journal entries of the 25th of *October* and 10th of *November,* according to Mr. *Mair.*

———————————*October* 25th.————————————

	l.	s.	d.
John Ward's accompt proper Debtor to ditto his accompt in company, for ¼ of 300 l. worth of hops, to pay in 3 months	150	0	0

————————————*November* 10th.————————————

	l.	s.	d.
John Ward's accompt in company Debtor to ditto his accompt proper, for ¼ sales of 9 puncheons of rum, due in 3 months	170	0	0

N. B.

N. B. Although the small distance of time between the several transactions here exemplified, and the inconsiderable amount of each, makes it appear a matter of very little consequence, whether the second Journal entries of the 25th of *October* and 10th of *November*, are made according to Mr. *Mair*, or agreeable to the rules I have laid down; yet in large concerns, and where the distance of time is greater, it becomes a very principal object, whether we consider it in point of convenience, or the interest of the sums advanced one for another.

On the other side, you have first, *John Ward's* accompt proper, with the Ledger posts of the six fore-mentioned cases, with the second Journal entries of the 25th of *October* and 10th of *November*, according to Mr. *Mair*; and secondly, you have *John Ward's* accompt proper, and his accompt on time, according to the rules which I have laid down: On which two methods, note well the six observations following the said Ledger posts.

		l.	*s.*	*d.*

According to Mr. *Mair's* method.

John Ward his accompt proper, Dr.

		l.	*s.*	*d.*
1777.				
Oct. 25	To *John Ward's* accompt in company, for his ½ fhare of 100 *cwt.* of hops —	150	00	00
Nov. 5	To cafh, paid him the ballance of his accompt in full — —	170	00	00
7	To *John Ward's* accompt in company, for ½ of 9 puncheons of rum — —	150	00	00
	To ballance due to him — — —	20	00	00
		490	00	00

According to my method.

John Ward his accompt proper, Dr.

		l.	*s.*	*d.*
1777.				
Nov. 5	To cafh, paid him the ballance of his accompt in full — —	170	00	00
7	To *John Ward's* accompt in company, for his ½ purchafe of 9 puncheons of rum —	150	00	00
		320	00	00

According to my method.

John Ward his accompt on time, Dr.

		l.	*s.*	*d.*
1777.				
Oct. 25	To *John Ward's* accompt in company, for his ½ purchafe of 100 *cwt.* of hops, due in 3 months — — —	150	00	00
	To ballance, due to him in 3 months —	20	00	00
		170	00	00

		l.	*s.*	*d.*

Contra,   *Cr.*

1777.

Nov. 3 | By *John Ward's* accompt in co. for his ½ share of sales of 100 *cwt.* of hops — | 170 | 00 | 00

10 | By ditto his accompt in company, for his ½ sales of 9 puncheons of rum — | 170 | 00 | 00

12 | By cash, received of him for his ½ share of 9 puncheons of rum —— | 150 | 00 | 00

                | 490 | 00 | 00

Contra,   *Cr.*

1777.

Nov. 3 | By *John Ward's* accompt in company, for his ½ of sales of 100 *cwt.* of hops — | 170 | 00 | 00

12 | By cash, received in full for his ½ share of 9 puncheons of rum —— — | 150 | 00 | 00

  | 320 | 00 | 00

Contra,   *Cr.*

1777.

Nov. 10 | By *John Ward's* accompt in company, for his ½ share of sales of 9 puncheons of rum, due in three months —— — | 170 | 00 | 00

  | 170 | 00 | 00

OBSERVATIONS.

Observation first, on the Ledger post of October 25th.

Here you see, that notwithstanding I bought the hops of *John Selby* at three months credit, yet (according to Mr. *Mair*) I make *John Ward's* (my partner's) accompt proper immediately Debtor for his half share of the purchase, viz. 150 *l.* by which it appears he *(John Ward)* owes me the said sum. Whereas (according to my method) *John Ward's* accompt on time, instead of his accompt proper, is charged Debtor ; and consequently it appears that he owes me nothing, till such time as I pay *John Selby* for the hops, provided there is no other transaction happen before that period.

Now let us suppose that, instead of three months credit, I had bought the hops at six months credit, which is very common ; and that no other transaction, either in buying or selling, had happened in the intermediate space of time. Let us likewise suppose *John Ward's* share of the purchase, instead of 150 *l.* to be 1000 *l.* *John Ward*, at the end of three months, comes to settle his accompt with me : I directly turn to his accompt proper, which (as has been often observed) should exhibit nothing but what is immediately due to or from the partner. It would there (according to Mr. *Mair*) appear that *John Ward* owed me 1000 *l.* besides three months interest for the said sum, which is 12 *l.* 10 *s.* more ; whereas, in reallity, he does not owe me a single shilling till the expiration of six months, which time of credit I had myself of *John Selby* : So that I have not only received 12 *l.* 10 *s.* for noaing, but by being paid his share, viz. 1000 *l.* three months before it became due, I thereby may gain 12 *l.* 10 *s.* interest more ; which together with three months interest of the 12 *l.* 10 *s.* makes in all 25 *l.* 3 *s.* 1¼ *d.* one penny of which I was not entitled to.

Observation second, on the Ledger post of November 3d.

This is both journalized and posted exactly alike in both methods here exemplified : Let us now examine how the ballance stands in each. *John Ward's* accompt proper (according to Mr. *Mair*) you see now stands debited on the 25th of *October* for 150 *l.* and on the 3d of *November* it is credited for 170 *l.* the ballance therefore in favour of *John Ward* appears to be 20 *l.*

Let us next take a view of *Ward's* accompt proper, according to my method. Here it stands credited on the 3d of *Nov.* 170 *l.* without the least charge against him on the debt side ; so that, instead of oweing him 20 *l.*, I, in reallity, stand indebted to him 170 *l.*

Observation third, on the Ledger post of November 5th.

This is journalized and posted alike by both of us ; but the two accompts exhibit a very different state of the matter : For notwithstanding this case in the Waste-Book of Mr. *Mair* would stand exactly as

I

I have it in mine, (viz. Settled accompts with *John Ward*, and paid him the ballance in full, 170*l.*) yet it appears by his method of keeping a partner's accompt proper, that he now owes me 150*l.* whereas, according to my method, the accompt stands now even, as it ought to do. Hence it is evident, that Mr. *Mair*, in order to difcover the true ftate of affairs between himfelf and partner, muft have recourfe to the perfon's accompt on whom he bought, or to whom he fold, the goods on credit, before he can exactly afcertain the fum immediately due to or from his partner; fo that I cannot fee what purpofe his keeping a proper accompt anfwers in fuch cafes, except as a correfpondent debt or credit to his partner's company accompt; which end is as effectually, and more properly anfwered, by keeping an accompt on time for your partner, by which means nothing will appear but what ought to be there, and confequently always exhibit a true ftate of affairs between you.

Note. Your partner's accompt on time ought to be made the fame ufe of in foreign trade. For inftance: In receiving advice from your factor abroad of the fales of goods in company, whether fold for ready money or on credit, in your fecond Journal entry, your partner's accompt on time, inftead of his accompt proper, muft be credited; except when your factor remits you at the fame time that he advifes you of the fales: But when this is not the cafe, and your partner's accompt on time is credited, and your factor afterwards remits you in bills or cafh, you muft then charge your partner's accompt of time Debtor to his accompt proper, for his fhare of the fum remitted; becaufe you are then (and not before) accountable to him for fuch returns.

Obfervation fourth, on the Ledger poft of Nov. 7th.

This is alfo precifely the fame as my method, and pofted alike in both.

Obfervation fifth, on the Ledger poft of November 10th.

If we confider this poft, and the preceding one of *November* 7th, diftinctly by themfelves, without regard to any of the former ones, according to Mr. *Mair*, it will appear that I owe *John Ward* 20*l.* for by giving his accompt proper (inftead of his accompt on time) immediate credit for his fhare of the fales, viz 170*l.* and the faid accompt proper only ftanding debited for 150*l.* his fhare of the coft, the ballance, as before obferved, is 20*l.* in *Ward*'s favour; whereas, in reality, he ftands indebted to me 150*l.* For as the goods were bought for ready money, and I paid both his fhare and my own, confequently he owed me 150*l.* for which his accompt ftood debited the 7th of *November*: And as the goods were fold at three months credit on the 10th of *November*, and of courfe nothing due to *John Ward* till I receive payment, confequently there is nothing appears on the credit fide of his accompt on the 10th of *Nov.* to counterballance the debt fide, and therefore the whole 150*l.* ftill ftands again him.

Obfer

Obfervation fixth. on the Ledger poft of November 12th.
This poft is alfo the fame in both.

Remarks on the final Ballance.

The goods I was concern'd with in company with *John Ward* being now all difpofed of, we fhall fuppofe the partnerfhip diffolved, and we come now to fettle our accompt: Let us therefore fee how matters ftand betwixt us. It appears by *John Ward's* accompt proper, (according to Mr. *Mair's* method) that I owe him a ballance of 20 *l.* immediately payable. By *Ward's* accompt proper (according to my method) I neither owe him, nor he owes me any thing. But by his accompt on time, I owe him a ballance of 20 *l.* due in three months.

The only difference then between Mr. *Mair's* method and mine, perhaps you will fay, is, That he, having the ballance in *Ward's* accompt proper, makes the faid ballance immediately due; and I, by having it in his accompt on time, make it due three months hence. But even that (efpecially when the ballance happens to be a large fum) may make a material difference in point of convenience to the perfon who has it to pay; befides the lofs of intereft for three months of fuch ballance. But that inconvenience and lofs will appear trifling, when compared with others of greater magnitude, which we fhall find by a nice inveftigation of the matter.

I muft not, however, forget to tell you, that I have ballanced *John Ward's* accompt on time in the common way, in order that the ballance might correfpond with his accompt proper by Mr. *Mair's* method; for otherwife I would have clofed it by a double ballance, by which means it would have appear'd in the new books, exactly as it did in the old ones, before fuch ballance was made. Let us then confider it as yet open, viz. 150 *l.* only on the debt fide, and 170 *l.* on the credit, with this difference only, that inftead of the 170 *l.* on the credit fide being due in three months, that it fhould not be due till the end of nine months, and then let us fee what you would lofe by paying *John Ward* the 20 *l.* immediately, agreeable to Mr. *Mair's* method of fettling the accompt.

In the firft place you would lofe the intereft of the faid 20 *l.* for nine months, as it was, in reality, not due before that time; and in the next place, the 150 *l.* which he ftands charged with, and which became due the 25th of *January*, you would not then be paid till you received payment of *Samuel Rich* for the rum fold him, and which we fuppofe not due till the 10th of *Auguft*; fo that you would lofe the intereft of 150 *l.* for about one hundred and eighty-one days, which amounts to 3 *l.* 14 *s.* which together with the intereft of the 20 *l.* for 9 months, (viz. 15 *s.*) make in all a lofs of 4 *l.* 9 *s.* befides the inconvenience (which it probably may be) of lying out of the money.

Thus

Thus you fee, that when the fum is large, and the diftance of time great, between that of the debt and credit fides being due, it then becomes an object of no fmall importance, and, at leaft, fo great, as to deferve the attention of thofe who would wifh to keep their books accurately.

Of BANKING BUSINESS in GENERAL.

AS this is a fubject entirely new to the generallity of people, and but very imperfectly underftood by many, who, in other refpects, may be tollerably well acquainted with mercantile affairs, I cannot, I think, be too particular in treating of it, as well that they may be able to diftinguifh between private bankers and public banks, as to fhew how the nature and bufinefs of both differ according to the particular place or town where fuch are eftablifhed. In order, therefore, that I may be as diftinct and clear as poffible, I fhall treat of them under the following heads: And firft of the

LONDON BANKERS.

With the bankers in *London* (who ought not only to be men of large property, but fair characters) the merchants generally lodge their cafh, it not only being much fafer in their hands than in their own houfes or counting-houfes, but alfo faves them a great deal of trouble in many other refpects. They, therefore, once a week, or whenever they have a pretty large fum by them, tell it carefully over at a leifure hour, and carry it to their banker; you at the fame time carry a little book with you, which you have for that purpofe; in this the banker figures the fum which you paid into him, and which ferves you as a voucher.

When therefore a bill is prefented for payment, or any other demand made upon you, (except it be too inconfiderable a fum to trouble your banker with) you give the perfon a checquered draft, (which you have always ready by you, and only wants filling up) upon your banker; this not only faves you a great deal of time and trouble, but prevents many miftakes which muft inavoidably happen in telling out large fums of money, and at a time perhaps when you are hurried with other bufinefs, and every one prefling equally for difpatch. There is yet another advantage, befides thofe already mentioned, in making ufe of a banker, which is this, all bills which you may have remitted you, either from any part of *Great-Britain*, or from abroad, your banker takes the trouble to collect for you, provided they be payable in *London*. I had almoft forgot to tell you, that it is cuftomary to fettle your banker's book with him once a month, or oftener as you chufe it, and the ballance remaining in his hands you carry for 4

This alfo prevents many miftakes which might happen by fetling it lefs frequently, or at leaft they are eafier difcovered, and fooner rectified.

You will now naturally expect I fhould inform you what the merchant allows the banker for all this trouble and expence; and, when I have told you not one fingle farthing, this queftion will as naturally follow, viz. what intereft then has the banker in ferving him?

This feeming myftery will be eafily unravelled, when I make it appear that the banker muft always have a very confiderable fum belonging to the merchants in his hands, which he employs in difcounting bills, notes, &c. buying of ftocks, or even lending, for a fhort time, at an exorbitant intereft: For trade is carried on there to fuch an extent, that a merchant worth fifty thoufand pounds, may fometimes be fo ftrait laced as to be obliged to borrow a few hundreds, to fatisfy fome immediate and unexpected demands, which may be made upon him. Thofe cafualties, with fome others, fuch as noblemen or gentlemen (who can give good fecurity) wanting a fum to difcharge a debt of honour, &c. affords him fufficient opportunities of employing that cafh t the utmoft advantage.

But perhaps you think I have not yet proved that circumftance clearly, on which depends all thofe advantages which I have been juft now enumerating, namely, that he muft have always a very confiderable fum of the merchants in his hands.

You will grant, I fuppofe, that it may fometimes happen fo; but then you fay again, How can he make ufe of that money freely, when he does not know how foon it may be called for?

I am therefore to make it appear that he muft always have a large fum by him. Let us then fuppofe a particular time, when he may have cafh by him to the amount of fixty or eighty thoufand pounds.

Now it would be very abfurd to fuppofe that all the merchants who kept their cafh with him fhould happen to bring it in on the fame day, or that each of them fhould chance to have the greateft quantity of ready money by him at that particular time, that he could poffibly be poffeffed of at any one time in the whole courfe of his trade; and it would be equally ridiculous to imagine that they fhould have all occafion to draw at the fame period for any part of it, much more for the whole. I think then we may very fairly prefume (upon an average) that what fums might be drawn for by fome, would be replaced by others; and confequently pretty nearly (I mean within a few thoufands) the fame money remain always in the banker's hands. When therefore I faid he might even lend money for a fhort time, I did not mean that the apprehenfion of its being called for unexpectedly fhould deter him from lending it for any confiderable time, or that it could even fubject him to the leaft inconvenience; but that the fhorter the time, the greater advantage to himfelf: For although the law ftrictly forbids any perfon to take above five *per cent.* for the loan of any fum of money for a year, or compound intereft for any number of years, yet he may take at the rate of five *per cent.* for any part of a year, and consequently, by lending cash, or discounting bills, or notes, at a short date, (suppose a month) he thereby, instead of receiving simple interest at five *per cent.* for a year, receives compound interest, as he might lend or employ the same sum twelve different times in the course of the year; and the last month's interest, still being added to the preceding one, together with the original sum, continually increases the principal for the succeeding month.

But when I mentioned five *per cent.* (for bills) being the common terms, I would be understood to mean those only as are deem'd good by the person who is to discount them; for their may be some circumstance attending the discounting of bills which might make it reasonable to take more: The law therefore does not determine any particular rate of interest in such cases, but leaves the person to take more or less, according as they can agree, and according to the risque he may apprehend he runs.

But as the least quibble or delay of payment would be attended with the most fatal consequences to a banker, it would be therefore highly imprudent in him to run himself too near. A few days observation will discover to him the general run that is made upon him, and then, by making a handsome allowance for extraordinary exigencies, the remainder he may safely employ in the manner afore-mentioned, or in any other way which he may find most to his advantage. Thus far for the *London* merchants and bankers mutual interests and connexions, I come next under the second head to shew the business and usefulness

Of COUNTRY BANKERS,
And how the nature of their business varies, according to their different situations.

By country bankers, I mean such as do not reside in the metropolis, but in most of the trading and manufactoring towns throughout the kingdom.

In manufactuturing towns, such as *Manchester, Leeds, Leicester, Coventry,* &c. the ballance of trade between them and *London* must be greatly in their favour, since the goods which each of them sends immediately there (independent of those which they send all over the kingdom, and which are commonly remitted to them in bills on *London*) must be considerably more in value than the goods which they are supplied with from thence; and consequently, *London* must owe them a large ballance in cash.

The principal business therefore of bankers in such places, is to supply the manufacturers with cash, either for their own drafts, or to discount other bills which they may have remitted them from their correspondents in different parts of the kingdom; but as the circumstances attending such transactions in the country differ greatly from those in *London*, so the terms on which they negotiate such business differ likewise.

G g 2

The

The common terms (as I obferved before) on which the *London* bankers difcount bills is at the rate of five pounds *per cent* for the bills being payable there, and generally accepted before they difcount them, they therefore know the precife time when they are to have a return of their money, and as they take care that the accepter is a good man, they run little or no rifque.

But with country bankers there can be no fixed rate of exchange, as not only one place varies greatly from another, but even the fame place at different times, according to particular circumftances. For, notwithftanding they will know the perfons well whofe drafts they take, and alfo know the precife time fuch bills have to run, yet the value they give for thofe bills being received by their agents in *London*, the cafh does not immediately return to them, but may be fooner or later according to the diftance they are from *London*, and the opportunities they may have of having it brought from thence by perfons whom they can depend on, being lefs or more frequent; as the nature of the connexions between the two places admits of no other way of having it returned.

For inftance, if the ballance of trade in favour of that particular place be very confiderable, then of courfe bills will be very plenty, and confequently the rate of exchange high: In fome places they give one half *per cent*. for a bill at thirty days, which is equal to fix *per cent*. *per annam*; and in others ⅜ *per cent*. which is equal to nine *per cent*. *per annum*; and fo more or lefs in proportion, as bills happen to be more or lefs plenty.

On the other hand: In all inland towns where there are no manufacturies carried on; it is evident that the goods they have from *London* muft be almoft an entire ballance againft them; and therefore, as the fhop-keepers, &c. want to remit to their merchants there, bills confequently will be very fcarce, efpecially if fuch place be any confiderable diftance from a manufacturing town.

The principal bufinefs therefore of a banker in fuch places, is to fupply the merchants with *London* bills for their cafh, for which he receives a premium, which ought to be in proportion to the demand there is for bills, and the means by which he can reimburfe his agent on whom he draws in *London*.

Here, as the banker runs no kind of rifque, (receiving always value in hand for his draft) it may not perhaps appear reafonable to you that he fhould receive the fmalleft premium for it: But you are to confider, that he cannot have cafh in his agents hands in *London* to anfwer all the drafts he may have occafion to give on him; he muft therefore allow him intereft for what cafh he advances for him, befides a fmall commiffion (of at leaft a quarter *per cent*.) for his trouble.

It is therefore his intereft to remit the cafh which he receives for his drafts with all convenient fpeed to his agent. The beft way of doing this is to have a correfpondent in fome manufacturing town, where it is moft convenient for him, to whom he can fend his cafh whenever

he

he finds it neceffary, and defire him to purchafe bills on *London* with it. By this means he gains a double advantage, viz. the premium which he received for his own draft, and the exchange upon what bills he buys.

But why, fay you, fhould the merchants, or fhop-keepers, give the banker a premium for bills, which they can purchafe themfelves by going to a manufacturing town, upon the fame terms that he can?

This queftion is eafily anfwered. For fuppofe fuch town to be but fifty or fixty miles diftant, it could not even then be worth any perfon's while who had but 50 or 100*l.* to remit, (much lefs 20 or 30*l.* which is more generally the cafe amongft fhop-keepers) to carry or fend fuch a fum fifty miles, for all he could both fave and get by it. Let us for inftance, even fuppofe the fum he wanted to remit to be 100*l.* and that the premium he muft give the banker at home, to be ½ *per cent.* and alfo what he would gain by going to fuch manufactoring town, ½ *per cent.* more; this makes a difference of one *per cent.* which is 20*s.* This I believe would fcarce defray the expence of his journey, befides neglecting his bufinefs, at leaft two days at home; much lefs would it be worth his while if the diftance was greater and the fum lefs.

But the cafe is different with a banker, for allowing he only fends 1000*l.* at a time, at ½ *per cent.* exchange, he would clear 5*l.* and fo in proportion for what he fent more.

From what has been faid in refpect to the ballance of trade being againft, or in favour of any particular place, and how fuch ballance neceffarily affects the rate of exchange; it naturally follows, that in all towns where the imports and exports are pretty near equal betwixt fuch towns and *London*, that bills will then be at par. That is, a bill at the common date of twenty or thirty days, will juft be worth fo much money in that place as it will anfwer in *London*. For the perfon who draws the bill (we fuppofe) is one who fends goods to *London* and wants to have his cafh from thence, and the perfon in whofe favour it is drawn, we may prefume is fome merchant or fhop-keeper who has goods from *London*, and wants to pay his credit there, confequently the obligation being mutual, there is no exchange on either fide.

Of PUBLIC BANKS.

In treating of public banks I fhall confine myfelf chiefly to thofe in *Scotland*, their bufinefs not only being the fame in common with thofe of *England*, but alfo admits of a much greater variety, and therefore beft anfwers my prefent purpofe.

Firft, I fhall fhew what a bank is.

Secondly, The particular bufinefs of it, and how their profits arife, with fome remarks on exchange.

Thirdly, How the feveral branches of it ought to be difpofed fo as to be any real advantage to the proprietors of it.

Fourthly

Fourthly, The fingular advantage which the trading part of the country derive from it.

Fifthly, How a perfon ought to keep his cafh accompt with the bank, or the bank with him, which is the fame thing. And

Sixthly, How a bank or any private merchant ought to keep their accompts with their agents in *London* or elfewhere; on, and to whom, they are occafionally drawing and making remittances; together with the method of cafting up the intereft, and finally ballancing the accompt. And firft

WHAT A BANK IS.

A bank is generally compofed of a great number of landed gentlemen, fubftantial merchants, and fometimes noblemen of large fortunes, which hold particular fhares, according to their abilities or inclinations, which like all other large companies go under a certain term or title. As for inftance, the firm of the late noted bank of *Ayre*, was *Douglas, Herring,* and *Co.* and that at *Newcaftle-upon-Tyne*, *Surtis* and *Burden;* and thofe gentlemen whofe names are particularly mentioned in the firm of any bank, are always underftood to be refponfable to the public for all its tranfactions; as it is on the credit of thofe people the public deem themfelves fecure in their dealings with it.

Of the BUSINESS of a BANK,

And how the profit arifes to the proprietors of it.

The principal profit of all banks arifes from two things; namely, the iffuing of their own notes, and the exchange on bills; in both which particulars the *Scots* banks have greatly the advantage over thofe in *England:* For firft, from the great fcarcity of real fpecie in that kingdom, they are able to fubftitute paper currency inftead of it with greater facility; and fecondly, the ballance of trade being fo confiderably againft them, the premium they take for *London* bills are very high; which laft advantage they avail themfelves of even to a degree of abufe; for I have heard that the bills of a late bank, at par, were fometimes drawn at fo long a date as fixty and feventy days.

As therefore the whole myftery of banking bufinefs depends upon a thorough knowledge of thofe two branches, I fhall point out, in as brief a manner as poffible, the true intereft of a bank refpecting thofe particulars, and alfo fhew how inconfiftent with thofe principals was the plan adapted by a late bank, ftill recent in every perfons memory.

Firft then, I fhall fhew how the profits arife from iffuing their own notes. To make this plain, let us fuppofe, that a particular bank lends, or otherwife circulates, their own notes, to the amount of five hundred thoufand pounds, which, befides the vaft number of notes circulat d by all the other banks in *Scotland,* is a very confiderable fum. Now it is generally allowed, that not more than one fifth of that fum in fpecie,

cie, would be neceffary to keep by them to take up thofe notes, which in the courfe of their circulation might be prefented for payment: Confequently, from a real capital only of one hundred thoufand pounds (for the five hundred thoufand in notes is merely an imaginary one) they are realizing an intereft of twenty five thoufand pounds *per annum*, which is twenty five pounds *per cent*.

But perhaps you will fay I have made to low an eftimate, as it is confidently afferted that a late S—*ts* B—k iffued their own notes to the amount of a million of money, which is twice the fum; and confequently, muft have cleared fifty thoufand pounds *per annum*.

But this is reafoning like a fchool boy, although it is pretty evident, that the managers of the b—k alluded· to had the fame conceptions, which proved the very rock on which they fplit.

In order to make this matter clear, let us fuppofe, for inftance, (it is not material whether too little or too much) the fum neceffary for the circulation of *Scotland* to be three millions: Let us fuppofe alfo, that of that three millions, there is only one million and a half in fpecie, the other million and half therefore only remains to be fupplied by paper currency. Now if we allow the feveral banks in *Scotland* (excepting one only) to fupply one million of this paper currency; then there remains but half a million, or five hundred thoufand pounds for the bank (before excepted) to compleat the three millions, which being the natural ·demand of the country, they would have circulated with the greateft facility; and in that cafe would (as I have before proved) at leaft cleared twenty five thoufand pounds *per annum*.

But, if inftead of five hundred thoufand pounds (which was only wanted) they fhould force five hundred thoufand more of their notes upon the public, the confequence is evident; for it being juft fo much more than is neceffary for the natural circulation of the country, they muft immediately return upon them; and therefore they muft have an additional fund in fpecie, equal to the whole of fuch unnatural circulation. So it is plain, that inftead of gaining twenty five thoufand pounds more intereft, they lofe twenty five thoufand upon this laft five hundred thoufand pounds, being the intereft which fuch fum would bring in, and which they are obliged to keep by them as· an additional dead ftock: So that it may be truly faid, that the late famous S—*ts* B—k (fuppofing the money to have been borrowed) were paying five *per cent*. for fix hundred thoufand pounds, and were only lending five hundred thoufand pounds of it again, at the fame rate of intereft, by which it is clear they muft lofe upon the whole five thoufand pounds. But you will perhaps afk me, how I make this lofs out, for as they gained twenty five thoufand pounds upon the firft five hundred thoufand, and loft the fame upon the fecond, they are then you will fay even hands. By no means; for you muft confider although they gain'd twenty five thoufand pounds upon the firft; yet the one hundred thoufand pounds in fpecie neceffary to have by them (being fuppofed borrowed,) they therefore had five thoufand pounds intereft to pay for it; and had it

been

been their own it is ftill the fame thing, as they could have made five thoufand of it by lending it out.

From what has been faid, I think it appears plain that one principal point in banking bufinefs, is to difcover the true criterion with refpect to the value in notes which they can circulate to advantage; and that I think (to any perfon of common underftanding) a few weeks obfervation would eafily point out.

I come now to treat of the other principal thing neceffary to be underftood in banking bufinefs, namely

*Of the EXCHANGE on BILLS.

This is another principal branch, in which the chief managers of a bank ought to be very converfant; but more efpecially fo in *Scotland*, as the advantage they have over the *Englifh* in this particular, ought to make it regarded by them as an object of the greateft importance.

I have before fhewn the caufes from which thofe advantages arife, namely, in refpect to the ballance of trade, and the diftance they are from manufacturing towns.

With refpect to the firft, it is greatly in favour of *England*; not only becaufe the goods they are fupplied with from thence are much more in value than thofe they fend thither, but alfo becaufe moft of their nobility and gentlemen of large fortunes refide there; and confequently have their annual incomes remitted them from *Scotland*. Thofe things, of courfe, make bills very fcarce; and the diftance they generally are from any manufacturing town, deprives them of any other means of procuring them, than by applying to a bank.

A bank fituated as above defcribed has no need of a capital for this branch of the bufinefs; for as the ballance of trade is greatly in favour of *London*, confequently the cafh they will receive for their drafts on it, muft be confiderably more than the cafh they will have to give for others bills, and therefore have only to eftablifh a credit with fome banker, or other perfon in *London*, who may act as an agent for them. Now as the bills which they will have occafion to draw upon their agent in *London*, will be more in value than thofe with which they can be furnifhed (in or near the place of their refidence) in order to reimburfe him, they ought therefore to confider of fome method by which fo material a point can be effected; for otherwife, inftead of gaining any thing by this branch, they will, as in the other, be confiderable lofers; for there will always be a heavy ballance againft them with their agent in *London*, for what he is in advance for them; which befides bearing intereft at five *per cent.* is fettled every three or fix months, and the intereft then due, added to the fum you are in arrear, is efteemed a new principal, which, together with one quarter *per cent.* for his trouble on the amount of what bills you draw upon him, muft in the courfe of a year greatly accumulate the intereft.

A bank fo fituated can therefore never give bills at par at any moderate date; nor do I fee any reafon why they fhould take bills fo, let the date be ever fo fhort, fince they may purchafe them on better terms, as I fhall make appear.

They fhould therefore have a premium for all bills they draw, which ought to be regulated according to the ballance of trade againft them, and the opportunities they have of reimburfing their agent in *London*, on whom they draw.

Suppofe then that the *S—ts* B—k alluded to, had fixed the premium at ⅛ *per cent.* for bills at thirty days, and had eftabifhed an agent, or office in fome manufacturing town in *England* to have counterballanced the ballance of trade againft them in *Scotland*; for inftance, *Manchefter*, (at which time I believe there was no bank there) where the manufacturers allow'd ⅛ *per cent.* for cafh for their bills, at three weeks date; here they gained ten days, and confequently by fending their cafh to *Manchefter* which they received for their drafts at home, and purchafing bills with it there, they not only kept their intereft accompt with their agent in *London* very low, but by this means gained one ⅛ *per cent.* for thirty days upon all the bills they drew, which is equal to fifteen pounds *per cent. per annum*.

Nor is this the whole advantage which they would have derived from fuch an intercourfe, for the vaft numbers of working people which the manufacturers pay weekly, would enabled them to have circulated a great quantity of their own fmall notes, a very few of which would return upon them, but paffed as current as cafh from one tradefman to another. I cannot pretend to give an exact eftimate what fuch circulation might amount to, but fuppofe it would be nearly equal to one half the returns of the whole town and neighbourhood for one month, which muft be a fum very confiderable.

I fhall now compare the method in which the late *S—ts* B—k conducted this branch of the bufinefs with that which I have laid down, and leave the public to judge which of the two is moft elligible.

Firft, Inftead of having an agent, or office, eftablifhed in fuch a town as *Manchefter* to counterballance their drafts they gave at home; the feveral towns in which they fixed them were all in *Scotland*, and each of them in the fame fituation with refpect to the ballance of trade; fo that they could anfwer no kind of purpofe, except it were to force the circulation of their notes, and to increafe the amount of their drafts, and thereby haften there own deftruction.

In the next place, they fixed the par of exchange at a certain date, and gave and took bills on the fame terms.

To any perfon of common underftanding, a few minutes confideration will difcover the impropriety of this meafure; for fuppofing even the ballance of trade to have been equal, then the bills remitted their agent juft paid of thofe which they drew upon him, and confequently, no intereft would be due on either fide, but the ⅛ *per cent.* which they allow their agent upon the whole amount of what they drew upon him, having nothing in their favour to counterballance it, would be a total lofs to them, and a very confiderable one too. But the ballance of trade was confiderably againft them, and therefore their plan ftill more ridiculous. Suppofe a merchant were to fell all the goods he bought at a quarter *per cent.* lofs, it would be eafy to foretel (without the gift of prophecy) that he muft foon impair his capital, and in the end become a bankrupt; but although this mode of proceeding would bring on inevitable ruin in the end, yet it thus muft haften to that period with a much greater rapidity. No doubt many people were aftonifhed what intereft they could have in giving one hundred pounds for a bill of the fame value, and felling it the next moment for the fame fum, (to fay nothing of the quarter *per cent.* to their agent, for tranfacting the bufinefs in *London.*) But rather than fuppofe any one individual (much lefs a body of men) fo exceedingly ftupid as uniformly to purfue a plan fo evidently tending to their own deftruction, they concluded there muft be fome myftery in banking which they could not comprehend.

But this was putting them only upon the fame footing with the above fuppofed merchant, viz. allowing the ballance of trade equal, whereas their fituation was much more defperate, for to what everamount the ballance was againft them, juft fo much were they paying their agent five *per cent.* for, over and above the quarter *per cent.* afore-mentioned. But you will perhaps fay, that thofe who had occafion to draw on *London,* being few in proportion to thofe wanted to remit, confequently, exacting a premium in either cafe, cannot be fupported on the fame principles of reafoning, without fuppofing this paradox, viz. that although cafh is plentier than bills, yet they are equally fcarce at the fame time. This, however ftrange it may feem, I fhall, notwithftanding, prove to be the cafe with refpect to the trading part of the people in the country where fuch bank is eftablifhed; for thofe who wanted to remit, would prefer the fecurity of a bank to that of a private tradefman or merchant, and confequently, thofe who wanted to draw, would be under the neceffity of giving the bank a fmall premium for cafh: But if they did not chufe this, it is a matter of no confequence to the bank, as they can (as I obferved before) purchafe bills on better terms.

Of the advantages which the trading part of the people derive from a bank properly conducted.

To prove this point, let us fuppofe a perfon, in order to increafe his trade, has occafion to borrow a thoufand pounds for a year or two. This would be found no eafy matter to be done, even on land, much lefs perfonal fecurity, efpecially in *Scotland,* where money is fcarce. But we fhall even leap over that difficulty, and fuppofe the loan can be procured.

In this cafe you are paying a certain intereft of five *per cent.* for the whole one thoufand pounds for the time agreed upon, whereas part of it often lyes by you unemployed.

For inftance, let us fuppofe a perfon to have only one thoufand
pounds

pounds capital, and he purchaſes a cargo to the amount of two thouſand pounds, one half of which he pays in ready money, and for the
other half has ſix months credit. In this caſe, the making good his
payment of one thouſand pounds at the end of ſix months, totally depends on the quickneſs of the ſale of his goods ; the uncertainty of
which, and the credit which he muſt give, would render his credit very
precarious, and of courſe a riſque which no prudent man would chuſe
to run: He therefore, on thoſe terms, ought not to have purchaſed to
above the amount of one thouſand five hundred pounds, by which
means, he would have had two hundred and fifty pounds remaining
in his hands, towards the payment of ſeven hundred and fifty pounds,
due in ſix months.

By this means he loſes the intereſt of two hundred and fifty pounds
for ſix months; ſo that he is paying intereſt for one thouſand pounds
for that time, and only employing ſeven hundred and fifty pounds of it.

But the manner in which you can be ſupplied with caſh from a bank
is this ; you open a caſh accompt with it for the ſum you want, (ſuppoſe a thouſand pounds) for which they only require another perſon's
joint bond with you. Now you are not obliged to take this thouſand
pounds all at once, but draw for it as you find you have occaſion ;
and conſequently, pays intereſt for no more than you realy employ ;
ſo that on the ſuppoſition before made, of a perſon buying a cargo to
the amount of one thouſand five hundred pounds, and paying ſeven
hundred and fifty pounds down, he thereby makes a reſerve of two
hundred and fifty pounds till he has occaſion for it, and conſequently
ſaves the intereſt of it for the ſaid time.

Not only that, but what caſh he receives in the courſe of his trade
need never lye dead by him, as he may pay it into the bank at twenty
or thirty pounds at a time, juſt as it happens to come in ; for which
he is allowed intereſt at five pounds *per cent.* according to the time,
ſtill drawing, or paying in, juſt as the nature of his trade requires.

The accompts to be opened betwixt a bank and you on this accompt,
are two, namely, one commonly called a progreſſive accompt, and the
other an accompt current.

The latter is managed in the ſame manner as any other accompt
current, viz. that kept by the bank, debited for all the caſh they advance you, and credited for all you pay in again; and ſo often as you
ſettle your progreſſive accompt with them, they alſo charge your accompt current debtor for the intereſt then due. It therefore only remains for me to explain the uſe

Of a P R O G R E S S I V E A C C O M P T.

This accompt is kept in a Ledger appropriated for that purpoſe, and
has no duplicate in your grand, or principal Ledger, which renders
an accompt current neceſſary to be kept, as a duplicate to the caſh accompt. I ſhall therefore ſuppoſe a few tranſactions between a bank
and

and a merchant, which I shall poft to this progreffive accompt, and will ferve as a fpecimen how it is to be kept.

As the cafes here are very fimple and eafy, I shall poft them immediately from the Wafte-Book, without making any Journal entry.

The method how a bank keeps a progreffive accompt.

	l.	*s.*	*d.*
————————*January* 1ft, 1777.————————			
This day opened a cafh accompt with *A B.* of *D——s*, on the faid *A. B.* and *C. D's* joint bond, for 1000 *l.* N. B. As *A. B.* has not yet acted upon this cafh accompt, there is confequently no entry made.			
————————————10th.————————————			
Paid *A. B's* draft on us, for — —	75	00	00
N. B. For this, and all the following tranfactions fee the progreffive accompt.			
————————————*February* 3d.————————————			
Received of *A. B.* on his cafh accompt — —	140	00	00
————————————17th.————————————			
Received of *A. B.* on his cafh accompt ——	50	00	00
————————————*March* 7th————————————			
Paid *A. B's* draft on us, for — —	20	00	00
————————————*April* 2d.————————————			
Received of *A. B.* on his cafh accompt ————	200	00	00
————————————30th.————————————			
Paid *A. B's* draft on us, for — — —	50	00	00
————————————*May* 15th.————————————			
Received of *A. B.* on his cafh accompt ——	100	00	00
————————————30th.————————————			
Received of *A. B.* on his cafh accompt — — —	80	00	00
————————————*June* 12th.————————————			
Paid *A. B's* draft on us, for — — —	150	00	00
————————————18th.————————————			
Received of *A. B.* on his cafh accompt ——	200	00	00
————————————25th.————————————			
Received of *A. B.* on his cafh accompt — — —	130	00	00
————————————*July* 10th.————————————			
Upon fettling accompts with *A. B.* there appears due for intereft — — —	11	09	6¼
which is added to the 200 *l.* the ballance of the progreffive accompt, and at the faid time his accompt current is charged debtor for the faid intereft.			

In order to render the following fpecimen of the progreffive accompt as little complex as poffible, I have fuppofed all the drafts of *A. B.* to be drawn upon the fpot where the bank was, and confequently, received the fame day, and likewife the money paid in in the fame manner,

manner. But had you been at any diftance from the place, and drawn upon the bank at any number of days after date, or remitted them in the fame manner, then the bank could not have made you debtor till they paid your bill, nor credited you till they received yours, except you remitted them a *London* bill, and then they ought to give you immediately credit for what fuch bill is worth.

1777.	*A. B's progreffive accompt.*	*L.*	*s.*	*d.*	Days Inte-reft.
Jan. 10 *Dr.* To cafh, paid his draft to *G. R.* at fight		750	00	00	24
Feb. 3 *Cr.* By ditto, received of him (fubtracted)		140	00	00	
		610	00	00	14
17 *Cr.* By ditto — — (fubtracted)		50	00	00	
		560	00	00	18
Mar. 7 *Dr.* To cafh, paid his draft on us (added)		20	00	00	
		580	00	00	26
April 2 *Cr.* By cafh, received of him (fubtracted)		200	00	00	
		380	00	00	28
30 *Dr.* To cafh, paid his draft on us (added)		50	00	00	
		430	00	00	15
May 15 *Cr.* By cafh, received of him (fubtracted)		100	00	00	
		330	00	00	15
30 *Cr.* By ditto, — — (fubtracted)		80	00	00	
		250	00	00	13
June 12 *Dr.* To cafh, paid his draft on us (added)		150	00	00	
		400	00	00	6
18 *Cr.* By cafh, received of him (fubtracted)		200	00	00	
		200	00	00	22
July 10 *Dr.* To intereft due to this day (added)		11	09	6¼	
Ballance due		211	00	6¼	

You fee by this fpecimen of the progreffive accompt, that the whole intereft of one thoufand pounds, for fix months, (in the manner it is there managed) does not amount quite to two one half *per cent.* whereas, had you borrowed one thoufand pounds of any private perfon, you would have paid, at five *per cent.* for fix months, twenty five pounds. I come now to fhew

How a bank, or any private merchant ought to keep their accompts with their agent in London, or elfewhere, on, and to whom they are cccafionally drawing and making remittances ; together with the method of cafting up the intereft, and finally to ballance the accompt.

The cafes relative to the tranfactions betwixt your agent and you, being equally fimple with thofe of the progreffive accompt, Journal entries of them in a fpecimen would be altogether unneceffary, I fhall therefore poft them to the feveral accompts immediately from the Wafte-Book. I muft likewife not forget to tell you, that I fhall fuppofe the bank, or merchant, to remit bills to their, or his agent, without accounting for the manner by which they obtain'd thofe bills, as the contrary would create a great number of Ledger accompts to be opened, not in the leaft effential to this part of the bufinefs.

The accompts neceffary to be kept with your agent on this account are three, Namely,

A. B. my accompt of bills drawn,

A. B. my accompt of bills remitted, and

A. B. my accompt current.

A. B. my accompt of bills drawn, is credited for all bills you draw upon your agent, and debited to *A. B.* my accompt current, as the faid bills become due.

A. B. my accompt of bills remitted, is debited for all bills you remit, and credited by *A. B.* my accompt current, as fuch becomes due.

To render it ftill more eafy, I fhall fuppofe all the bills which the bank either grants, or takes, to be received and drawn at par.

DUMFRIES, *January* 1ſt. 1777.

		L.	s.	d.
✓	Drawn on *A. B.* our agent in *London*, at 30 days, payable to *G. R.* or order, for　　— 　—	100	00	00
	————————15th.————			
✓	Remitted *A. B.* a bill drawn by *T. W.* on *R. B.* in *London*, dated the 10th inſtant, at 30 days, for	50	00	00
	————————*February* 3d.————			
✓	Drawn on *A. B.* in *London*, at 30 days, payable to *I. D.* or order, for　　— 　—	450	00	00
✓	It appears by our bill-book, that our draft on *A. B.* dated the 1ſt of *January*, to *G. R.* or order, at 30 days, becomes due this day, for　　— 　—	100	00	00
	————————12th.————			
✓	Remitted *A. B. I. C.*'s draft on *K. L.* in *London*, dated this day, payable at 30 days, for　　—	300	00	00
✓	It appears by our bill-book, that *T. W.*'s draft on *R. B.* which we remitted *A. B.* becomes due this day	50	00	00
	————————*March* 5th.————			
✓	Drawn on *A. B.* in *London*, at 30 days, payable to *A. R.* or order, for　　— 　— 　—	250	00	00
✓	Drawn on *A. B.* in *London*, at 30 days, payable to *S. T.* or order, for　　— 　—	200	00	00
	————————8th.————			
✓	By our bill-book it appears, that our draft on *A. B.* dated *February* 3d, at 30 days, becomes due this day, for　　— 　— 　—	450	00	00
	————————12th.————			
✓	Remitted *A. B.* in *London*, *F. Z.*'s draft on *H. T.* dated the 8th inſtant, at 35 days, for　　—	300	00	00
	l.			

		L	s.	d.
———————March 12th.———————				
✓	I. C.'s draft on K. L. dated the 12th of *February,* at 30 days, remitted *A. B.* becomes due this day, for	300	00	00
————————April 4th.————————				
✓	Drawn on *A. B.* in *London,* at 30 days, payable to *D. U.* or order, for ——— ——— —	500	00	00
———————————7th.———————————				
✓	Our dr ft on *A B.* dated the 5th of *March,* pay-able to *A. R.* or order, at 30 days, becomes due this day ——— ——— —	250	00	00
——————————— 8th. ———————————				
✓	Our draft on *A. B.* dated the 5th of *March,* at 30 days, to *S. T.* or order, due this day, for —	200	00	00
———————————— 8th. ————————————				
✓	Drawn on *A. M.* in *London,* at 30 days, payable to *A. M.* or order, for ———————— —	180	00	00
——————————19th.——————————				
✓	F Z.'s draft on *H. C.* dated the 8th of *March,* at 35 days, remitted *A. B.* due this day ———	300	00	00
——————————— 30th. ———————————				
✓	Remitted *A. B.* in *London,* *H. K.*'s draft on *B. M.* dated this day, at 30 days, for ———	150	00	00
✓	Remitted *I. O.*'s draft on *N. C.* dated the 12th in-stant, at 30 days, for ——— ———	200	00	00

N.

N. B. In order to avoid miftakes, which might eafily happen in pofting from different books, I would recommend it to you to examine carefully your bill-book every morning, and what bills you find becomes due that day (either drawn on or remitted to your agent) enter in your Wafte-Book; by which means they will be regularly pofted, and thereby prevent confufion, which would inevitably be the confequence of fuch neglect.

On the other fide you have the Ledger pofts of the feveral preceding cafes in the Wafte-Book, in which you will pleafe to obferve, that A. B. our accompt of bills drawn is always credited by cafh, which we fuppofe to be received for fuch bills refpectively granted; and A. B. our accompt of bills remitted, is debited fuccettively to bills receivable, for what bills we remitted him; and confequently, cafh ought to have been debited to the former for the refpective fums of the credit fide of that accompt, and bills receivable credited by the latter for thofe on the debt fide of it: But as this would have occafioned two more accompts to be opened, which were not in the leaft effential to my prefent purpofe, I have therefore omitted them.

Year & Month.	A. B. *our accompt of bills* } Drawn, Dr.	Fo	l.	s.	d.
1777.					
Feb. 3	To *A. B.* our accompt current, for our draft } to G. R. due this day .———— {	1	100	00	00
Mar. 8	To ditto, for our draft to *J. D.* due this day	1	450	00	00
Apr. 7	To ditto, for ditto to *A. R.* due this day	1	250	00	00
	To ditto, for ditto to *S. T.* due this day —	1	200	00	00
	To ballance unpaid by him ————		680	00	00
			1680	00	00

	A. B. *our accompt of bills* } remitted, Dr.	Fo	l.	s.	d.
1777.					
Jan. 15	To bills receivable, for *T. W.*'s on *R. B.* } remitted him ———— {		50	00	00
Feb. 12	To ditto, for *J. C.*'s on *K. L.* remitted him } at 30 days ———— {		300	00	00
Mar 12	To ditto, for *F. Z.*'s on *H. T.* remitted him		300	00	00
Apr. 30	To ditto, for *H. K.*'s on *B. M.* remitted him		150	00	00
	To ditto, for *J. O.*'s on *N. C.* remitted him		200	00	00
			1000	00	00

	A. B. *our accompt current,* Dr.	Fo	l.	s.	d.
1777.					
Feb. 12	To *A. B.* our accompt of bills, remitted } for *T. W.*'s on *R. B.* due ———— {	1	50	00	00
Mar 17	To ditto, for *J. C.*'s on *K. L.* ————	1	300	00	00
Apr. 19	To ditto, for *F. Z.*'s on *H. C.* ————	1	300	00	00
	To ballance due to him in cash ————		355	11	06
			1005	11	06

Year & Month.	Contra, Cr.	L.	s.	d.
1777.				
Jan. 1	By cash, for our draft on him to G. R. or order, at 30 days ———	100	00	00
Feb. 3	By cash, for our draft on him to J. D. or order, at 30 days ——— ———	450	00	00
Mar. 5	By ditto, for ditto to A. R. or order, at 30 days	250	00	00
	By ditto, for ditto to S. T. or order, at 30 days	200	00	00
Apr. 4	By ditto, for ditto to D. U. or order for —	500	00	00
8	By ditto, for ditto to A. M. or order, at 30 days, for ———	180	00	00
		1680	00	00

Year & Month.	Contra, Cr	L.	s.	d.
1777.				
Feb. 12	By A. B. our accompt current, for T. W.'s on R. B. due ——— ———	50	00	00
Mar 17	By A. B. our accompt current, for J. C.'s on K. L. due ———	300	00	00
Apr. 19	By ditto, for F. Z.'s on H. C. due this day	300	00	00
	By ballance, not yet received by him —	350	00	00
		1000	00	00

Year & Month.	Contra, Cr.	L.	s.	d.
1777.				
Feb. 3	By A. B. our accompt of bills drawn, for one to G. R. due ———	100	00	00
Mar. 8	By ditto, to J. D. due ——— —	450	00	00
Apr. 7	By ditto, to A. R. due ———	250	00	00
	By ditto, to S. T. due this day ———	200	00	00
	By profit and lofs, for a ballance of intereft for cash advanced ——— ———	3	01	06
	By ditto, for ¼ per cent. commiffion on 1000 l.	2	10	00
		1005	11	06

A. B. our accompt of bills drawn, you fee, exhibits on the credit fide, the number of bills drawn upon him, together with the amount. The debt fide of the faid accompt, fhews what of thofe bills he has paid; confequently, the ballance is what remains of thofe bills yet unpaid by him,

A. B. our accompt of bills remitted, contains on the debt fide, the number of bills remitted to him, with the amount. And the credit fide of that accompt, fhews what of thofe bills he has received payment of; of courfe, the ballance is what remains yet unreceived by him.

A. B. our accompt current, fhews on the credit fide, thofe of your bills on him which are become due, and what he is (of courfe) fuppofed to have paid. The debt fide fhews which of thofe bills you remitted him are become due, and which (we fuppofe) he has received for. The difference, therefore, between thofe two fides, is the ballance due to, or from him in real cafh. But before we proceed to clofe this accompt, we muft firft fee what intereft is due on either fide, which is done in this manner: Firft multiply the refpective fums on the credit fide by the number of days from the date of each particular poft to the time of fettling the accompt, and then add the feveral products together. Next, proceed in like manner with the debt fide; fubtract the one from the other, and the difference divide by 7300, and that will give you the ballance of intereft due to, or from your agent. Make then this accompt Debtor to, or Creditor by profit and lofs (or intereft accompt) for fuch intereft. Having done this, you next credit it by profit and lofs for commiffion, at $\frac{1}{4}$ *per cent.* on the whole amount of the debt fide of *A. B.* our accompt of bills remitted, which you allow him for his trouble in collecting the cafh for the faid bills; the difference then of thofe two fides, will be the ballance due to, or from your agent in cafh.

N. B. Some (inftead of charging commiffion on the amount of the debt fide of the accompt of bills remitted) charge it on the whole amount of the credit fide of bills drawn; but I do not think this method in the leaft equitable, for it is prefumed as there is no trouble in paying the bills, further then telling out the cafh, or giving a draft upon their banker, that the intereft fufficiently repays that; and therefore, to me it appears more reafonable to charge it on the accompt of bills remitted, as there is fome trouble and expence attending the collecting the cafh for them.

How Manufacturers are to keep their books by Double Entry.

IF the firſt ſet of books, conſiſting of domeſtic trade (only) are well
underſtood, there will be very little difficulty in managing the accompts of manufacturers.

The ſpecimen I ſhall give is in the thread-hoſiery branch; and altho
I am not acquainted with all the various branches of it, nor with the
particular prices paid to workmen for each, yet miſtakes or ignorance
in thoſe things can in no meaſure affect the general plan.

The firſt article neceſſary to begin this branch of buſineſs, viz. flax,
I ſhall ſuppoſe the manufacturer to' buy ready dreſs'd; and then ſhew
the ſeveral proceſſes from that ſtate, in a regular progreſſion, to the
compleat finiſhing of the hoſe.

I ſhall likewiſe (that this ſpecimen may appear as little complex as
poſſible) ſuppoſe all the flax bought to be of the ſame quality and price,
and alſ that the hoſe are all made of one ſize.

The ſubſidiary books neceſſary to be kept on this occaſion, are only
two, viz.

The Spinners Book, and
The Weavers Book.

The reaſon for keeping thoſe two books are, becauſe the great number which you employ of each would render it not only troubleſome,
but alſo fill up your Ledger, by opening an accompt with each; and
therefore we only open a general accompt for each in our Ledger, viz.
Spinners accompt and Weavers accompt, and refer to the aforemen-
tioned ſubſidiary books for particulars; but as one dyer, one trimmer,
&c. may probably be ſufficient, we ſhall open an accompt in our
Ledger for each of thoſe reſpectively.

N. B. I ſhall ſuppoſe the ſpinners, weavers, trimmer, and dyer,
to bring in their work every week, and the bleacher once in a month.

W A S T E-

		l.	s.	d.

―――――――― *April* 1ſt, 1777.――――――

Bought for reidy money 5 *cwt.* of ready dreſſed flax, at 5 *l.* 12 *s. per cwt.* comes to ― ― 28|00|00

―――――――――――2d.―――――

✓ Delivered out to ſpin to ſundry perſons, as *per* ſpinners book, 100 *l.* flax, at 1 *s. per lb.* ― 5|00|00

―――――――――9th.――

✓ Received of ſundry perſons (as *per* ſpinners book)

l. s. d.

200 hanks of linen yarn for 50 *lb.* of flax, va- ⎫ lued to them at 1 *s. per. lb.* ― ⎬ 2 10 0

Paid them for ſpinning the ſame, at 1 *s.* 4 *d.* ⎫ *per lb.* ― ― ― ⎬ 3 6 8

Paid them likewiſe for ſcowering and boiling, ⎫ at 1 *d. per* hank ⎬ 0 16 8

Amounting in the whole at about 8 *d. per* hank, to ―― 6|13|04

l. s. d.

✓ Received alſo 200 hanks for 50 *lb.* of flax, ⎫ 2 10 0 at 1 *s. per lb.* ― ― ⎬

Paid for ſpinning ― ― ― 3 6 8

Amounting in the whole at 7 *d. per* hank to ――― 5|16|08

✓ Delivered out to ſpin 100 *lb.* of flax, at 1 *s. per lb.* 5|00|00

✓ Delivered to *James Green* (dyer) to dye blue

l. s. d.

100 hanks of ſcowered yarn, at about 8 *d. per* ⎫ 3 6 8 hank ― ― ⎬

And to the weavers

100 hanks ditto at the ſame price ― 3 6 8

6|13|04

✓ Delivered to *Thomas White*, bleacher

200 hanks of unſcowered linen yarn, at 7 *d. per* hank 5|16|08

―――――――16th.――――――

✓ Received of ſundry perſons (as *per* ſpinners book)

l. s. d.

200 hanks of yarn for 50 *lb.* flax, delivered ⎫ 2 10 0 at 1 *s. per lb.* ― ― ⎬

Paid for ſpinning do. at 1 *s.* 4 *d.* ⎫ *per lb.* ― ⎬ 3 6 8 ⎫

Ditto for ſcowering and boiling, ⎫ 0 16 8 ⎬ 4 3 4 at 1 *d.* ― ― ⎬ ⎭

Amounting in the whole to about 8 *d. per* hank ――― 6|13|04

April

——————————*April* 16th.——————————

		l.	s.	d.
✓	Received alfo 200 hanks for 50 *lb.* flax, at 1 *s. per lb.*	2	10	0
	Paid for fpinning at 1 *s.* 4 *d. per lb.* —	3	6	8
	Amounting in the whole to about 7 *d. per* hank	5	16	08

		l.	s.	d.
✓	Received of *James Green* (dyer) 100 hanks of blue yarn, for 100 hanks fcowered ditto, valued at	3	6	8
	Due to him for dying, at 2 *d. per* hank	0	16	8
	Amounting to about 10 *d. per* hank	4	03	04

		l.	s.	d.
✓	Received of weavers (as *per* weavers book)			
	5 dozen 2 pair of men's hofe, for 99 (in part of 100) hanks of yarn delivered to them, valued at 8 *d. per* hank	3	6	0
	Paid for weaving ditto, at 1 *s.* 4 *d. per* pair	4	2	8
	Amounting in the whole to about 2 *s.* 5 *d. per* pair	7	08	08

		l.	s.	d.
✓	Delivered to *George Forfter* (trimmer) 5 dozen 2 pair of hofe, valued at near 2 *s.* 5 *d. per* pair	7	08	08

		l.	s.	d.
✓	Delivered to fundries (as *per* fpinners book) 200 *lb.* of flax, valued at 1 *s. per lb.* —	10	00	00

		l.	s.	d.
✓	Delivered to fundry perfons (as *per* weavers book) 200 hanks of fcowered yarn, valued at about 8 *d. per* hank	6	13	00

——————————23d.——————————

		l.	s.	d.
✓	Received of *George Forfter* (trimmer)			
	5 dozen 2 pair hofe, valued at —	7	8	8
	Paid him for trimming, at 2 *d. per* pair —	0	10	4
	Amounting now to about 2 *s.* 7 *d. per* pair	8	18	00

		l.	s.	d.
✓	Received of fundry perfons (as *per* fpinners book)			
	400 hanks of yarn, equal to 100 *lb.* of flax, valued to them at 1 *s. per lb.* —	5	0	0
	Paid for fpinning, at 1 *s.* 4 *d. per lb.* — 6 13 4	8	6	8
	Ditto for fcowering, &c. at 1 *d. per* hank 1 13 4			
	Amounting in the whole to about 8 *d. per* hank	13	06	08

		l.	*s.*	*d.*
————————*April* 23d.———				
✓ Received (as *per* weavers book				
	l. *s.* *d.*			
10 dozen 6 pair of men's brown hose, for 200 ⎫ hanks of yarn, delivered to them at 8 *d.* ⎬ 6 13 4 *per* hank ⎭				
Paid for weaving ditto, at 1 *s.* 4 *d. per* pair 8 5 4				
Amounting in the whole to about 2 *s.* 5 *d. per* pair ———		14	18	08
✓ Delivered (as *per* weavers book)				
400 hanks of scowered yarn, valued at 8 *d. per* hank ⟶		13	06	08
✓ Delivered to *George Forster* (trimmer)				
10 dozen 6 pair of men's brown thread hose, at about				
2 *s.* 5 *d. per* pair —		14	18	08
———————————*May* 9th.———				
✓ Received of *Thomas White* (bleacher)				
	l. *s.* *d.*			
200 hanks of white yarn, for 200 hanks of ⎫ brown ditto, valued at 7 *d. per* hank — ⎬ 5 16 8				
Paid him for bleaching, at 2 *d. per* hank — 1 13 4				
Amounting to 9 *d. per* hank ———		7	10	00
✓ Received (as *per* weavers book)				
	l. *s.* *d.*			
21 dozen pair of men's brown thread hose, ⎫ for 400 hanks of yarn, delivered out to ⎬ 13 6 8 them at 8 *d. per* hank ⎭				
Paid for weaving ditto, at 1 *s.* 4 *d. per* pair 16 10 8				
Amounting in the whole to about 2 *s.* 5 *d. per* pair ———		29	17	04
✓ Received of *George Forster* (trimmer)				
	l. *s.* *d.*			
10 dozen 6 pair of men's brown thread hose, ⎫ valued to him at ⎬ 14 18 8				
Paid him for trimming, at 2 *d. per* pair — 1 1 0				
Amounting to about 2 *s.* 7 *d. per* pair ———		15	19	08
————————————16th.				
✓ Delivered to *George Foster* (trimmer)				
10½ dozen of men's hose, valued about 2 *s.* 5 *d. per* pair		14	18	08
———————————25th.———				
	l. *s.* *d.*			
✓ Twisted 50 hanks of blue yarn, about 10 *d. per* hank 2 1 8				
With 100 ditto of white ditto, at 9 *d. per* hank 3 15 0				
The mixture amounting to about 3 *s.* 3½ *d. per lb.* for				
27½ *lb.* ———		5	16	08

		l.	s.	d.
	April 1ft, 1777.—			
1	Flax Debtor to cafh, 28 *l.*			
0	Paid for 5 *cwt.* at 5*l.* 12*s. per cwt.* —	28	00	00
	————2d.————			
1	Spinners accompt Debtor to flax, 5 *l.*			
1	Delivered 100 *lb.* at 1*s. per lb.* to fundry perfons, as *per* fpinners book — —	5	00	00
	————9th.————			
	Brown linen yarn, (fcower'd) Debtor to fundries, 6*l.*			
1	13*s.* 4*d.*			
	l. s. d.			
1	To fpinners accompt, for 200 hanks, received } 2 10 0 in exchange for 50 *lb.* of flax —			
	To cafh, for fpinning and fcowering — 4 3 4			
	Amounting in the whole to about 8*d. per* hank ——	6	13	04
1	Brown linen yarn, (unfcowered) Debtor to fundries, 5 *l.* 16*s.* 8 *d.*			
	l. s. d.			
1	To fpinners accompt, for 200 hanks, received } 2 10 0 in exchange for 50 *lb.* of flax, at 1*s. per lb.*			
0	To cafh, for fpinning, at 1*s.* 4*d. per lb.* — 3 6 8			
	Amounting now in the whole to 7 *d. per* hank ——	5	16	0?
1	Spinners accompt Debtor to flax, 5 *l.*			
1	Delivered 100 *lb.* to fundries, as *per* fpinning book, at 1 *s. per lb.* — — —	5	00	00
	Sundries Debtors to brown linen yarn, (fcower'd) 6*l.* 13 *s.* 4 *d.*			
	l. s. d.			
1	*James Green,* for 100 hanks to dye at 8 *d.* — 3 6 8			
2	Weavers acc. for 100 ditto, as *per* weavers book 3 6 8			
1	——	6	13	04
1	*Thomas White* Debtor to brown linen yarn, (unfcowered) 5*l.* 16*s.* 8 *d,*			
1	Delivered him 200 to bleach, at 7 *d. per* hank —	5	16	08
	————16th.————			
1	Brown linen yarn (fcower'd) Dr. to fundries, 6*l.* 13*s.* 4*d.*			
	l. s. d.			
1	To fpinners accompt, for 200 hanks, received } 2 10 0 in exchange for 50 *lb.* of flax —			
0	To cafh, for fpinning and fcowering — 4 3 4			
	Amounting in the whole to about 8*d. per* hank ——	6	13	04

		l.	s.	d.
———————*April* 16th.———————				

1	Brown linen yarn (unfcower'd) Debtor to fundries, 5*l.*			
—	16 *s.* 8 *d.*	*l. s. d.*		
1	To fpinners accompt, for 200 hanks, in exchange for 50 *lb.* of flax ———— } 2 10 0			
0	To cafh, for fpinning, at 1 *s.* 4 *d. per lb.* — 3 6 8			
	Amounting now to 7 *d. per* hank. ————	5	16	08

2	Blue linen yarn Debtor to *James Green*, 4 *l.* 3 *s.* 4 *d.*			
2	For 100 hanks received dyed, valued at 10 *d. per* hank	4	03	04

2	Brown thread hofe (undrefs'd) Debtor to fundries, 7 *l.*			
—	8 *s.* 8 *d.*	*l. s. d.*		
2	To weavers accompt, for 5 *doz.* 2 *pr.* in exchange for 100 hanks of fcower'd yarn } 3 6 0			
0	To cafh, for weaving, at 1 *s.* 4 *d. per* pair — 4 2 8			
	Amounting in the whole to about 2 *s.* 4 ¼ *d. per* pair ———	7	08	08

2	*George Forfter* Dr. to brown thread (undrefs'd) hofe,			
	7 *l.* 8 *s.* 8 *d.*			
2	Delivered him 5 *doz.* 2 *pr.* to trim, at near 2 *s.* 5 *d. per* pair	7	08	08

1	Spinners accompt Debtor to flax, 10 *l.*			
—	Delivered to fpin to fundries as *per* fpinners book, 200 *lb.*			
1	valued at 1 *s. per lb.*	10	00	00

2	Weavers ac. Dr. to brown linen yarn (fcower'd) 6 *l.* 13 *s.*			
1	Delivered to fundries as *per* weavers book, 200 hanks	6	13	00

———————23d.———————				

2	Brown thread hofe (drefs'd) Debtor to fundries, 8 *l.* 4 *d.*			
		l. s. d.		
2	To *George Forfter*, for 5 dozen 2 pair — 7 8 8			
0	To cafh, paid him for trimming, at 2 *d. per* pair 0 10 4			
	Amounting now to about 2 *s.* 7 *d. per* pair	7	18	08

1	Brown linen yarn (fcower'd) Debtor to fundries, 13 *l.*			
—	6 *s.* 8 *d.*	*l. s. d.*		
1	To fpinners accompt, for 400 hanks, received in exchange for 100 *lb.* of flax — } 5 0 0			
	To cafh, for fpinning and fcowering — 8 6 8			
	Amounting now to about 8 *d. per* hank ————	13	06	08

2	Brown thread hofe (undrefs'd) Debtor to fundries, 14 *l.*			
—	18 *s.* 8 *d.*	*l. s. d.*		
2	To weavers accompt, for 10¼ dozen, in exchange for 200 hanks of fcower'd yarn — } 6 13 4			
0	To cafh, for weaving at 1 *s.* 4 *d. per* pair — 8 5 4			
	Amounting to about 2 *s.* 5 *d. per* pair ————	14	18	08

		l.	*s.*	*d.*
	———————*April* 30th.———————			
2 / 1	Weavers accompt Debtor to brown linen yarn (fcow-er'd) 13*l.* 6*s.* 8*d.* Delivered as *per* fpinners book, 400 hanks, at 8*d. per* hank	13	06	08
2 / 2	*George Forfter* Dr. to brown thread (undrefs'd) hofe, 14*l.* 18*s.* 8*d.* Delivered him 10 ½ dozen to trim ———	14	18	08
	——————*May* 9th.——————			
2	White linen yarn Debtor to fundries, 7*l.* 10*s.*			
		l.	*s.*	*d.*
2	To *Thomas White*, for 200 hanks, received in ⎰ exchange for the fame quantity of brown ⎱	5 16 8		
0	To cafh, paid him for bleaching, at 2 *d. per* hank	1 13 4		
	Amounting now to 9 *d. per* hank ———	7	10	00
2	Brown thread hofe Debtor to fundries, 29*l.* 17*s.* 4*d.*			
		l.	*s.*	*d.*
2	To weavers accompt, for 21 dozen, in ex- ⎰ change for 400 hanks of fcowered yarn ⎱	13 6 8		
0	To cafh, paid for weaving, at 1 *s.* 4 *d. per* pair	16 10 8		
	Amounting in the whole to about 2*s.* 5*d. per* pair ———	29	17	04
2	Brown thread hofe (drefs'd) Debtor to fundries, 15 *l.* 19 *s.* 8*d.*			
		l.	*s.*	*d.*
2	To *George Forfter*, for 10 ½ dozen —	14 18 8		
0	To cafh, paid for trimming, at 2 *d. per* pair	1 1 0		
	Amounting to about 2 *s.* 7 *d. per* pair ———	15	19	08
	——————16th.——————			
2 / 2	*George Forfter* Debtor to brown thread hofe, (undrefs'd) 14*l.* 18*s.* 8*d.* Delivered him 10 ½ dozen to trim ———	14	18	08
	——————25th.——————			
2	Mix'd thread (twifted blue and white) Debtor to fundries, 5*l.* 16*s.* 8*d.*			
		l.	*s.*	*d.*
2	To white thread, for 100 hanks, at 9 *d. per* hank	3 15 0		
2	To blue do. for 50 ditto, at about 10*d. per* hank	2 1 8		
	Making 27¼ *lb.* twifted, amounting to near 3 *s.* 1¼ *d.* *per lb.* ———	5	16	08

N. B. In pofting to the Ledger I have opened no accounts but what were abfolutely neceffary to fhew the true
ftate of your goods, according to the feveral degrees of
improvement which they were arrived at, and confequently, the cafh has no credit to correfpond with the feveral
other accounts which are debited to fundries, of which
the cafh accompt is one of the Creditors.

Year & Month.		Fol	l.	s.	d.
	Flax, (ready drefs'd) Dr.				
1777.	cwt. lb.				
April 1	To cafh, at 5l. 12s. per cwt. for — 5	560	28	00	00
		560	28	oc	00
	Spinners accompt, (as per ⎱ *fpinners book)* ⎰ Dr.				
1777.	lb.				
April 2	To flax, at 1s. per lb. for — — —	100	1	5	00	00
9	To ditto, at 1s. per lb. for — — —	100	1	5	00	00
16	To ditto, at 1s. per lb. for — — —	200	1	10	00	00
		400	20	00	00
	Brown linen yarn, (fcower'd) Dr.				
1777.	bks.				
April 9	To fundries as per Journal, at 8 d. per hank, for	200	6	13	04
16	To ditto, as per ditto, at 8 d. per hank, for —	200	6	13	04
23	To ditto, as per ditto, at 8 d. per hank, for —	400	13	06	08
		800	26	13	04
	Brown linen yarn, (unfcower'd) Dr.				
1777.	bks.				
April 1	To fundries as per Journal, at 7 d. per hank —	200	5	16	08
16	To ditto, at 7 d. per ditto — — —	200	5	16	08
		400	11	13	04
	James Green, Dyer, Dr.				
1777.	bks.				
April 9	To brown linen yarn, (fcower'd) at 8d. per hk. for	100	1	3	06	08
	To ballance, due to him for dying — —			16	08
		100	4	03	04
	Thomas White, Bleacher, Dr.				
1777.	bks.				
April 9	To brown linen yarn, (unfeower'd) at 7 d. per hk.	200	1	5	16	08

Year&		Fo	l.	s.	d.
Month.	*Contra,* Cr.				

1777. cwt. lb.

April 2	By spinners accompt delivered, at 1s. per lb.	100	1	5	00	00
9	By ditto, at 1s. per lb. — — —	100	1	5	00	00
16	By ditto, at 1s. per lb. — —	200	1	10	00	00
	By ballance, at 1s. per lb. — —	160		8	00	00
		5 : 560		28	00	00

1777.	*Contra,* Cr.				

lb.

April 9	By brown linen yarn (scower'd) in return for flax, at 1s. per lb. for — — — }	50	1	2	10	00
	By ditto, (unscower'd) at 1s. per lb. for —	50	1	2	10	00
16	By do. (scower'd) return for flax, at 1s. per lb. for	50	1	2	10	00
16	By do. (unscower'd) return for flax, at 1s. per lb. for	50	1	2	10	00
23	By do. (scower'd) return for flax, at 1s. per lb. for	100	1	5	00	00
	By ballance, at 1s. per lb. for — —	100		5	00	00
		400		20	00	00

1777.	*Contra,* Cr.				

hanks

April 9	By sundries as per Journal, at 8d. per hank, for	200		6	13	04
16	By weavers accompt (as per weavers book) delivered at 8d. per hank — — }	200	2	6	13	04
30	By ditto, (as per ditto) delivered at 8d. per hank	400	2	13	06	08
		800		26	13	04

1777.	*Contra,* Cr.				

bks.

April 9	By T. White, bleacher, delivered him at 7d. per hk.	200		5	16	08
	By ballance remaining, at 7d. per hank —	200		5	16	08
		400		11	13	04

1777.	*Contra,* Cr.				

bks.

Apr.16	By blue linen yarn, at 10d. per hank —	100	2	4	03	04
		100		4	03	04

1777	*Contra,* Cr.				

bks.

May 9	By linen yarn, (white) received back bleached	200	2	5	16	08

Year & Month.	Weavers accompt, (as per weavers book) Dr.		Fo	L	s	d
1777.		bks.				
April 9	To brown linen yarn, (scower'd) at 8d. per hank	100	1	3	06	08
16	To ditto, ditto, at 8d. per hank — —	200	1	6	13	04
30	To ditto, ditto, at 8d. per ditto — —	400	1	13	06	08
		700		23	06	08
	Blue linen yarn, Dr.					
1777.		bks.				
Apr. 16	To J. Green, (dyer) received of him dyed at 10d.	100	1	4	03	04
		100		4	03	04
	George Forster, (trimmer) Dr					
1777.		doz.	pr.			
Apr. 16	To brown thread hose (undress'd) delivered to trim, valued at about 2s. 5d. per pair, for	5	2	2	7	08	08
30	To ditto, (undress'd) delivered him to trim —	10	6	2	14	18	08
May 16	To ditto, ditto, delivered him to trim —	10	6	2	14	18	08
		26	2		37	06	00
	White linen yarn, Dr.					
1777.		bks.				
May 9	To sundries as per Journal, at 9d. per hank —	200		7	10	00
		200		7	10	00
	Mix'd thread, (blue and white twisted) Dr.					
1777.		lb.	oz.			
May 25	To sundries as per Jour. at neat 3s. 1½d. per lb.	27	8	5	16	08
	Brown thread hose, (undress'd) Dr					
1777.		doz.	pr.			
Apr. 16	To sundries as per Jour. at neat 2s. 5d. per pr.	5	2	7	08	08
23	To sundries as per do. at about 2s. 5d. per pair	10	6	14	18	08
May 9	To sundries as per do. at about 2s. 5d. per pair	21		29	17	04
		36	8	52	04	08
	Brown thread hose, (dress'd) Dr.					
1777.		doz.	pr			
Apr. 23	To sundries as per Jour. at about 2s. 7d. per pr.	5	2	7	18	08
May 9	To sundries as per do. at about 2s. 7d. per do.	10	6	15	19	08
		15	8	23	18	04

Year & Month.	Contra,	Cr. bks.	Fo	L.	s.	d.
1777- Apr. 16	By brown thread hose, (undress'd) received for	99	2	3	06	00
23	By ditto, ditto, received for — —	200	2	6	13	04
May 9	By ditto, ditto, received for — — —	400	2	13	06	08
	By ballance remaining, as per weavers book —	1				08
		700		23	06	08

Year & Month.	Contra,	Cr. bks.	Fo	L.	s.	d.
1777. May 25	By mix'd thread (blue and white) at 10d. per hk. for	50	2	2	01	08
	By ballance, at 10 d. per hank, for — —	50		2	01	08
		100		4	02	04

Year & Month.	Contra,	doz.	pr.	Fo	L.	s.	d.
1777. Apr. 23	By brown thread hose, (dress'd) received —	5	2	2	7	08	08
May 9	By ditto, ditto, received — —	10	6	2	14	18	08
	By ballance remaining in his hands —	10	6		14	18	08
		26	2		37	06	00

Year & Month.	Contra,	Cr. bks.	Fo	L.	s.	d.
1777. May 25	By mix'd thread, (blue and white) at 9d. per hk. for	100	2		15	00
	By ballance, at 9d. per hank — —	100		3	15	00
		200		7	10	00

Contra,	Cr. lb.	oz.	Fo	L.	s.	d.
By ballance, at near 3s. 1½ d. per lb. for —	27	8		5	16	08

Year & Month.	Contra,	doz.	pr.	Fo	L.	s.	d.
1777. Apr. 16	By George Forster, delivered him to trim —	5	2	2	7	08	08
30	By ditto — — — —	10	6	2	14	18	08
May 16	By ditto — — — —	10	6	2	14	18	08
	By ballance, at about 2s. 5 d. per pair, for	10	6		14	18	08
		36	8		52	04	08

Contra,	doz.	pr.	Fo	L.	s.	d.
By ballance, at about 2s. 7 d. per pair, for	15	8		23	18	04
	15	8		23	18	04

For Product Safety Concerns and Information please contact our EU
representative GPSR@taylorandfrancis.com
Taylor & Francis Verlag GmbH, Kaufingerstraße 24, 80331 München, Germany

www.ingramcontent.com/pod-product-compliance
Ingram Content Group UK Ltd.
Pitfield, Milton Keynes, MK11 3LW, UK
UKHW021831240425
457818UK00006B/155